Abbas Kiarostami and Film-Philosophy

Abbas Kiarostami and Film-Philosophy

Mathew Abbott

EDINBURGH
University Press

Edinburgh University Press is one of the leading university presses in the UK. We publish academic books and journals in our selected subject areas across the humanities and social sciences, combining cutting-edge scholarship with high editorial and production values to produce academic works of lasting importance. For more information visit our website: edinburghuniversitypress.com

Edinburgh University Press Ltd
The Tun – Holyrood Road
12(2f) Jackson's Entry
Edinburgh EH8 8PJ

First published in hardback by Edinburgh University Press 2017

Typeset in 11/13 Garamond MT Pro by
Servis Filmsetting Ltd, Stockport, Cheshire,
and printed and bound in Great Britain by
CPI Group (UK) Ltd, Croydon CR0 4YY

A CIP record for this book is available from the British Library

ISBN 978 0 7486 9990 2 (hardback)
ISBN 978 1 4744 3229 0 (paperback)
ISBN 978 0 7486 9991 9 (webready PDF)
ISBN 978 1 4744 0467 9 (epub)

Contents

Acknowledgements

The conversation, arguments, criticism, insight, and editorial guidance of the following people have made important contributions to this book: Robert Arculus, Amir Ahmadi Arian, Rex Butler, Edward Cavanagh, Bruin Christensen, Eileen Clements, Lisabeth During, Gregory Flaxman, Hamish Ford, Michael Fried, Richard Hammond, Melanie Hughes, Fiona Jenkins, David Macarthur, Stephen Mulhall, Emilie Owens, Robert Sinnerbrink, Babak Tabarraee, Lisa Trahair, and Dominic Williams. As well as the ones listed here, I would like to thank members of the Cinematic Thinking Network, without whose input this would have been a weaker book. I would also like to thank Carol Macdonald, James Dale, and other staff at Edinburgh University Press with whom I have worked, on this and my last book project. I would like to extend special thanks to Robert S, for your ongoing support of my work; to Fiona, for teaching me film and philosophy; to David, for teaching me Wittgenstein; to Amir, for showing me Tehran; and to Eileen and Richard, for your friendship in Ballarat. Most of all I would like to thank Emilie, for all that you do. This book is dedicated to you, Em.

Material from this book was first published in *SubStance: A Review of Theory and Literary Criticism* and *Senses of Cinema*.

Abbas Kiarostami died while this book was in its proofing stages. May it honour his memory, and the profound, compassionate, and attentive films he left us.

Introduction: *Abbas Kiarostami and Film-Philosophy*

Abbas Kiarostami's 1997 film *Taste of Cherry* follows the middle-aged Badii as he drives around the outskirts of Tehran trying to enlist strangers in the task of helping him commit suicide. His plan is to take sleeping pills and lie down to die in a grave he has dug on a hillside. He wants someone to come by the next morning to fill it with earth or, if he is still alive, help him out.

As is quite typical of Kiarostami, the nature of Badii's plan is revealed piecemeal through his conversations with the people he encounters.[1] The first exchange is with a man he overhears on a public telephone haggling over money, and who rebuffs him with a threat before he has time to make his offer (apparently mistaking Badii for someone cruising for sex). Then Badii encounters a man picking through trash for plastic bags to sell, refusing his proposition before really hearing it because, he says, he won't know how to help. The next exchange – which takes place after the opening titles – involves a young Kurdish soldier. Badii picks him up and drives him to show him the hillside on which he wants to die; when they arrive, the soldier runs for it. Badii encounters his next would-be assistant in the form of a security guard watching over what looks to be a quarry; he refuses Badii too, saying he cannot leave his post. Now Badii tries to convince the Afghan guard's friend; the young man – a seminarist – is disturbed by Badii's plan ("My hands do God's justice. What you want wouldn't be just"). A bizarre and unsettling sequence then ensues: Badii steps out of his car and wanders around the quarry, staring with vacant intensity as mounds of dirt are dropped by earth-movers and rocks are conveyed and sorted by large machines, the images and sounds all taking on a strangely sickening material quality.[2] After becoming almost entirely enveloped in a cloud of thick orange dust, Badii returns to his car at the urgings of a worried worker. When he closes the door we are surprised to see him start speaking to a passenger. As we soon realise, however, there has been a startling temporal shift – Badii is no longer at the quarry, but is parked near his grave, and is speaking to a new character, who has agreed to help him die. They discuss the specifics of the plan and come to an agreement regarding payment. But the man also tries to convince Badii not to kill himself. He tells Badii that his troubled relationship with his wife once led him to decide on suicide: he travelled out to a mulberry plantation with the intention of hanging himself from a tree, but found his rope wouldn't hold; he climbed the tree in order to retie it, brushing his hand against some mulberries; he tasted them; he looked up to notice the sunrise; he decided not to kill himself. It is unclear what effect the story has on Badii. Later, we see him in his apartment getting dressed to leave, and he heads out to the hillside in a taxi.

As Badii lies in his grave, a storm brews overhead; cloud blocks out the moon and, save the light cast by four flashes of lightning, all goes dark for a minute and a half (yet not all is silent: after forty-five seconds, the rain starts). At some stage during the darkness there is an infamous cut in which film switches to video, and when light returns we find that the scene has changed dramatically. It's greener (as Michael Price points out,[3] the season has changed: now it looks like spring). We see a film crew with cameras and other equipment, and find that Badii is no longer in his grave, but walking up the hill with a cigarette. He hands it to another man who, we soon see, is actually Kiarostami himself. The two engage in what appears to be idle conversation, and we hear Louis Armstrong (it is the only non-diegetic music in the movie). We are then treated to a remarkable handheld sequence mostly featuring soldiers at ease, and which includes the young man who ran in fear. It is like a curtain call, except the movie isn't over: it has just changed in a beguiling way.

I take it as the paradigmatic instance of Kiarostami's characteristic gesture (and in that sense, as a kind of watershed in his artistic development, definitively marking his arrival as a great filmmaker). In such moments, one's claims to knowledge – to tell the difference between the real and the fake, the authentic and the artificial; to claim a basic level of insight into a film's characters, their motivations and eventual destiny; to understand the meaning and dramatic stakes of what one is watching – are paralysed by the emergence of a disorienting reflexivity. Yet this disorientation is not simply a distancing: in certain important respects – and this is part of what is remarkable about it – it draws the viewer more deeply into the films. In the case of *Taste of Cherry*, the 'reveal' at the end does not cancel or even dampen my response to the movie. If Price is right to say that it gets the audience waking from its "two-hour slumber" – that now it "has to rise and account for itself"[4] – then this accounting is no Brechtian chore: with its colour and sudden music, the scene throws new light on the rest of the film; we wake bewildered, but with fresh eyes. There is something affirmative about Kiarostami's gesture, which is especially pronounced given the film's grim plot.[5]

Consider 1990's *Close-Up*. It is about real events: impersonating Mohsen

Makhmalbaf, Hossein Sabzian conned a Tehrani family into letting him film their domestic life; he was eventually found out, and put in jail under suspicion of planning robbery. Kiarostami not only gained permission to film the trial (and indeed to 'recreate' it afterwards in the court room[6]); he also arranged a re-enactment of the deception that led to it, filming Sabzian in the family's home pretending to be pretending to be Makhmalbaf.[7] In the final scene of the film, the viewer has difficulty finding firm ground: we watch Makhmalbaf and Sabzian meeting from the perspective of what is supposedly a hidden camera; Makhmalbaf is miked up, but the sound cuts out as they ride a motorcycle to the house Sabzian deceivingly entered. Yet the final shot is a close-up of Sabzian's face from an entirely new angle; the 'hidden camera' theatrics are revealed as just that. But this does not take away from the scene, or make Sabzian's gesture – he arrives at the door with a pot of flowers – less striking. As Jean-Luc Nancy writes:

> In this film, what could have been the story of gentle madness or a denunciation of the cinematographic illusion leads to the contrary in the end . . . a return to the real that a progressive fading away of the movie signals . . . a bunch of red flowers, explicitly chosen for their color, stands out against the blue-grey of the noisy street . . . [8]

The complexity of the set-up, in which the real and the artificial nearly become indistinguishable, does not detract from the gesture. Rather, it heightens it (after all, part of the sweetness of the act of giving flowers is bound up with the fact that its status *as a gesture* is so clear).

We could also turn here to the Koker Trilogy.[9] The narrative of 1987's *Where is the Friend's Home?* turns on a mix-up: Ahmad, the eight-year-old protagonist, mistakes his classmate Mohammad's exercise book for his own and takes it home from school. Knowing that Mohammad – who has recently drawn their (authoritarian and cruel) teacher's ire for failing to do his homework – is in danger of expulsion if he fails again to complete it, Ahmad sets off in search of his house in order to return the book. The simplicity of the film is part of its appeal, but it prefigures the crucial problem of Kiarostami's later cinema: the question of the real and its relation to the fake (a relationship complicated by the film's ending, in which Ahmad gets Mohammad off the hook by copying his own work into his book[10]).

On hearing the news of the earthquake that devastated northern Iran in 1990, Kiarostami travelled with his son to the town of Koker – where parts of *Where is the Friend's Home?* were shot – to try and locate his two child actors. Kiarostami was unable to find the boys, but returned some months later to make 1992's *Life and Nothing More*, a semi-fictional feature about a director and his son (played by Farhad Kheradmand and Buba Bayour) visiting Koker after the quake in order to track down two child actors.[11] The film is remarkable for its handling of the disaster, which it never sensationalises, and for how it tracks what happens to the ordinary in such exceptional circumstances. One of the film's most interesting scenes involves a young couple who had decided to get married shortly after the earthquake – a scene which then became crucial in 1994's *Through the Olive Trees*. This film depicts the real-life romance that unfolded between the two non-actors during the filming of *Life and Nothing More*. Kiarostami arranges a re-enactment of their courtship featuring one of the original cast members, who plays himself falling in love while playing himself in a fictional romance. Meanwhile the actor who played the director of *Where is the Friend's Home?* in *Life and Nothing More* is now cast as himself playing his original role, while another actor plays the real director of the 1992 film. It is impressive that these reflexive games never collapse into knowing irony or detached, cerebral mannerism: at its heart the film is a story of quixotic love told with tenderness and gentle humour.[12] As Nancy acknowledges, the meta-cinematic element itself only "introduces a new story, neither more nor less effective than the first one, just showing another angle of what is real and therefore many-faceted".[13]

So the question is clear: how do these techniques – which in theory should produce distancing, alienation, *ostrananie*, *Verfremdungseffekt*, etc. – manage to draw us further into the films? How is it that, in Chris Lippard's phrase,[14] the real in Kiarostami is both disappearing into the distance and getting closer all the time? And what does this say about the so-called 'suspension of disbelief' and its alleged role in our absorption in movies? As I show in this book, asking these questions opens fundamental problems in the philosophy of cinema. What is film's connection to the real world? What happens to reality when we screen it? How does film create problems of knowledge? Might it help us solve them? How can film make moral or political claims on us? What is the difference between documentary and fiction? How do fictional films move us, when we know that happens in them isn't real? What is a film genre, and what does it mean to claim a film as a member of one? What does it mean to say that a film is 'philosophical'? Is there a way of supporting the idea that films can do philosophical work? As I hope to show, thinking through Kiarostami's recent movies will allow us to shed new light on these questions. This book uses philosophy and the films of Kiarostami for their mutual illumination, turning to the Iranian director in an attempt at finding and clarifying a form of cinematic thinking.[15]

Stanley Cavell's writings on the philosophical (and cinematic) problems of scepticism will play an important role here. His best-known book – *The Claim of Reason* – is remarkable for the obsessive way in which it follows up on these problems, yet it does so without the intent of solving them. Part of the uniqueness of Cavell's work (although he is also indebted to Ludwig Wittgenstein and Martin Heidegger on this) consists in this very particular understanding of the nature and function of philosophy: unlike so many of his Anglo-American contemporaries, Cavell does not think it should be concerned primarily with the task of defending sets of beliefs about how it is with the world, or trying to justify our claims to know it. Instead he takes the task of philosophy to be a therapeutic one. The implications of this are difficult and far-reaching, but what's particularly relevant for us is the connection between philosophical therapy and the problems of modern scepticism, which Cavell sees as running more deeply into 'ordinary' or 'non-philosophical' life than we tend to assume. Cavell is following the later Wittgenstein, but in a way that complicates him. Here is a passage from the *Philosophical Investigations*:

> But can't I imagine that the people around me are automata, lack consciousness, even though they behave in the same way as usual? – If I imagine it now – alone in my room – I see people with fixed looks (as in a trance) going about their business – the idea is perhaps a little uncanny. But just try to keep hold of this idea in the midst of your ordinary intercourse with others, in the street say! Say to yourself, for example: 'The children over there are mere automata; all their liveliness is mere automatism.' And you will either find these words becoming quite meaningless; or you will produce in yourself some kind of uncanny feeling . . . [16]

Wittgenstein is right: we tend to forget such sceptical worries in ordinary life. But the uncertainty that makes it impossible for a philosopher simply to dismiss such a sceptical problem plays itself out in far more mundane situations: in the fear and feeling of being unintelligible to another, such that one's words do not mean what one thinks they do, or do not mean at all; in the feeling that another self can be or become opaque to one, such that the other is unintelligible and/or impossible to respond to rightly; in the possibility that the way one takes the world, and so the way one lives, could be misguided or fantasmatic in some fundamental sense; in the potential for insanity that subsists within some or all of us (insanity is actually internal to philosophy for Cavell, and Wittgenstein too: not through the blunt claim that philosophy is insane, but in the sense that it is haunted by a sort of linguistic madness). Crucially, these can all be framed as problems of knowledge, experiences of not being able to know.

Obviously Descartes is important here (the above quote from the *Investigations* chimes, I presume deliberately, with the Second Meditation's worry about hats and cloaks covering clockwork machines[17]). And of course, Descartes does reach certainty after negotiating his sceptical quagmires, famously finding his Archimedean point in the indisputable fact of his own existence. He goes on to try and save the rest of our knowledge by proving the existence of God. Descartes's idea is that God is good, and wouldn't subject us to life in a world where our claims to knowledge are ungrounded. Yet of course, if we think the ontological proof of God fails, then we are left in a difficult spot. We get the self – the one certainty of the Cartesian system – but without all the extra claims that would 'reconnect' that self to the world and other selves outside it. One might say, then, that the certainty that Descartes gave us was ambiguous. He found us a little piece of firm epistemological ground, but in doing as he bequeathed to us (or discovered for us) a potential for absolute isolation, for entrapment in subjectivity (to push the above metaphor a bit too far, we might say that we've been marooned on little Cartesian islands). As Cavell puts it: "At some point the unhinging of our consciousness from the world interposed our subjectivity between us and our presentness to the world. Then our subjectivity became what is present to us, individuality became isolation."[18] As this passage makes clear, Cavell sees this problem as inherent in modernity, as the age in which the criterion of knowledge takes on new significance. It is as though we find ourselves trapped by the demand for certainty it sparks. He says we have suffered a

> fall into skepticism, together with its efforts to recover itself, events recorded variously in Descartes and Hume and Kant and Emerson and Nietzsche and Heidegger and Wittgenstein . . . It is in modern philosophical skepticism . . . that our relation to the things of the world came to be felt to hang by a thread of sensuous immediacy, hence to be snapped by a doubt. The wish to defeat skepticism, or to disparage it, has been close to philosophy's heart ever since.[19]

To summarise a little violently, for Cavell, modern philosophical scepticism is simultaneously correct and confused: correct because it intuits that the human relation to the world is epistemically unassured; confused because it takes this as a problem to be solved. The former claim is ontological; it is what Cavell calls the "truth of scepticism".[20] The latter claim is historical; it is that philosophical modernity is characterised by a rage to know. This rage sees us distort the truth of scepticism: by raging against it, we fail to acknowledge it; we come to take it as a deficit in our knowledge. This is why the philosophical task for Cavell is not to solve the problems of scepticism, but to reorient us in relation to them, to loosen their grip by transforming our sense of them. The task is to own up to the fact that "the human creature's basis in the world as a whole, its relation to the world as such, is not that of knowing".[21]

What is the relevance of this for film? Cavell sees it as both alleviating and exasperating scepticism. The key claim in *The World Viewed,* which was Cavell's first monograph and which, as William Rothman and Marian Keane point out,[22] can be strikingly inexplicit in its treatment of these issues, is that film is a "moving image of scepticism".[23] What Cavell means is that film draws part of its power from the sceptical threat: film finds itself naturally drawn to the depiction of (the implications of) our lack of epistemic assurance.[24] If this is true, it is not just in virtue of film's purported status as 'the' modern art form, but because of how the camera can seem to take on the basic standpoint of the sceptical theorist, viewing the world from a detached position, recording events happening before it in a way that makes its own connection to those events seem ambiguous (yet at the same time, raising a nearly unshakable thought: that what happens in front of it just *is* 'real' in some sense of the word). On the one hand, photography, film, and video seem to be indexical: we *use* them to tell us things about what happens (think of CCTV, footage from which can happily stand in court). We tend to feel that this ability to record the real is a function of the automatism of photographic apparatuses: the fact that they – unlike say, paintbrushes – produce images of the world the nature of which is wholly or strongly dependent on what actually happens in it, rather than on what their makers want to depict.[25] On the other hand, coming up with a successful philosophical account of this feature of photographic media is very difficult.[26] For isn't our sense of a particular image or scene's bearing a direct relationship to the real a function of artistic or directorial fiat as much as of its having automatically reproduced reality? Doesn't this undermine the key condition we had in mind: that photographic apparatuses record what happens regardless of the wills of their human users? What about the case of digital video files, which are not the results of literal imprints of light on film, and which can be manipulated easily with computer software? And of course, from bitter experience we know that being surrounded by images of the real does not bolster as much as undermine our conviction in it (think of arriving at a tourist destination only to find it appears less vibrant than in the images you saw of it online). This is part of why Cavell can read the films of the Hollywood golden age as working in a sceptical register – arguing for instance that "the overcoming of skeptical doubt can be found in all remarriage comedy . . ."[27] – and finding in them real philosophical depth: this is the case in virtue of the tendencies of the medium. For Cavell, we go to the movies to experience a reconnection to the world, a connection we feel has been severed in modernity. Cinema simultaneously screens the world before and from the viewer; it presents an uncannily literal version of the truth of scepticism. Film allows us to *view the world*, to take views of it. Film toys with, undermines, and restores our confidence in it. As Cavell writes: "The basis of film's drama, or the latent anxiety in viewing its drama, lies in its persistent demonstration that we do not know what our conviction in reality turns upon."[28]

Think here of Walter Benjamin's understanding of the experiential effects of technologies of reproduction, which stems from broader quasi-Marxist claims regarding the historicity of not only experience but sense perception as well. Benjamin puts it clearly:

> *Just as the entire mode of existence of human collectives changes over long historical periods, so too does their mode of perception.* The way in which human perception is organized – the medium in which it occurs, is conditioned not only by nature but by history.[29]

This comes in 'The Work of Art in the Age of its Technological Reproducibility', where Benjamin famously claims that "what withers in the age of the technological reproducibility of the work of art is the latter's aura"[30] (where 'aura' is something like the authentic presence of the original, and its being embedded in a fabric of tradition). The idea is that our ability to make copies of artworks rips them from their social contexts, which allows for their wider dissemination while simultaneously undermining our faith in originals and the very idea of authenticity. I want to make a quasi-phenomenological point in order to connect this to Cavell's claims about film. It is that one's memories of events can be infiltrated by the images we produce of them. I have had the experience of finding that some of my vivid 'memories' are not really memories at all. It is the experience of going through family photos or videos, or perhaps of looking at photographs of a holiday: one realises that something one has taken as a memory is actually a memory of a photograph or video recording. This isn't to say that there is no real memory, but rather that one's memory has been infiltrated and even supplanted, and cannot be accessed without the mediation of that image. The media of photography, film, and/or video can get inside one's experience in this way (I also think here of the studies which have shown that people who grew up in the age of black and white film reported dreaming in black and white, while more recently people have reported dreaming in colour[31]). In *Vertigo*, W. G. Sebald writes of Stendhal's shock when he came to realise that one of his most vivid memories had been infiltrated like this:

Beyle writes that for years he lived in the conviction that he could remember every detail of that ride, and particularly of the town of Ivrea, which he beheld for the first time from some three-quarters of a mile away, in light that was already fading. There it lay, to the right, where the valley gradually opens out into the plain, while on the left, in the far distance, the mountains arose . . . It was a severe disappointment, Beyle writes, when some years ago, looking through old chapters, he came across an engraving entitled *Prospetto d'Ivrea* and was obliged to concede that his recollected picture of the town in the evening sun was nothing but a copy of that very engraving. This being so, Beyle's advice is not to purchase engravings of fine views and prospects seen on one's travels, since before very long they will displace our memories completely, indeed one might say they destroy them.[32]

With characteristic scholastic horror, Sebald hits here on a common experience, and perhaps we could say that in the twentieth century this problem became endemic (and that now it is practically impossible for us to avoid it by refusing to purchase engravings of fine views). Of course, the problem also works in reverse (this is the sense that most interests Benjamin): seeing an image of something before actually encountering it can influence our experience of, and distance us from, the object in question. The easy example is the *Mona Lisa*: one might say that it is now impossible really to see this painting (this is almost literally true, in that it attracts massive crowds of tourists, many of whom, interestingly, will be taking photos of the painting), that there is a disappointment that comes with encountering it, a feeling of not having encountered the real thing. Photographic and cinematic reproductions of reality have a paradoxical effect on us: they simultaneously offer us views of reality, of the world as it is in itself, while also working to remove those things from us, making an unmediated experience of reality impossible. The ubiquity of images characteristic of our culture is both a cause of and response to our desire for reality; in being given what we want, we are distanced from it. The pleasures and anxieties of film and photography are bound up with how they purport to solve problems of knowledge while simultaneously exasperating them.

These understandings of philosophy and film allow me to pitch the idea of 'film as philosophy' in a particular way. Like Paisley Livingston, I think there are reasons to be dubious of certain of the claims that have been made for film-philosophy. I am unconvinced, for instance, of the full philosophical usefulness (if not the accuracy) of the idea one finds, for example, in Julian Baggini[33] and Jerry Goodenough[34] (and also with a more pedagogical slant in works by Chris Falzon[35] and Mary Litch and Amy Karofsky[36]): because of its imagistic, narrative, sonic, and other powers, film is able to present ideas with greater affective force than written texts have often been able to achieve; thus films can provide an important supplement to philosophical argument, helping to illustrate – or even provide a certain kind of experiential evidence for[37] – philosophical theses. This notion (which often relies on a rough and ready version of Wittgenstein's say/show distinction[38]) is itself somewhat Platonic, relying as it does on an opposition between artistic *mythos* and philosophical *logos* (even as it gives it the contrary evaluative spin, regarding the affective powers of cinema as something to be welcomed rather than rejected[39]); thus it flirts with admitting that the medium specific propensity of film is just to provide an affective accompaniment to 'real', in principle discursively paraphrasable, philosophical work, and so maintaining the distinction between thinking and feeling that film-philosophy, in its most compelling moments, has promised to overcome. Unlike Livingston[40] (and others such as Thomas Wartenberg[41]), however, I am also wary of the idea that a film's philosophical interest is to be found in the ideas or problems with which its directors and/or writers have imbued it.[42] First and most obviously, such intentionalist theories tend to raise problems of authorship (problems that are particularly intense in the case of the inherently collaborative process of filmmaking); secondly, and as Damian Cox and Michael Levine point out,[43] restricting ourselves to this notion effectively shuts down the possibilities that arise as a direct result of what *exceeds* authorial intention, those aspects of a film which call out for philosophical reflection not because but *in spite* of what a director or writer may have intended (*Taste of Cherry* actually presents a useful example: given the film's title and Kiarostami's handling of Badii's conversation with him, it may be plausible to imagine the director himself 'sides with' the man who tells the humanistic story about mulberries – yet this is perhaps not the most interesting way of understanding what the film has to say and show philosophically); third and most importantly, this understanding of the film-philosophy relationship does not get at the *specifically cinematic nature of cinematic thinking* (as Livingston himself is very happy to acknowledge). To put all this another way: I want to regard film as having more than the mere capacity to illustrate – or provide an affective (or simply more entertaining) supplement to – philosophy, yet I want to resist the notion that film's philosophical power consists in its ability to present theoretical content that could itself be fully paraphrased in written philosophical discourse. Cinematic thinking is a specific kind of thinking (and it really is thinking).

This would seem to commit me to what Livingston has influentially called the 'bold thesis' in the philosophy of film: "the conjunction of the idea that films can make an original contribution in philosophy, and the idea that this contribution can be achieved primarily if not entirely through means exclusive to the cinematic medium".[44] And this would, in turn, seem to pin me on the horns of the dilemma he claims it raises:

> either support for the bold thesis depends on a claim about a cinematic contribution that cannot be paraphrased and so can be reasonably doubted, or it rests on a contribution that can be paraphrased, in which case the clause about medium specificity is betrayed.[45]

For Livingston, the idea that has been so attractive to film-philosophers – that cinema has a special propensity for thought – is actually the Achilles heel of their entire programme. If the thinking that goes on in film is specific to the capacities of the medium, then how could it be made discursive? And if it can't be made discursive, then what use is it to philosophy, whose medium is language? The film-philosopher who wants to insist on medium specificity will end up committing himself to a kind of obscurantism, insisting on some ineffable experience of thinking that takes place exclusively in films. And as Livingston says, "it is fair to ask whether such appeals to experience can offer good grounds for believing that a significantly new idea, general thesis, or argument has emerged".[46]

Yet of course, it is possible to question Livingston's characterisation of the 'bold thesis', which smacks of philosophical entrapment. One of his explicit targets here is Stephen Mulhall, whose *On Film* is in some ways a foundational text for the programme of film-philosophy, at least as it has been practised over the past decade. Perhaps the first thing to note is that Mulhall does not formulate his own understanding of film-philosophy quite as 'boldly' as Livingston implies he does. Here is one such formulation from Mulhall's book (and which Livingston himself quotes):

> I do not look to these films as handy or popular illustrations of views and arguments properly developed by philosophers; I see them rather as themselves reflecting on and evaluating such views and arguments, as thinking seriously and systematically about them in just the ways that philosophers do. Such films are not philosophy's raw material, nor a source for its ornamentation; they are philosophical exercises, philosophy in action—film as philosophizing.[47]

It is a provocative passage, but look at the descriptions of film-philosophical practice: Mulhall writes of film as 'evaluating' and 'reflecting on' philosophy, as 'thinking seriously and systematically', and of 'philosophy in action'.

Compare this with Livingston's query as to how, given the condition of medium specificity and the problem of paraphrase, we could ever really know whether a film presents a 'new idea', 'general thesis', or 'argument'. Livingston, as is clear enough, is working with a relatively traditional idea of philosophical work, understood as the articulation of arguments regarding how it is with the world: philosophy as theory building. Mulhall, on the other hand – and this is part of his own inheritance from Cavell – has a broader and in many ways subtler notion of it.[48] In the reply to his critics included in the most recent edition of *On Film*, he asks: "must our acknowledgment of reason's claims on us always take the specific form of giving reasons in support of our opinions or our 'symbolic representations' (which I take to mean something like our 'view' or 'vision') of the world?"[49]

Now we can see the ambiguity in Livingston's term 'original contribution'. If an original contribution is a new theory or argument for a particular view of the way things are, then it is pretty easy to see how the bold thesis founders; however, things are far less obvious if 'contribution' could mean, say, an instance of therapeutic philosophical practice founded on "the wager . . . that we can inhabit our life of and with language otherwise".[50] Here it is worth invoking Mulhall's useful distinction between philosophy understood as the provision and assessment of reasons for and against particular views, and philosophy understood as reflection on the very "shared space of thought" in which disagreements arise in the first place. "Sometimes", he writes,

> we want to, or need to, or simply do, reconceive that space, by finding a new way of thinking about the topic – one that reorients both participants to the dispute by altering their sense of what stances are available to them with respect to its topic.[51]

Such a conception of philosophy should deflate the bold thesis and shift the terms of the debate on cinematic thinking. The problem of paraphrase will no longer seem so intractable, as we are no longer committed with the same force to the idea that there is some philosophical 'content' to be found in a particular film (a content that will have to be 'translated' into language in order to become properly philosophical), the previously so intuitive notion that a philosophical film must been seen as proposing new ideas or theses that it is the film-philosopher's job to discover and somehow translate. Yet we can remain committed to a version of the thesis of medium specificity, holding that the kind of thinking that can happen in films remains specifically cinematic – and indeed that this is precisely why it is of such interest to philosophy, why the creation of film somehow seems to have been "meant for philosophy".[52] I should emphasise that this must be understood as a type of philosophical practice: the therapeutic contribution of a film is not a content to be extracted and paraphrased but something the film *does*, something it achieves on and with us. Bringing this out in philosophical writing is a matter of attentive description: rather than capture in language the new idea or theory a film has put forward, the task is to give an elucidatory account of the work the film has done on one in provoking, rebuking, and deflating sceptical theorising.

This is not to deny the importance of narrative and character; nor is it to ignore the political and cultural contexts of films. It is simply to say that these are not the domains in which the medium specific philosophical propensity of film does its work. And this, of course, is not to deny that these domains can be philosophically salient. It is just to say that when they are, this salience is not medium specific (because of how it deploys narrative and character, some novels have profound philosophical significance, but they are less equipped for the type of philosophical work that films can carry out).[53] In the following pages, then, I will make a number of arguments regarding the philosophical salience of narrative and character, as well as the political and cultural contexts of Kiarostami's films. My claim will be that, by following up on the connection between film and problems of knowledge, Kiarostami is able to draw a particular kind of philosophical significance out of narrative and character, and to undo philosophical commitments and fantasies with significant political and cultural purchase. This requires interpretive accounts of narrative and character, as well as philosophically attentive description of a film's philosophical effect. (The exception that proves the rule here is *Five*, which does away with narrative and character, thus isolating the anti-theoretical philosophical propensity of film with particular clarity.)

It may seem that saying film has a medium specific philosophical propensity born of its relationship to reality implies accepting old-fashioned and/or implausible claims regarding the nature of cinema. In particular it may seem to require accepting a strong claim regarding the essence of film, of the necessary and sufficient conditions of something's being a film – necessary and sufficient conditions which, moreover, would have to be located in the physical nature of the cinematographic apparatus (whether in cameras, film stock, or whatever), and its attendant capacity to record what happens automatically.[54] But my account of the philosophical propensity of film relies on no such claim. It relies on our beliefs and practices regarding film and its relationship to reality. More specifically, it relies on the fact that film has a problematic relationship to reality: that we (sometimes) treat cinematic images as though they possess an indexical relationship to what happens, yet cannot come to a convincing general account of precisely how and why. Imagine a world where our beliefs and practices regarding cinematic images have changed so substantially that we no longer regard them as bearing any significant relationship to reality, any tendency to record what happens in it (though I would suggest it is more difficult than many seem to think, perhaps one can imagine such a state of affairs emerging out of the pressure of digital technologies). In such a world, there would not be film-philosophy in my sense, because film would not provoke sceptical or anti-sceptical theorising. So this account relies on the *tension* between film and reality, such that if the tension were to be released, it would no longer stand. This is why I do not take this account to trouble my claim to be doing anti-theoretical philosophy. The account does not require a convincing overarching theory of the relationship between film and reality. On the contrary, it relies on there being no such theory.

Some may wonder what is left for philosophy if it pulls out of the game of theory building. And to certain ears, the above claims about how it can reorient us, transform our sense of the possible, or open up new paths for thinking may sound a bit romantic, woolly, or even empty. Part of what I want to demonstrate in this book, then, is exactly what an explicitly anti-theoretical film-philosophy *can* do. Kiarostami's films do not really present a "systematic vision of the world".[55] Rather, the thinking we can bring out of them is deflationary or even destructive: it wants to get us reflecting on our very desire for an overarching vision (and, one might say, get us *looking* instead). I will not be trying to unearth a robust philosophy from Kiarostami's films as a whole or any of his films in particular; instead I want to think with his films about the practice of philosophising itself, about what it can and can't achieve. Throughout this book, I want to remain open to the possibility that film may actually challenge or even rival philosophy, and thus – like any true rival – that it could provoke philosophy into changing itself. The philosophical significance of film consists less in its ability to make a positive contribution to philosophical theorising than in how it challenges, beguiles, goads, and resists it. And this general tendency or power of cinema, I hope to show, has been exploited in a fascinating, charming, and often devastating way by Kiarostami.[56]

I say 'devastating' in part because philosophical therapy carried out in the spirit of Wittgenstein must be distinguished from what could be called *consolation*. It is very easy to caricature (whether intentionally or otherwise, whether as a detractor or supporter) the motivations and stakes of philosophical therapy. To console is to give solace – to soothe or to comfort – and especially to alleviate grief or disappointment. Kiarostami's films are not consoling in this way. Indeed the films achieve what they do precisely in virtue of their *capacity to disappoint*, setting us up with a desire they end up liquidating. Yet they do not simply show us how to come to terms with our epistemological limitedness, or how to adjust to the fact that we will never find the philosophical peace we seek, or whatever. The disappointment in question is not simply the result of having what we want withheld – our being shown that we're not going to get it – but of a demonstration that we didn't really know what we wanted, because what we (thought we) wanted was always already chimerical. It is not that we do not need or can do without the purchase on reality we were seeking (that we should happily remain sceptics, or at least get used to it), but that it is unclear what it would mean to get such purchase in the first place, and so that the sceptic's words (and those of his opponent) do not make the sense he thinks they do. This explains why the destruction is enlivening and freeing. At the risk of paradox, we could describe it as a destruction that destroys by not destroying, or in Wittgenstein's terms, as a destruction that destroys only *Luftgebäude* (literally: air-buildings).[57] In this context, the problem with consolation is that it leaves intact – assumes the meaningfulness and solidity of – the structures in which it offers solace.

What does it mean to say the sceptic's words do not make the sense he thinks they do, or that philosophical therapy works by destroying what we had wrongly thought was meaningful? There is a tradition in Wittgensteinian philosophy in which claims like this are deployed with great self-assurance, where philosophers become something rather like nonsense cops, bent on policing authoritatively the border between sense and meaninglessness. In his attack on Cavell – which, it should perhaps be said, appears not to have been made in bad faith – Malcolm Turvey takes the philosopher to task for his understanding of Wittgenstein. Specifically the critique centres on Cavell's claims about scepticism, which Turvey says he sets up as "an underlying principle of *all* of Wittgenstein's later philosophy".[58] Now in a certain sense Turvey is perfectly correct, as Cavell does think problems of scepticism are basic for the later Wittgenstein. But this is not necessarily the same thing as saying, as Turvey wants to say Cavell does, that it is an *Urphänomen* in Wittgenstein's own sense of the term: a "preconceived idea that takes possession"[59] of the person using it, such that it comes to "describe any and all phenomena, whether or not such phenomena are suitable candidates for such a description".[60] For Turvey, Cavell's fixation on problems of scepticism actually demonstrates just how untrue to Wittgenstein he is, for the aim of his later philosophy was to break our attachments to full-blown theorising of this sort. Now this is roughly fair, as far as it goes, as an account of the later Wittgenstein, but it is not fair to Cavell.

Turvey's critique appears to turn on Cavell's phrase 'the truth of scepticism', which he interprets uncharitably and quite literally to mean something like 'scepticism is true'. But it should be obvious that Cavell does not mean it like this; a better way of understanding it would be to say that Cavell uses 'the truth of scepticism' similarly to someone using a phrase like 'there is truth in every joke' or 'well, there may be a grain of truth in that' (Turvey also writes of Cavell's tendency to refer to scepticism as 'undeniable', once again crudely equating this with 'truth' *tout court*). It is not that 'scepticism is true' is true; rather, it is that scepticism contains a grain of a truth that it ends up distorting, which is that the human relation to the world is epistemically unassured, or (put another way) that our relation to the world *as such* is "not one of knowing"[61] (if you want to push the metaphor further, imagine an oyster which, irritated by a grain of sand, secretes calcium carbonate around it in an attempt at quarantining it: the grain remains, but it has become unrecognisable). If scepticism is *undeniable*, it is not because it is true, but because it is beguiling and (in certain contexts, particularly philosophical contexts) seemingly unshakable – and so impossible to deny satisfactorily. Of course, this is not to say that 'scepticism is false' is true either, for the very attempt to deny that scepticism is true already cedes too much. Turvey writes:

> it is very hard to find anywhere in Wittgenstein's later writings – and certainly in the *Investigations* – where Wittgenstein argues that scepticism is either 'true' or 'false' (or a combination of the two). And the reason why it is so hard, I suspect, is because Wittgenstein's overwhelming and repeatedly stated (and enacted) concern in his later writings is with questions of sense and meaning, *not* with making arguments about what is true or false.[62]

Once again, this is fair enough as an account of Wittgenstein, but all of it is also true of Cavell, whose own overwhelming and repeatedly stated concern is with sense and meaning over truth and falsity, too. The difference between Turvey's Wittgensteinianism and that of Cavell hinges on the nature of this concern: for Turvey, it appears, the task of the therapeutic philosopher is to know the difference between sense and nonsense, and call out the latter when he sees it (hence his own dismissals of Cavell's lapses into alleged senselessness); for Cavell things are more complex. As Conant writes in an article on Cavell's reading of Wittgenstein:

> according to Cavell, what the early Wittgenstein calls the logic of our language and what the later Wittgenstein calls grammar is not the name for a grid

of rules we lay over language in order to point out where one or another of its prescriptions are violated.[63]

For Cavell, there is no pre-determinable set of criteria that we can apply to sentences in order to sort the meaningful from the meaningless. Further, we cannot simply dismiss scepticism as nonsense and expect it to go away – in a sense, we have to start by taking it seriously, and in particular by acknowledging the hold it has on us, which cannot be loosened so brusquely. Conant describes the reader of Wittgenstein as moving from "a psychological experience of entertaining what appears to be a fully determinate thought . . . to the experience of having that appearance (the experience of there being any such thought) disintegrate".[64] What Turvey's approach ignores, we might say, is the first stage in this process: the reader has to entertain genuinely a sceptical thought if its disintegration (or as I have termed it, liquidation or destruction) is to have force. This is why Cavell writes in the way he does (and Turvey is not alone in finding him opaque), why he spends so much time in *The Claim of Reason* entertaining thoughts that, by Wittgensteinian lights, we may have to regard as properly meaningless. Yet this is also true of Wittgenstein's own writing, and in particular of the role of the interlocutor in the *Investigations*, who responds again and again to Wittgenstein's statements with incredulity, defiance, and disbelief, never satisfied with the philosopher's procedures. Yet the interlocutor plays a crucial role in the book; he is more than a foil; he gives voice to the disquietudes that grip philosophers, oscillating between certainty and defeat. As an example, consider the interlocutor's exasperation during one of Wittgenstein's famous excurses on the concept 'game' (where he shows that we cannot delimit the set of necessary and sufficient conditions for gamehood): "But if the concept 'game' is uncircumscribed like that", the interlocutor responds, "you don't really know what you mean by a 'game'."[65] The aim, as usual, is that the reader will come to recognise herself in the interlocutor here: that he says precisely what the reader cannot help but think. This is why it is not enough simply to dismiss scepticism as nonsense. The reader must come to see just how seductive nonsense can be, how inclined she is to entertain it. As Mulhall writes, "[w]hat Wittgenstein detects in his interlocutor's impatience is the influence of a false necessity";[66] we need to do something more than simply point out the falsity in order to loosen the sense of necessity. This is what both the *Investigations* and *The Claim of Reason* are designed to achieve. It is also what I take Kiarostami's films to achieve.

To be fair to Turvey, he does identify a potential problem in his attack on Cavell. This is not the place to construct a full defence of Cavell's philosophy, but the problem is worth acknowledging, because it is one that could conceivably be raised against my own programme in this book. It is that it is possible to be disingenuous in one's claim to be doing non-doctrinal, anti-theoretical philosophy. This, I take it, is really at the root of Turvey's criticisms of Cavell: for the former, the latter claims to be forgoing theoretical commitments, yet his work – and this may seem especially true of *The Claim of Reason* – appears to advance a theory of scepticism. Obviously very much hangs on just how we interpret the word 'theory' here. Cavell does not claim, and I do not claim, to be doing philosophy without advancing any general claims at all. Indeed, partly following Cavell, I want to advance a number of claims about philosophical scepticism: that it contains a grain of truth; that we have a tendency to deny and, as a result, distort this truth; that this tendency takes a virulent and desperate form in modernity; that film, because of its specific features, has a particular capacity to provoke sceptical theorising; that for this very reason film, at least some of the time, can provide a singularly powerful rebuke to such theorising; that film can thus be regarded as doing real philosophical work. The point is that these are claims about the limits of – and the unacknowledged forces driving – philosophical theorising. Saying that scepticism has a deep hold on us, that sceptical or anti-sceptical theorising leads us to speak or write words that lack purchase on the world, or that film has a special relationship to sceptical problems, is not the same as advancing a full-blown sceptical theory (or a full-blown anti-sceptical theory). This is how I understand Wittgenstein when he writes that "[i]f one tried to advance *theses* in philosophy, it would never be possible to debate them, because everyone would agree to them."[67] The remark strikes as counterintuitive because we are used to philosophers debating each other endlessly; it implies that philosophers who take themselves to be advancing theses are not really doing so at all, and so must instead (unbeknownst to each other, and presumably themselves) be speaking emptily. If this claim is itself a thesis, then it is a thesis about philosophers, not a thesis of the type philosophers mistakenly take themselves to debate – which is to say, not a thesis *in* philosophy. Wittgenstein does not argue against philosophical theses or philosophical claims to truth, but rather wants to show, through philosophical analysis of a different and non-theoretic sort, that they are not substantial enough to debate in the first place, not solid enough to pit oneself against. This is a way of explaining why Mulhall expresses such disappointment in certain of the replies to the first edition of *On Film*, writing that "even those responsive to its concerns tend not to engage in any detail with the specific readings of particular films that make up the bulk of the book itself . . .".[68] If one claims to be doing film-philosophy non-doctrinally – and to have identified in certain films non-doctrinal insights of deep philosophical significance – then the real weight must be placed on one's engagements with the films themselves. The proof of the claim, in other words, will be in the doing – and the doing, by its nature, must be attentive to the specificities of the individual case. "It is not that philosophy is to be brought as such to an end", Cavell writes, "but that in each case of its being called for, it brings itself to an end".[69] My readings of Kiarostami's films get their bearings from certain (sceptical) philosophical problems, but they are not meant simply to show how the films illustrate those problems – they are not primarily *interpretive* in quite that way. I want to account philosophically for what happens in them, and for what happens to those problems in them.[70] This means attending to how each film calls for philosophy, and its end, in its own way. The dissolutions of sceptical problems I want to claim these movies achieve will never be fully binding or definitive for philosophy: all they can do is repeatedly bring it to its own limits. Yet this repetition is neither compulsive nor monotonous. By their nature as anti-theoretical, the philosophical achievements of these films are irreducibly specific.

In Chapter 1 I turn to 1999's *The Wind Will Carry Us*, Kiarostami's first (and perhaps best) film after *Taste of Cherry*. This movie – which follows a filmmaker and his crew as they try to make a documentary in Siah Dareh, a village in Iranian Kurdistan – intensifies Kiarostami's trademark reflexivity, following up complexly on the question of what it means to document reality on film, and problematising our desire for the exotic and the authentic. This is an especially interesting move given that Kiarostami was rapidly gaining recognition in 'the West' when he made the movie; it is particularly relevant for me as a white, English-speaking philosopher claiming to have found something important in the work of an Iranian filmmaker. Extending and critiquing Nancy's work on Kiarostami, I argue that the unsettling power of this film stems not from its ability to return us to some (purportedly) pre-modern experience, but from how it undermines modernity's fantasies about itself (and indeed about pre-modernity). It thus provides a subtle but decisive rebuke to orientalist tendencies on display in the international reception of Kiarostami's films, as well as the claims from some Iranian critics – including Hamid Dabashi and Azadeh Farahmand – that they deliberately perform a kind of exoticism. Kiarostami's cinema presents an education in looking, in seeing things differently. It can help us think what it would be to stop wavering between a fantasy of unmediated access to reality and horror at finding it lacking.

After finishing *The Wind Will Carry Us*, Kiarostami made two feature-length movies on video: *ABC Africa* in 2001, and *Ten* in 2002. The films stand out among his works because of how political they are. At the same time, these films are marked by an idiosyncratic blend of the factual and the artificial, documentation and experimentation: they are neither 'mockumentaries' nor 'docudramas', yet they are far from being traditional documentaries. *ABC Africa*, to which I turn in Chapter 2, is about the AIDS crisis in Uganda and its devastating effects on children. As I try to show, part of the philosophical interest of the film consists in how it refuses standard tropes of political documentary cinema and the conceptual vocabulary of much of documentary theory. Indeed Kiarostami claims to have discovered the video camera's capacity to record 'absolute truth' while making *ABC Africa* – a surprising claim that I want to make sense of. While deeply reflexive, the movie is not content merely with demonstrating the partiality of the documentarian's claim to truth; rather, it works to dissolve metaphysically inflated oppositions between subjectivity and objectivity, partiality and neutrality. This allows it to evoke a rare kind of solidarity.

I turn to *Ten* in the third chapter. Working through the political complexities of Iranian society via stunning performances from non-actors playing themselves, *Ten* is interested in a particular kind of moral claim: one that emerges out of Kiarostami's crafty handling of questions regarding the reality of what happens in the film. Through a series of intrusive formal techniques, Kiarostami creates a sense of intense realism while troubling the very category, such that the viewer is consistently unable to say whether or not what is conveyed on screen is real or staged. Are we watching people playing roles or going about their daily business? Is what is said scripted or unscripted? Are the situations depicted on screen real, or has Kiarostami arranged them? The film evokes the ordinary with a singular intensity: not through (the pretension of) eliminating artifice, but through a complex foregrounding of it. It can help us clarify the connection between moral claims and propositions, imagination, and belief.

In Chapter 4 I turn to 2003's *Five*. Shot on digital cameras, the movie is split into five episodes, each (or so it seems) consisting of a single long take. At first blush, the film appears to add weight to the canonical reading of Kiarostami as a filmmaker concerned with the dignity and drama of the quotidian. I do not reject this reading, but refine it by following up on the questions *Five* raises about its own status: what was arranged here, and what was genuinely 'discovered'? Further, what is the difference between arrangement and discovery, the staged and the natural? What is contemplation in cinema, and what is its relation to realism? Complicating Roland Barthes's notion of *punctum* and Michael Fried's concept of theatricality, I argue *Five*'s foregrounding of artifice allows it to achieve a certain kind of realism: one attentive to the non-epistemic nature of the claim reality makes on us.

Chapter 5 is about 2008's *Shirin*, the final instalment in the experimental period that opened with *ABC Africa*. It consists almost entirely of shots of the faces of women as they appear to watch a film in a cinema. The women seem intently rapt in the film they are apparently watching: an adaptation of the twelfth-century Persian tragedy *Khosrow and Shirin*.[71] Working to clarify how *Shirin* treats absorption, I want to bring out the grounds and stakes of a provocative claim by Fried regarding cinema and theatricality. Connecting Fried's argument to a central idea from Negar Mottahedeh's remarkable study of the visual logic of Iranian cinema – that a significant (albeit unintended!) effect of rules regarding modesty and the depiction of women in Iranian film has been to render it a "woman's cinema"[72] – I develop an account of how *Shirin* upsets sceptical fantasies of voyeuristic spectatorship.

Chapter 6 turns to 2010's *Certified Copy*. This relatively (and deceptively) 'mainstream' film – which begins with a lecture on the importance of repro-ductions of works of art – raises philosophical questions regarding love, mar-riage, reality, and artifice. It shows the relationship between these questions and film's connection to problems of scepticism, specifically in this case the problem of other minds. Inviting while simultaneously refusing the possibil-ity of our taking it as a member of what Cavell has called the 'comedy of remarriage', *Certified Copy* also asks what it means for a film to be a member of any particular genre, and of the remarriage comedy in particular. With this reflexive aporia – as well as its deliberate narrative incoherence and refusal to answer basic questions regarding the protagonists – the film leads the viewer into an epistemological impasse. Yet from here we can perhaps be granted a new perspective on scepticism, and the loss it seems to figure.

The final chapter turns to 2012's *Like Someone in Love*. Against Gilles Deleuze's claim that the task of modern cinema is to restore our belief in the world, I suggest that modern scepticism stems not from a lack of belief, but more fundamentally from a kind of belief in belief. Drawing on John McDowell's recent work, I develop an account of cinematic absorption that does not rely on the idea that, to be moved by cinematic images, we must somehow be led to entertain their propositional content. The problem with such a claim is not simply that it falsifies our relationship to cinematic images: it is also that it falsifies our relationship to reality. The film follows a Japanese call girl as she develops an unlikely relationship with a man old enough to be her grandfather. It finishes abruptly. It shows that that our relation to the film image is not primarily one of supposing, believing, imagining, or knowing, but something uncannier.

It was not feasible to treat all of Kiarostami's features, so a word is in order regarding my choice of films. There are three reasons for my decision to focus on his recent cinema. First and least interestingly, it has allowed me to write about movies that – simply in virtue of their recentness – have been given less attention in the extant English-language literature on Kiarostami,[73] and which the reader will find easier to obtain. Second, there is the fact that treating films made sequentially – rather than chopping between different moments in Kiarostami's career – allows me to do greater justice to the links between them, and so to the iterative process of inquiry at the heart of the filmmaker's project. I alluded to the aesthetic commitment motivating the third reason earlier in my discussion of *Taste of Cherry*, when I described its infamous coda as a kind of watershed. Without wanting to discount the significance of a masterpiece like *Close-Up*, the films of the Koker Trilogy, interesting works from the 1980s such as such as '83's *Fellow Citizen* or '89's *Homework*, or remarkable pre-Revolutionary films like 1977's *The Report*, it may be worth distinguishing between an 'early' and a 'mature' Kiarostami. By 'early' I have in mind all those works leading up to and including *Through the Olive Trees*; by 'mature' I have in mind those works from *Taste of Cherry* onwards. *Taste of Cherry* can rightly be regarded as crucial not only because of its inherent brilliance and importance but because of the light its coda throws on the filmmaker's wider project. It definitively shows he is interested in something much more than rehashing neo-realism in an Iranian context.[74] Indeed this is why it so divisive: it is an aesthetic point of no return after which we can no longer simply regard his films as poignant studies of the life and struggles of ordinary Iranians. Complicating these tendencies, it shows the depth of Kiarostami's interest in the philosophical enigmas that turn up in the act of filming the world.

Notes

1. The in-car dialogues that form the core of the film were never carried out between the film's actors; rather, the scenes were filmed separately, with Kiarostami himself standing in (or really, sitting in) for Badii or the relevant passenger, working in a partially improvised fashion to lead his interlocutors in conversation (see Saeed-Vafa and Rosenbaum, *Abbas Kiarostami*, 31–2 and Naficy, *A Social History of Iranian Cinema Volume 4*, 191–2; Kiarostami would use a similar technique again in *The Wind Will Carry Us* (see Saeed-Vafa and Rosenbaum, *Abbas Kiarostami*, 36 and the interview with Kiarostami later in the book (111)). Apparently Kiarostami also used another method for the sake of greater naturalness and realism: terrifying the actor playing the young soldier by hiding a gun in the glovebox, before asking him to open it (109). Yet we should probably be a little careful of such stories: in an interview with *Indiewire*

in 1998, Kiarostami told Anthony Kaufman that he had him discover a knife covered in pomegranate juice! Kiarostami said there:

> Whatever reaction you see from him is a true reaction. Including when I wasn't telling him what we wanted him to do. Including one time where in the dashboard of the car, I told him, "Could you give me a box of chocolates from the dashboard," and there was a knife in there with some pomegranate juice on it, so he thought we had killed someone – so that was how we got the kind of horrified reactions you see from him in the film. ('Abbas Kiarostami Speaks about *Taste of Cherry*')

As Alberto Elena notes (see *The Cinema of Abbas Kiarostami*, 13–16), Kiarostami seems to like making misleading – or at least, inconsistent – statements in interviews.

2. Hamish Ford ably captures the strange horror of this scene:

> An absolute evacuation of hopefulness and immobilising lack of purpose is suggested, more abstract than embodied despite the always 'real' nature of the entirely unglamorous portrayal of 'being-in-the-world' on screen. The sequence is most centrally suggestive of ruins through an enormous and poetic opening out of the symbolic death imagery already so strong in the film, reaching a point of self-conscious plasticity. Here are a flood of images more clearly than ever now intimating entropy and earthly material burial: the unusually bold and clear shadow-play on the dust-covered quarry wall of Badii's body in spectral form being eaten up by the earth-moving machinery; our observation of his gaze, first from outside then entering it as a point-of-view shot, into a grilled trap through which fall rocks in a seemingly random and 'meaningless' process; the human shadow-figure now explicitly cast across, and therefore associated with, the vertiginous ground of rubble, bars and invisible abyss; the dominance of autumnal oranges and browns thanks to the ubiquitous dusty, 'lifeless' earth; and finally, the almost complete envelopment and gradual disappearance of our human figure as the air fills with yellow dust, coming to erase Badii and then the camera's entire field of vision. ('Driving into the Void', 13)

3. Price, 'Imagining Life'.
4. Price, 'Imagining Life'.
5. As Rosenbaum puts it:

> Though it invites us into the laboratory from which the film sprang and places us on an equal footing with the filmmaker, it does this in a spirit of

collective euphoria, suddenly liberating us from the oppressive solitude and darkness of Badii alone in his grave. (Saeed-Vafa and Rosenbaum, *Abbas Kiarostami*, 30)

6. See Elena, *The Cinema of Abbas Kiarostami*, 87–8.
7. As Dabashi puts it (in a book named after the movie):

> The spectator is . . . put in the bizarrest of situations, a succession of fact and fantasy, in which one knows one is watching a fiction (Kiarostami's *Close-Up*) that is based on fact (Sabzian's real story) that is based on fiction (Sabzian pretending to be Makhmalbaf) that is based on fact (Makhmalbaf as a leading Iranian filmmaker) that is based on fiction (Makhmalbaf making fictional stories in film) that is based on fact (the reality that Makhmalbaf transforms into fiction). (*Close Up*, 67)

8. Nancy, *The Evidence of Film*, 22.
9. Though the term is widely used by critics, Kiarostami rejects it. See Elena, *The Cinema of Abbas Kiarostami*, 107–8; see also Cheshire, 'Taste of Cherry', which notes that Kiarostami sees the grouping as arbitrary because it is based on an "'accident' of place" alone; see also the remark in Saeed-Vafa and Rosenbaum, *Abbas Kiarostami*, 23.
10. The film presents a number of these ontological mix-ups of type and token. For example, Ahmed also mistakes a pair of trousers on a washing line for an identical pair owned by his friend, and encounters a man who shares his friend's name but turns out not to be his father.
11. Here is Kiarostami on the making of the film:

> In June 1990, an earthquake of catastrophic proportions jolted northern Iran, killing tens of thousands of people and causing unbelievable damage. Immediately, I decided to make my way to the vicinity of Koker, a village where four years earlier I shot *Where Is the Friends House?* My concern was to find out the fate of the two young actors who played in the film but I failed to locate them. However, there was so much else to see . . . I was observing the efforts of people trying to rebuild their lives in spite of their material and emotional sufferings. The enthusiasm for life that I was witnessing gradually changed my perspective. The tragedy of death and destruction grew paler and paler. Towards the end of the trip, I became less and less obsessed by the two boys. What was certain was this: more than 50,000 people had died, some of whom could have been boys of the same age as the two who acted in my film (the two boys at the end of this film may be taken as substitutes for the

original pair). Therefore, I needed a stronger motivation to go on with the trip. Finally, I felt that perhaps it was more important to help the survivors who bore no recognizable faces, but were making every effort to start a new life for themselves under very difficult conditions and in the midst of an environment of natural beauty that was going on with its old ways as if nothing had happened. Such is life, it seemed to tell them, go on, seize the days . . . (quoted in Elena, *The Cinema of Abbas Kiarostami*, 92–3)

12. Elena's wider discussion of the trilogy in *The Cinema of Abbas Kiarostami* is invaluable (see 92–117).
13. Nancy, *The Evidence of Film*, 26.
14. Lippard, 'Disappearing into the Distance and Getting Closer All the Time'.
15. I have borrowed this phrase from Robert Sinnerbrink and his excellent *New Philosophies of Film*.
16. Wittgenstein, *Philosophical Investigations*, §420; 107e.
17. See Descartes, *Discourse on Method and the Meditations*, 100.
18. Cavell, *The World Viewed*, 22. Rothman – who writes on Cavell on film but who is arguably (and perhaps for this reason) one of the most effective interpreters of his philosophy of scepticism – puts it like this:

    The 'unhinging of our consciousness from the world' is a historical event and also a mythical event, like the biblical fall from grace, the social contract (or, for that matter, Jacques Lacan's mirror stage). Picture it as a spiritual and psychological and political cataclysm that presents us with a new fact, or a new consciousness of an old fact, about our condition as human beings. We now feel isolated by our subjectivity. It is our subjectivity, not a world that we objectively apprehend, that appears present to us. ('Film, Modernity, Cavell', 320)

19. Cavell, *Philosophy the Day after Tomorrow*, 245.
20. Cavell, *The Claim of Reason*, 241.
21. Cavell, *The Claim of Reason*, 241.
22. Rothman and Keane, *Reading Cavell's* The World Viewed, 261.
23. Cavell, *The World Viewed*, 188.
24. This chimes with a claim from Philipp Schmerheim: that "the very process of filmmaking as well as the ontological constitution of the film medium already raises questions about the relation between the so-called 'reality' of filmic worlds and the (physical) reality their creator and spectators are a part of" (*Skepticism Films*, 8). Alongside this ontological

claim, Schmerheim offers another explanation for contemporary manifestations of the sceptical impulse in cinema, arguing they are responses to "the manipulative power of digital technology, computer-generated imagery, and comprehensive control of worldwide information flows" (11).

25. André Bazin gives voice to this intuition in one of his remarks on painting: "No matter how skillful the painter, his work was always in fee to an inescapable subjectivity. The fact that a human hand intervened cast a shadow of doubt over the image" ('The Ontology of the Photographic Image', 12).

26. For a survey of various attempts at developing such an account in the philosophy of photography, see Costello and Phillips, 'Automatism, Causality, and Realism'.

27. Cavell, *Contesting Tears*, 90.

28. Cavell, *The World Viewed*, 189.

29. Benjamin, 'The Work of Art in the Age of its Technological Reproducibility', 255 (original emphasis).

30. Benjamin, 'The Work of Art in the Age of its Technological Reproducibility', 255.

31. The experimental philosopher Eric Schwitzgebel is interested in the vagaries and inaccuracies of the reports we make of our subjective experiences. In 'Do People still Report Dreaming in Black and White?' Schwitzgebel tried to replicate findings from studies in the 1940s and 1950s which showed people reported dreaming in black and white, and found an increase in reports of coloured dreams. Instead of taking the reports at face value, however, he concludes that subjects must be mistaken about this feature of their dreams. Whether this is right or not, the change calls out for explanation.

32. Sebald, *Vertigo*, 8.

33. Baggini argues for this in 'Alien Ways of Thinking', his sympathetic yet in some ways highly critical review of Mulhall's *On Film*. He writes:

> Film, like philosophy, can represent reality to us truthfully in such a way as to make us understand it better or more accurately than before. Film can achieve this through fictions which can include non-literal modes of representation such as metaphor, whereas philosophy usually achieves the same goal through more literal modes of description.

34. Goodenough develops such an understanding of film-philosophy in his introduction to his *Film as Philosophy* collection. One of his examples is

Alain Resnais's *Last Year at Marienbad*, which he claims refutes Cartesian scepticism "not by *telling* us, not by demonstrating the falsity of a proposition involved or the invalidity of a logical move, but by *showing* us, by showing us solipsism in action" ('A Philosopher Goes to the Cinema', 25).

35. See *Philosophy Goes to the Movies*, which Falzon bills as "an introduction to philosophy that turns to films in order to illustrate and discuss philosophical ideas and themes" (1).

36. See their *Philosophy through Film*, which introduces a series of problems in philosophy on the basis of the idea that "a film . . . may be used to present philosophical positions and arguments in a way that is both rigorous and entertaining" (2).

37. This is how Baggini understands the philosophical power of Kurosawa's *Rashomon*. He claims the film

> demonstrates the possibility of what might, simply described, seem impossible, and in showing it in the context of a story that is all too believable – all-too human in its moral and emotional projection, fallibility, and self-serving bias – it provides evidence that this is actually the way the world is. ('Alien Ways of Thinking')

38. Baggini writes: "Philosophy thus *says* while film *shows*, its form of showing being distinct from more literal forms, such as demonstration" ('Alien Ways of Thinking'). Goodenough puts it similarly in reference to *Blade Runner*:

> Film leads us into the lives of the replicants and the humans, and makes us realise that the former are closer to our real life than the latter, and thus it tells us something about ourselves and *our* world. (It approaches the problem cinematically via Wittgenstein's insistence on showing rather than telling.) ('A Philosopher Goes to the Cinema', 23)

39. This is clear enough in Goodenough's account of *Blade Runner*:

> *Blade Runner* does not just make us intellectually aware that the replicants satisfy many possible conditions for personhood. Rather, by sharing this portion of their lives, by seeing their quest for life, the way they relate to each other, by comparing it with Deckard's job of termination, we must inevitably come to *feel* for them, anger, fear, lust at one particular point, and, at the end, perhaps a profound pity and admiration . . . The film allows us to perceive

and to feel, to experience what is happening at a deeper and more persuasive level than any mere written account could manage. ('A Philosopher Goes to the Cinema', 4; original emphasis)

40. For Livingston, "some film-makers indeed use the cinematic medium to express philosophical ideas of sufficient complexity to be of interest in the context of philosophical teaching and research" (*Cinema, Philosophy, Bergman*). He cashes out this claim with a detailed and quite compelling reading of Bergman's project in later chapters (see 125–200). For a powerful critique of Livingston's intentionalism, see Sinnerbrink, *New Philosophies of Film*, 129–31.

41. Wartenberg writes: "When I say that a film philosophizes, it is really a shorthand expression for stating that the film's makers are the ones who are actually doing philosophy in/on/through film" (*Thinking on Screen*, 12). However, he also allows that film is capable of carrying out a type of thinking that is specifically cinematic. In particular he argues films have the ability to set up thought experiments, writing for instance of "film's deployment of widely recognized and quite standard philosophical techniques – most notably the thought experiment – to justify seeing the artform as capable of philosophical thinking" (136).

42. In *Philosophy of the Film*, which was written well before the current wave of scholarship on film-philosophy, Ian Jarvie puts this slightly differently. He argues that a film's philosophical content is not to be found on the level of authorial intention but rather in the culturally inherited philosophical presuppositions that are unwittingly installed into it via its makers. He writes:

> Why do writers, directors, etc. put philosophy on to film? The answer is simple: they do not. *Philosophy puts itself in their films.* That is to say, behind such a work there always lurk the personal or cultural presuppositions about reality, morality, etc. implicit in our thought and action. One job of philosophy is to expose and to criticize those presuppositions. (26)

43. See Cox and Levine, *Thinking Through Film*, 13–15.
44. Livingston, *Cinema, Philosophy, Bergman*, 4–5.
45. Livingston, *Cinema, Philosophy, Bergman*, 5.
46. Livingston, *Cinema, Philosophy, Bergman*, 23.
47. Mulhall, *On Film*, 3–4.
48. See Sinnerbrink, *New Philosophies of Film*, 141.
49. Mulhall, *On Film*, 89.

50. Mulhall, *Philosophical Myths of the Fall*, 112. Sinnerbrink finds another way out of Livingston's dilemma, insisting (surely with great plausibility) that film-philosophers can be understood not as paraphrasing the philosophical content of films, but as advancing philosophical *interpretations* of them (see *New Philosophies of Film*, 132–5).
51. Mulhall, *On Film*, 90.
52. Cavell, *Contesting Tears*, xii.
53. This is a way of differentiating my account of film-philosophy from more expansive and pluralist accounts developed by authors such as Sinnerbrink and Steven Rybin. For Sinnerbrink, resistance to the idea of film-philosophy is indicative of a "too-narrow or reductive conception of what counts as philosophy", and an overly "hierarchical" understanding of the "relationship between philosophy and art" (*New Philosophies of Film*, 117). Following Mulhall, he argues films can contribute to philosophy through

> questioning, reflecting, or disclosing through vivid redescription salient aspects of a situation, problem or experience, typically through the artful use of narrative, performance or cinematic presentation (montage, performance, visual style or metafilmic reflection). Film contributes to questioning or rendering problematic the background assumptions that we draw upon in framing specific arguments or making philosophical claims, whether on generally recognized themes or on what we might understand film to be. (133)

While I find these claims compelling, my account of film-philosophy insists more trenchantly on medium specificity. On Sinnerbrink's account, it appears it is not easy to draw a strong or qualitative distinction between the philosophical contributions of films and the philosophical contributions of (say) novels, insofar as both can "disclose novel aspects of experience, question given elements of our practices, and open up new paths for thinking" (141). This is not to say that Sinnerbrink neglects medium: for him it seems that cinema's immersive and affective qualities grant it particular philosophical powers too, by making its world-disclosures more engaging and so potentially more transformative. Once again, I find nothing to disagree with here (except to say that novels can also be immersive and engaging). But I am arguing that cinema has a *distinctive* philosophical propensity born of its connection to problems of knowledge, and its tendency to provoke and rebuke sceptical theorising: a deflationary propensity that can work in concert with the transformative aesthetic and philosophical potentials of works of art in general.

Rybin develops an account of the philosophical significance of

Malick's cinema in similar terms. Citing Sinnerbrink's claim that Malick's work calls upon film-philosophers "to experiment with the aesthetic disclosure of alternative ways of thinking and feeling, acting and being, in our relations with nature and culture" (Sinnerbrink, 'Re-enfranchising Film', 43; quoted in Rybin, *Terrence Malick and the Thought of Film*, xix), Rybin writes: "In Malick's films, traces of other possible ways of doing and making, and of thinking and feeling, open up for his dedicated viewers an engagement with the philosophical ways of thinking and feeling and doing and making, that we bring to the screen" (xix). It is notable that, in setting up these claims, Rybin weakens the condition of medium specificity. He writes:

> Works of film-philosophy almost always buttress their analyses of favoured filmmakers with speculation on the nature of the film medium, and philosophical aesthetics, more generally, often aims at situating artistic mediums through their timeless essences. But film, an inherently unstable object, resists such efforts. (xvii)

As I argue in the next paragraph, there should be no problem with making strong claims regarding medium specificity while accepting that media 'essences' are not timeless, stable, or ahistorical.

54. For a fascinating treatment of these and related intuitions, see Doane, 'The Indexical and the Concept of Medium Specificity'. Doane writes:

> indexicality has become today the primary indicator of cinematic specificity, that elusive concept that has played such a dominant role in the history of film theory's elaboration, serving to differentiate film from the other arts (in particular, literature and painting) and to stake out the boundaries of a discipline. (129)

55. Falzon, *Philosophy Goes to the Movies*, 12. In this respect, Kiarostami's films are unlike those of someone like Ingmar Bergman, which (as Livingston shows quite convincingly) can be read as the creations of a filmmaker who was concerned to articulate a particular philosophical worldview (see *Cinema, Philosophy, Bergman*, 125–60).

56. This is to say that Kiarostami's movies

> 'resist theory', evoking an experience that is aesthetic and reflective . . . Such films communicate an experience of thinking that resists philosophical translation or paraphrase; thus they are films where we encounter what I am calling

> *cinematic thinking* in its most intensive and dramatic forms. (Sinnerbrink, *New Philosophies of Film*, 142)

57. Wittgenstein, *Philosophical Investigations*, §118; 41e.
58. Turvey, 'Is Scepticism a "Natural Possibility" of Language?' 119.
59. Wittgenstein, quoted in Turvey, 'Is Scepticism a "Natural Possibility" of Language?' 118.
60. Turvey, 'Is Scepticism a "Natural Possibility" of Language?' 118.
61. Cavell, *The Claim of Reason*, 45.
62. Turvey, 'Is Scepticism a "Natural Possibility" of Language?' 123.
63. Conant, 'Stanley Cavell's Wittgenstein', 63–4.
64. Conant, 'The Method of the *Tractatus*', 423.
65. Wittgenstein, *Philosophical Investigations*, §71; 29e.
66. Mulhall, *Inheritance and Originality*, 82.
67. Wittgenstein, *Philosophical Investigations*, §128; 43e.
68. Mulhall, *On Film*, 88.
69. Cavell, 'Declining Decline', 263.
70. Wittgenstein:

> we may not advance any kind of theory. There must not be anything hypothetical in our considerations. We must do away with all explanation, and description alone must take its place. And this description gets its light, that is to say its purpose, from the philosophical problems. (*Philosophical Investigations*, §109; 40e)

71. The film had a precedent for Kiarostami: *Where is My Romeo?*, a short he made for the 2007 Cannes-commissioned anthology *To Each his Own Cinema*. This film uses the same technique, yet here the women are apparently watching the final scene from Franco Zeffirelli's *Romeo and Juliet*.
72. Mottahedeh, *Displaced Allegories*, 5.
73. The filmography included in *Abbas Kiarostami*, the book co-authored by Mehrnaz Saeed-Vafa and Jonathan Rosenbaum, concludes in 2003; the one included in Elena's *The Cinema of Abbas Kiarostami* concludes in 2002; Nancy's study of the Iranian director was completed in January of the year 2000; few academic articles have been published to date on *Shirin* and *Certified Copy*; at the time of writing none have been published focussing on *Five* or *Like Someone in Love*; the only article focussing exclusively on *ABC Africa* was an earlier version of the chapter included in this book.
74. Kiarostami's cinema has often been read in neo-realist terms. For one important recent example, see Weinberger, 'Neorealism, Iranian Style'.

CHAPTER 1

The Wind Will Carry Us: Cinematic Scepticism

The Wind Will Carry Us opens with long takes of a car zigzagging down a road in the Iranian countryside. This is to say it opens with a sequence that, to anybody who knows Kiarostami's work, will be immediately recognisable as typical of it: *Life and Nothing More* returns repeatedly to such sequences, and ends with a brilliant one; similar sequences turn up in *Taste of Cherry*; *Through the Olive Trees* concludes with a long shot of its protagonists zigzagging across a field; we see the hero of *Where is the Friend's Home?* meandering in a similar pattern on more than one occasion.[1] The opening of *The Wind Will Carry Us* is intriguing and, with its muted semi-screwball feel, a little funny.[2] By the time of this film's release, however, the car on the screen was bringing this cinematic history with it. Thus there is something self-aware or even self-effacing about these opening shots: Kiarostami seems to be referring here not only to his previous works but also perhaps to himself, and to the by then internationally recognisable figure called 'Kiarostami'. So if Nancy is right to say that long aerial takes are Kiarostami's "signature"[3] – that "a person or a car's zigzagging path on the background of an unchanging landscape traverses, like a single trajectory, five movies . . . and turns into an emblematic summary of all the films"[4] – then perhaps this is complicated here by a certain irony. We might say that in the opening sequence of this film Kiarostami *cites his own signature*, with all the philosophical complications such a gesture entails.

For what is it to cite one's signature? As Jacques Derrida argues, there is an ontological tension in the very idea of a signature, insofar as it is both an "absolute singularity" – a means by which we secure the identity of a particular person, plus a singular event of writing – and an eminently "repeatable, iterable, imitable form".[5] Despite the fact that it is singular, a signature is also a repetition of previous signatures, and it becomes what it is through iteration (such that, for instance, one's first ever signature cannot really qualify as such). But how much iteration does it take? And won't each iteration also be a unique, singular event? To clarify this problem, suppose someone untrained in forgery has a stamp made of a handwritten example. If fraudulence were to be suspected, the fact that the signature being employed is always exactly the same could give the game away: the signature, if it is to convince, must be more than a mere replica (we might say that it has to have life in it). Yet of course, an untrained attempt at forging by hand will not convince either, because it will be insufficiently similar to the original. To be convincing a signature must be both singular *and* an imitation. So what is the difference between a signature and the citation of one? The meandering car is a giveaway that we are watching a Kiarostami film yet – deployed as it is with such deliberateness at the very beginning of *The Wind Will Carry Us* – it also gives away the fact that Kiarostami's signature is, like any signature, a technique that can be repeated, indeed mimicked or parodied. Importantly, however, this self-effacing gesture is not *simply* ironic, and it is not only in spite but also partly because of its reflexivity that the opening sequence of this film in particular is intriguing and gently funny. After all, gestures of self-effacement – ironic nods to the mediality of cinema – are perhaps as typical of Kiarostami's films as long aerial takes of zigzagging cars. If Kiarostami is citing his own signature, then that is also his signature.

Thus I want to disagree with Nancy when he writes that "there is no room for reflexivity"[6] in Kiarostami. Yet I share the intuition that appears to be guiding Nancy's statement. For what's remarkable about Kiarostami's films is how his relentless problematisation of the real, his dogged insistence on the mediality of the cinematic image, does not leave us in a free play of significations unmoored from their referents: if the opening sequence of this film is an example of 'intertextuality', it is not because Kiarostami is spruiking some pop postmodernism. Further, his repeated attempts at turning our attention to his medium do not produce a *Verfremdungseffekt*. Or if they do, this distancing is highly absorbing. Note that this is not really paradoxical: my argument is that it is through undoing our desire for access to the world that Kiarostami can reconnect us with it. It is like being brought back to reality, though an epistemologically deflated, mundane one (which is to say, not the one we were wishing for). Kiarostami evokes the real – or as Nancy wants to say, provides a certain kind of *evidence* for it – in upsetting our claims to know it with certainty and security.

As the car rolls along, we hear a conversation between its passengers. The men are arguing over directions, looking for a single tree that should mark the point at which they need to turn. This is a bit comedic, for of course there are many 'single' trees on these hills.[7] When the characters see the tree (they do so before we do), there seems to be no mistaking it: someone exclaims, "It's so big!" about ten seconds before a large tree appears on screen. A couple of minutes into the sequence the shot changes, and we are given views from the side windows of the car: farmers are working in the open field. If these are point of view shots, they are multiply framed and reframed: we are watching a screen, seeing through the eyes of characters who are themselves viewing the field through the frames of the windows. Add to this the fact that this shot – the view out the side window from the interior of a moving car – is another of Kiarostami's signatures (as is the fact that our characters are lost and need to ask for directions): we are not only viewing the point of view of the characters as they view the scene through a window; we are also provoked to recall a series of similar views from Kiarostami's other films. The dialogue during the sequence is remarkable not only for its humorous repetitiveness, but also for how that repetition has the weird effect of getting what is said to seem to address the viewer. Here are some of the phrases we hear during this sequence:

> This is the winding road. We're on it.
> I'll tell you what there is.
> It says a tall, single tree. There are a lot on this hillside.
> There it is. There, look, a single tree!
> Jahan, take a look. Up there!
> What a big tree! Look at it.
> Two more up there. It's beautiful!
> Slow down a bit.
> Someone's been sleeping!

On the one hand, then, we have extreme reflexivity: self-effacement; self-reference; views of views of views of views. Mobilising the unique powers of film to raise questions of knowledge, Kiarostami goads us into the epistemological quagmires characteristic of modern scepticism, in which our claims to know the world – indeed our very sense of being connected to it – are called into doubt. On the other hand, we have a demand being made of the viewer: *look!* It is a call to presentness; it demands you wake up and pay attention (in his essay on Kafka, Benjamin quotes Malebranche: attentiveness as the "natural prayer of the soul"[6]). At one stage during the sequence someone quotes a poem:

> Near the tree is a wooded lane,
> greener than the dreams of God.

The couplet is taken from Sohrab Sepehri's 'The Token', a line from which provided the title for *Where is the Friend's Home?* Yet the reference to the earlier film does not undermine this film's poetics (on the contrary). Once again the same confluence is at work: Kiarostami is both reminding us of the constructedness of his images, and demanding that we attend to them intensely. As Elena puts it: "The complex mirror game created by Kiarostami . . . consistently breaks away from the mannerist dimension from which these experiments with form usually suffer."[10] If Kiarostami distances us from the real, it is a distancing that draws us into new intimacy with it.

The film follows its protagonist as he takes a film crew to the village of Siah Darreh in Iranian Kurdistan. They are there to shoot what is apparently some kind of documentary, intending to record the traditional funeral and mourning rites surrounding the death of an elderly woman, rites in which female mourners use their fingernails to scar their own faces. This is disclosed very slowly, however. At first all we know is that they have some kind of arrangement to meet a local man, who has sent his young nephew out to intercept them on the road. The boy says he knows why they are in town, but they request he keeps it secret, chucklingly telling him to tell anyone who asks that they are looking for lost treasure. The decision to withhold vital information is characteristic of the film, which also never shows us the faces of a number of important minor characters (including those of the protagonist's crew), and never quite takes us into the interior of a house. Problems of knowledge are thus reflexively foregrounded from the start: just as the protagonist and his crew do not know where they are in the opening sequence, we spend much of the film in the dark as to who they are, what they are doing, and why. The narrative of the film turns on a non-event, for the men quickly realise that the old woman whose funeral they have come to shoot is sick, but not quite dying. So they are forced into morbid waiting, the crassness of which underlines their haughtiness, their tendency to regard the village and its people with a kind of detached arrogance. Much of the 'action' (if that is the right word) thus centres on the filmmaker's time in the village, and how he slowly comes to acknowledge the lives going on around him and the strange beauty of his surrounds. This is punctuated by a number of phone calls from his impatient Tehrani producer, which require him to jump in his car and drive up a nearby hill to get phone reception. A man – whose face we never see – is digging what looks like a grave up there.[11]

One of the most important scenes comes when the filmmaker picks up the local schoolteacher, and speaks with him about the real reason for his presence in the village. Things are ambiguous. The protagonist gives the schoolteacher a ride on the return leg of one of the drives he takes uphill; he has on his dashboard the human femur he found on the hill and, for reasons that aren't clear, decided to keep. This is part of their conversation:

> Schoolteacher: You seem to have problems. One problem!
> Protagonist: Any affair has its own problems.

> S: Anything over a hundred years old is considered an antique.
> P: What are you talking about?
> S: You don't work underground?
> P: Because of this bone, you think we're looking for treasure or antiques?
> S: I don't think that. I'm almost sure of it. You haven't come for the ceremony?

What's strange about the exchange is how the schoolteacher seems simultaneously to affirm two mutually exclusive theories: that the men are in town looking for treasure or underground artefacts; that the men are in town to film the local ceremony. Of course, we don't take him to believe the childish cover story, but he appears to think there is truth in it. In my reading, he is right: the men are in town to film the ceremony, but they have projected something onto it, something that sets it up as treasure-like. For in a sense what they are after is an archaeological remnant – follow Benjamin and call it aura, or follow Cavell and call it an unbreakable connection to the world – a pre-modern way of experiencing, living, and dying. And you might say that this is precisely what they don't get (at least in the form in which they were expecting it), because they eventually leave without obtaining what they (thought they) wanted. For at the end of the film the woman does finally die, but the filmmaker seems to have lost interest in whatever it was that was originally driving his project. He watches part of the ceremony, snaps a few photographs, then drives away, stopping to throw the bone into a stream. The film closes abruptly now, and once again with another signature: its only non-diegetic music starts up in this closing sequence. The key question of the movie seems to be: what happens to the filmmaker such that he loses interest in his project? Why does he abandon his plans to film the ceremony?

I take the conversation with the schoolteacher to have been crucial (and in this scene he really is an educator, not only for the local children but for the filmmaker and by extension us the audience; note that Kiarostami himself cut his teeth as an educational filmmaker working for Kanoon, or Iran's Institute for the Intellectual Development of Children and Young Adults[12]). In particular I am referring to what the schoolteacher says when asked of his opinion of the ceremony. He tells a story about his own mother, who participated in the ceremony after the death of her husband's boss's cousin. The woman ended up competing in a game of one-upmanship with the other women whose husbands were employed at the factory – she was left with two terrible scars as a result. And of course, it was for show, not what we would usually take as a real expression of grief (for the schoolteacher's mother had no connection to the dead man), but rather a desperate attempt to preserve her husband's job by winning favour with the factory owner: the ceremony is, as the schoolteacher puts it, "connected to the economy". "There was a lot of competition at the factory between the men to hold onto their jobs . . .", he says. "[E]veryone displayed themselves, pushed themselves forward to please the boss." So the ceremony the filmmaker came to document is – no doubt like his own work as a filmmaker – compromised by its position in an economic system predicated on the exploitation of abstract labour, in which people appear to one another not as subjects but as objects, and in which one subset of people – those who do not own the means of production – must sell their labour power to the subset of those who do to survive. This world puts serious pressure on the very possibility of authenticity, understood as a commitment to living for oneself rather than acting for the eyes of others. Robert Pippin characterises it in terms of a worry "that everything that one does might not be one's own but rather everywhere already has taken account of others", a worry about "social independence and genuine individuality".[13] What I take the filmmaker to have learned, then, is that his own idea of a village populated by locals living in an entirely different world was a projection: that the image of tradition with which he was working – a particular image of a pre-modern experience of meaning, perhaps even a mythical experience of it – is a kind of fantasy. It is not quite that the villagers are inauthentic, but that they too are subject to the same pressures and worries, and so that they live in his world.

Interestingly, a similar projection appears to be at work in Nancy's own reading of the film (his refusal to acknowledge the reflexivity in Kiarostami is probably symptomatic of it). At a few moments in *The Evidence of Film*, he opposes "worlds where presence . . . is first of all given (as it is in the symbols and rites of traditional bereavement) . . ." to "the world that is ours", a world in which "the given is withdrawn".[14] While Nancy is undoubtedly right to say that Kiarostami is interested in the "relation between ancient Iran and modern Iran"[15] (indeed it is useful to read the whole film in terms of the problem of modernity, or of so-called 'modernisation'), it seems to me that part of what makes this work so compelling is how it gets us thinking about the modern image of tradition. Things are more complicated than Nancy makes out. Arguably what Kiarostami shows is that there really is no completely unmediated experience of the world, no world where "meaning is given"[16] in the way Nancy implies; rather, this is a fantasy internal to our own world, in which we feel that things have become irremissibly mediated. This is not to say that things weren't different in pre-modernity. It is to say that the image we project onto pre-modernity is a fantasy of capitalist modernity, perhaps one that is constitutive of it. There is something like a myth of myth at work here: an idea that there are people out there who live without distance from themselves, who are fully immersed in some communally based system of meaning. What the filmmaker wanted, and us with him, is not necessarily belief itself, but the belief that others believe, the certainty that others have the certainty he feels he lacks (in psychoanalytic terms, this would be a form of fetishism). What the filmmaker gets instead – both in this scene and over the course of the film – is a lesson about his own desire to capture tradition on film, about his own fantasy of what it is and where to find it. Indeed the schoolteacher's lesson places the protagonist and his camera in a curious proximity to the factory owner, as the 'audience' for the staging of the ceremony. In a certain sense the protagonist is positioned not only as having projected his own desire onto the villagers who were to perform for his camera, but also as complicit in the destruction of its object, insofar as his desire for authenticity will effectively turn the villagers into performers, if he is to pursue his project.[17] (Consider here how the factory owner may have responded to the women participating in the ceremony at his cousin's funeral, for one imagines he was aware they were performing for him. Was he impressed by their ceremony in spite of this fact? Or perhaps impressed *because* of it?[18])

It should go without saying that this is our education too, and the filmmaker stands in for our own desire as viewers attracted to – or perhaps indeed repelled by – a certain type of film. Remember that this movie followed *Taste of Cherry*, which won the Palme d'Or, marking an important moment in the Western reception of Kiarostami, as well as for his standing in his home country.[19] As he accepted the prize on stage at Cannes, Kiarostami received a kiss on the cheek from Catherine Deneuve – an event that saw him condemned by conservative critics in Iran[20] (timing was no doubt an important factor here, as debate had already been developing on the place of Iranian films in Western festivals,[21] and Khatami – former Minister for Culture and political moderate with a policy of entering into dialogue with the West – was about to be elected as President of the Republic, despite fierce opposition to him in Parliament[22]). Yet Kiarostami's Iranian detractors are by no means all conservatives. Placing Kiarostami's reception in the context of the country's domestic politics, the tastes of international art house audiences, and the new economic and diplomatic ties established in the late 1990s between Iran and the West, Farahmand argues that Kiarostami's films betray "political escapism".[23] For Farahmand, their detached protagonists disavow "equal exchange and a compassionate involvement"[24] with other characters, standing in for Western viewers and their aloof enjoyment of exotic subjects and locations. Kiarostami's cinema thus protects its Western viewer from "any shock, unpleasant encounter or guilty conscience. He can maintain his distance and remain uninvolved, be fascinated, securely appreciative of the exotic locales, as though viewing an oriental rug, whose history he does not need to untangle."[25] She goes on: "the internationally adored Iranian auteur is not popular in his home country, where he is commonly suspected of 'making films for foreigners'".[26] I want to read *The Wind Will Carry Us* – with its reflexive critique of the desire to capture authentic, pre-modern culture on film – as a rebuke to certain orientalist tendencies in the international reception of Kiarostami, and a riposte to his Iranian critics, especially those who see him as deliberately performing an ethnographically inclined 'Third World' exoticism.

This polemical aspect of the film is perhaps at its clearest – and most equivocal – during the underground sequence, where the protagonist pursues a young woman into the dark space beneath her home, ostensibly in search of the milk she has been providing to the worker on the hill, who appears to be her lover. As the young woman milks her cow for him, she silently refuses his repeated requests that she step into the light and show him her face – a loaded demand for unveiling made all the more questionable in coming from a relatively wealthy and powerful Tehrani man.[27] As Dabashi registers, the scene is especially significant in the context of Kiarostami's wider body of work, which has often insisted on "not showing . . . private moments . . .".[28] Perhaps we should also read it as a deliberately ambiguous challenge to censors,[29] toying with restrictions on the depiction of unveiled women (for we never quite see her face[30]), and women indoors with men to whom they are not married or related (for are they really indoors?).[31] In any case, the scene is charged to say the least, which may explain Dabashi's own remarkably hostile reaction to it. Taking the protagonist – I would say rightly – as a "vulgar man intruding into the private passions of young woman", he describes the scene as a "brutally accurate picture of dehumanization",[32] and even as "one of the most violent rape scenes in all cinema".[33] Thus for Dabashi *The Wind Will Carry Us* is the film in which Kiarostami "sealed his own doom":[34] a "nightmarish negation of every film he ever made . . .".[35] Coming as it does from a critic who elsewhere praises Kiarostami in equally extreme terms,[36] one wonders how to explain this reaction. Less surprising – because consistent with her other claims – is Farahmand's critique of the protagonist as a "tourist/reporter peeping into holes and caves while awaiting a woman's death".[37] On my reading, Dabashi and Farahmand are right in their judgements, but they do not really apply to Kiarostami's film. Rather, *they are judging the film its protagonist is trying to make*, which is precisely an "ethnographic study of a village" carried out by a "First World anthropologist".[38] While misdirected, then, the responses are quite understandable, insofar as

the protagonist's film is where Kiarostami stages just the kinds of fantasies –
and one can see how they could appear nightmarish to an Iranian – that these
critics rightly attack. As Mottahedeh puts it, specifically in the context of a
discussion of *The Wind Will Carry Us*:

> It is evident . . . in the multiple reflexive moments that refer to questions of
> ethnographic fetishism and in representations of 'the exotic' throughout his
> work that Kiarostami is resistant to, and indeed critical of, any posture that
> attempts to situate his characters as ethnographic tallies of dress and custom
> among primitive culture in the Third World.[39]

In missing this film's critical and reflexive, anti-ethnographic edge, Dabashi
and Farahmand have really sided with Kiarostami himself. Part of the philosophical and political value in *The Wind Will Carry Us* consists in the links
it draws between the orientalist, indeed colonial desire to capture an exotic
culture on film and the sceptic's desire for certainty, as two inflections of our
craving for the real. When he stops projecting onto the villagers, the protagonist is giving up an attachment that is not merely metaphysical.

This is achieved through an education in looking. The protagonist learns
that what he was looking for does not exist, or does not exist in the form he
thought it did. In learning this, he also learns to look differently at what is
right in front of him. What's interesting about the filmmaker's education is
that it seems to be coextensive with the breakdown of his fantasy: as he stops
projecting onto the villagers, he starts to see the world rightly (and vice versa).
This is a look that can take place after the desire for unmediated access has
been given up. In Nancy's parlance, what the filmmaker comes to learn is "a
possibility of looking that is no longer exactly a look at representation or a
representative look".[40] I am referring to the moments in the film in which the
filmmaker's attention is captured by events that, at least in terms of the narrative, are insignificant: a busy dung beetle; mongrel dogs playing in a field; a
boy chasing a soccer ball; an apple as it rolls with haphazard grace; a woman
hanging out her clothes to dry. These moments call out for the filmmaker's
attention, and they do so insofar as they are unimportant or peripheral to
what he wants, incidental to his desire for unmediated access. And again,
what happens to the filmmaker happens to the viewer too: Kiarostami's
strategy, in this film and in his work more generally, is to effect a breakdown
in the viewer's ability to tell the difference between the real and the artificial,
a signature and its citation, the original and the copy, the important and the
peripheral, and so on. The neat trick of his cinema is that it is only by para-
lysing our claims to knowledge in this way that he can bring us out of our

scepticism. Or rather: not out, but through, and all the way to the presentness of the world, unrepresentable – for existence is not a predicate; it is no fact *in* the world; it is not *about* it – but not for that reason ineffable – for it just *is* the world; it is mundane.

This is why I want to resist Nacim Pak-Shiraz's reading of Kiarostami's project, which is also indebted to Wittgenstein, and which also tries to take his films not as illustrations of pre-existing philosophical ideas or theories, but as doing a certain kind of philosophical work of their own.[41] Leaning very heavily on Wittgenstein's infamous conclusion to the *Tractatus*, Pak-Shiraz claims the Viennese philosopher as a proponent of a form of mysticism predicated on drawing a strict border between what can be said and what can only be shown.[42] The problem is not just that this account has been demonstrated to be internally incoherent, relying as it does on claims that it must, by its own lights, regard as nonsensical.[43] It is also that reading Kiarostami as bringing our attention to the limit of the sayable (and in doing so, perhaps, as pointing or hinting beyond that limit) is to inflate his work metaphysically, and in such a way that fails to get at the very ordinariness of what he really has to show. I do not read Kiarostami's as a cinema of the ineffable, and do not see it as proceeding via some cinematic equivalent of the *via negativa* of apophatic theology. He is interested not in ultimate reality but in plain reality. As Dabashi says, what compels in his work is its "stripping of the real from all its violent metaphysical claimants".[44] Placing this in the context of the quasi-neo-Platonism underlying the official ideology of the Islamic Republic, Dabashi writes that "[a]t a time when our entire culture was inundated with the most pernicious consequences of metaphysical violence, [Kiarostami] made the sensual simplicity of the real shine through every distorting layer of metaphysics superimposed on its evident matter-of-factness".[45] To say that Kiarostami educates us in a mode of looking that is not representational is not to say that he teaches us to glimpse unutterable truths. What he gets us to see is just the ordinary itself – or, if you like, life. Nancy puts it quite evocatively:

> The evidence of cinema is that of the existence of a look through which a world can give back to itself its own real and the truth of its enigma (which is admittedly not its solution), a world moving of its own motion, without a heaven or a wrapping, without fixed moorings of suspension, a world shaken, trembling, as the winds blow through it.[46]

In Kiarostami, this mundane and wholly secular world is what we are called upon to acknowledge. As he shows, it is only after our letting go of the desire to know it with certainty, to possess and be possessed by it – which in the filmmaker's case was enacted through a projection of such certainty and possession onto those that were to become his subjects – that acknowledgement can occur.

If acknowledgement is a mode of knowledge, then it is one that brings its limits to light. This is the basis of Wittgenstein's interest in statements of the order of 'I am in pain': it is a quirk of philosophers to take such statements simply as expressing a claim about how things are, and so a claim that could be doubted, as though the proper response to such a sentence is something like 'I believe you.' As Cavell puts it in 'Knowing and Acknowledging': "your suffering makes a claim upon me. It is not enough that I know (am certain) that you suffer — I must do or reveal something (whatever can be done). In a word, I must acknowledge it . . .".[47] In *The Wind Will Carry Us*, the filmmaker learns something similar of the world: that it is only when he has jettisoned his desire to possess it – to have his scepticism cured – that he can come to attend to its presentness to him. Because if the sceptic is right to point out I do not really know if the world exists outside of me, or if others exist, or if my words mean what I take them to, then this lack of surety forms the condition of the possibility of my being surprised by it in the first place (and by others, and by myself).[48] This is not a solution of the sceptical problems characteristic of modernity, but another way of responding to them; to employ Heideggerian terms, it is an ontic modification of the ontological truth that the human relation to the world *as such* is epistemically unassured. It is a modification in which the world is not taken as something in which we believe, and thus as something for which our belief needs philosophical justification – or bolstering through a fetishised relation to an exotic other who believes – but as something with a form and sense of its own, as something that makes a claim on us. If Cavell is right to understand philosophy as "the education of grown-ups"[49] then Kiarostami's is a lesson in looking at the world, and letting it make that claim.

Notes

1. Aerial tracking shots of cars return in *Certified Copy* and *Like Someone in Love*. Devin Orgeron provides an account of Kiarostami's films as exemplars of the road movie genre (see *Road Movies*, 183–99). Elena shows how the motif of the road has been crucial for Kiarostami since his first experiments as a filmmaker (see *The Cinema of Abbas Kiarostami*, 20–1). However, Farhang Erfani argues quite persuasively that things are more complex, reading Kiarostami in Deleuzian terms in order to complicate the notions of movement and journeying in his work (see *Iranian Cinema and Philosophy*, 24).

2. Such sequences in Kiarostami could perhaps be taken as highly subdued – if such a thing is possible – instances of the aesthetic of the "zany" so brilliantly analysed by Sianne Ngai (see *Our Aesthetic Categories*, 174–232). These zigzagging cars and persons may be participating in something like a slowed down, indeed contemplative form of zaniness.

3. Nancy, *The Evidence of Film*, 10.

4. Nancy, *The Evidence of Film*, 24. The five movies Nancy has in mind are *Where is the Friend's Home?*, *Life and Nothing More*, *Through the Olive Trees*, *Taste of Cherry*, and *The Wind Will Carry Us*.

5. Derrida, 'Signature Event Context', 20.

6. Nancy, *The Evidence of Film*, 18.

7. There is probably a joke to be made here about Nancy's *Being Singular Plural* (the central idea of which actually trades on just this paradox).

8. Benjamin, 'Franz Kafka', 812.

9. See Zanganeh, *My sister, guard your veil; my brother, guard your eyes*, 97–8.

10. Elena, *The Cinema of Abbas Kiarostami*, 89.

11. The man – played by Bahman Ghobadi, who worked as Kiarostami's assistant before embarking on his own remarkable filmmaking career – tells the protagonist he is digging a hole for "telecommunications". Though it is not clear exactly what he means by this, I take it as referring to the encroachment on the village of technological modernity (and as such, as another instance of the threat also represented by the protagonist himself).

12. Rosenbaum writes: "Practically all of [Kiarostami's films] qualify in one way or another as didactic works, analogous to what Bertolt Brecht called *Lehrstücken*, or learning plays" (Saeed-Vafa and Rosenbaum, *Abbas Kiarostami*, 9).

13. Pippin, *After the Beautiful*, 92.

14. Nancy, *The Evidence of Film*, 34.

15. Nancy, *The Evidence of Film*, 36.

16. Nancy, *The Evidence of Film*, 40.

17. It may be worth invoking Robert Flaherty's 1922 film *Nanook of the North* here, which records the daily life of an Inuit man and his family. The movie is famous not only for being perhaps the first documentary, but also for how its director staged certain important scenes. As Rothman puts it:

> Flaherty did not, in the manner of a cinéma-vérité filmmaker, simply film Nanook and his family going about their lives. Many actions on view in the film were performed for the camera and not simply "documented" by it. The

filmmaker actively involved his subjects in the filming, telling them what he wanted them to do, responding to their suggestions, and directing their performance for the camera. (*Documentary Film Classics*, 1)

Rothman goes on to argue that the film "is implicated" in the destruction of "Nanook's way of life" because it was sponsored by a French fur company, and so participates in importing into it "the social and economic structures of Western civilization" (2). I wonder, however, if some might regard Flaherty's acts of filming in similar terms, as they effectively required Nanook and his family to perform – rather than simply live – their lives. As I believe Rothman demonstrates, however, this would be an oversimplification, insofar as "Nanook's relationship to the camera, the camera's relationship to him, is part of his reality, part of the camera's reality, part of the reality being filmed, part of the reality on film, part of the reality of the film" (3). Regardless, something profound – and deeply relevant to Kiarostami's own concerns – is captured in that very oversimplification. The field of problems that Rothman is both invoking and attempting to demystify here is like a synecdoche of the metaphysical attachments and desires – as well as the anti-metaphysical lessons – displayed and undergone by the protagonist of *The Wind Will Carry Us*.

18. If the latter, then he must possess a particularly sadistic version of what Fried calls a "sensibility or mode of being . . . corrupted or perverted by theater" ('Art and Objecthood', 168). I treat Fried's concept of theatricality in Chapters 4 and 5.

19. Initially it had been held back from Cannes, apparently on the grounds that it had not already been shown at Tehran's Fajr Film Festival, then a condition of submission (see Elena, *The Cinema of Abbas Kiarostami*, 123). After some negotiation between the Iranian Foreign Minister Ali Akbar Velayati and Cannes director Gilles Jacob, the film was eventually submitted, arriving after the official deadline (see Farahmand, 'Perspectives on Recent (International Acclaim for) Iranian Cinema', 95). Farahmand goes on to highlight a wider issue: "Iranian filmmakers cannot independently submit their work to international festivals and film companies. The task is handled by Iran's public and private sectors through the ultimate authority of FCF" (93). The FCF is the Farabi Cinema Foundation, a state-run non-profit that works under the auspices of the Ministry of Culture and Islamic Guidance. It advises screenwriters on producing scripts for review by inspectors, plays a role in the allocation of production equipment and film stock, controls the acquisition of rights for foreign films, and provides subsidies for select Iranian projects (see 90).

20. Hamid Sadr writes:

> This two-second transgression of Islamic propriety instantly set off a polemical firestorm in Iran. On Kiarostami's return from France a welcoming reception at the airport was derailed by angry fundamentalists; Kiarostami was spirited through customs and out through a side door. (*Iranian Cinema*, 238)

    See also Pak-Shiraz, *Shi'i Islam in Iranian Cinema*, 173.
21. See Devictor, 'Classic Tools, Original Goals', 73–4.
22. For an excellent account of the liberalisation of Iranian cinema during the Khatami period, see Sadr, *Iranian Cinema*, 237–52.
23. Farahmand, 'Perspectives on Recent (International Acclaim for) Iranian Cinema', 101.
24. Farahmand, 'Perspectives on Recent (International Acclaim for) Iranian Cinema', 100.
25. Farahmand, 'Perspectives on Recent (International Acclaim for) Iranian Cinema', 101.
26. Farahmand, 'Perspectives on Recent (International Acclaim for) Iranian Cinema', 103. For a more detailed account of negative responses to Kiarostami in Iran, see Saeed-Vafa, *Abbas Kiarostami*, 50–1.
27. Mottahedeh provides unparalleled analyses of the scene in her fascinating *Displaced Allegories* (see 91–6, 128–30).
28. Dabashi, *Close Up*, 253.
29. For an excellent discussion of the complex role of censorship "as both a prohibitive, excisionary power and a productive, generative one" (173) in pre- and post-Revolutionary Iranian cinema, see Khosrowjah, 'Unthinking the National Imaginary', 128–83. I return to the issue of censorship in Chapters 3 and 5.
30. As Mottahedeh argues, the cinema screen in Iran is regarded as a public space, even when it depicts women in private, such that women must appear covered even when depicted at home (see *Displaced Allegories*, 8–10).
31. This speculation has some weight behind it: censors delayed the film before it was shown at the Fajr Film Festival (see Mottahedeh, *Displaced Allegories*, 96). As Khosrowjah acknowledges, while the new regime augured more moderate cultural policies, censorship codes remained in place, coming instead to be interpreted more liberally (see 'Unthinking the National Imaginary', 171).
32. Dabashi, *Close Up*, 253.
33. Dabashi, *Close Up*, 254.

34. Dabashi, *Close Up*, 252.
35. Dabashi, *Close Up*, 254.
36. Just a few pages earlier Dabashi writes: "In the long and illustrious history of Iranian cultural modernity, from poetry to drama, from fiction to every kind of performing art, no one came close to what Kiarostami ultimately achieved in teaching us *to be* otherwise" (*Close Up*, 251–2).
37. Farahmand, 'Perspectives on Recent (International Acclaim for) Iranian Cinema', 101–2.
38. Dabashi, *Close Up*, 254.
39. Mottahedeh, *Displaced Allegories*, 100. Later she writes that "the decisive underlay of Kiarostami's cinema is a critique of the morbid effects of ethnography . . ." (138).
40. Nancy, *The Evidence of Film*, 10.
41. See Pak-Shiraz, *Shi'i Islam in Iranian Cinema*, 170–2.
42. See Pak-Shiraz, *Shi'i Islam in Iranian Cinema*, 177–80, 183–4.
43. Cora Diamond and James Conant have done the most to challenge such readings, presenting in their stead exemplary accounts that 'resolutely' insist on taking Wittgenstein's statements about nonsense seriously. See Diamond, 'Throwing Away the Ladder' and 'Ethics, Imagination and the Method of Wittgenstein's *Tractatus*'; see Conant, 'Must We Show What We Cannot Say?', 'Throwing Away the Top of the Ladder', 'Elucidation and Nonsense in Frege and Early Wittgenstein', and 'The Method of the *Tractatus*'.
44. Dabashi, *Close Up*, 252.
45. Dabashi, *Close Up*, 251.
46. Nancy, *The Evidence of Film*, 44.
47. Cavell, 'Knowing and Acknowledging', 263.
48. As Cavell puts it in his essay on King Lear: "since we cannot know that the world exists, its presentness to us cannot be a function of knowing" ('The Avoidance of Love', 324). Or as Mulhall writes: "the world's existence – unlike the existence of a given object in the world – is not something in which we 'believe,' not an 'opinion' that we hold on the basis of evidence" ('Can There Be an Epistemology of Moods?' 33).
49. Cavell, *The Claim of Reason*, 125.

CHAPTER 2

ABC Africa: Apparition and Appearance

In *Ten on Ten*, a 2004 documentary featuring ten short scenes in which Kiarostami speaks in a car on his work in filming 2001's *Ten* – itself a ten-part movie featuring short video sequences shot entirely inside a car – the film-maker makes a series of highly provocative statements. This occurs in the context of a discussion of the radical possibilities that he claims opened to him when, starting with that beguiling sequence at the end of *Taste of Cherry*, Kiarostami started using digital cameras. Referring to the production of *ABC Africa* – his first feature-length digital production, and which was shot in Uganda – he says:

> I felt that a 35 mm camera would limit both us and the people there, whereas the video camera displayed truth from every angle, and not a forged truth. To me this camera was a discovery. Like a God it was all encompassing, omnipresent. The camera could turn 360 degrees and thus reported the truth, an absolute truth.[1]

I want to take seriously Kiarostami's claim that his move to digital – which resulted in two of his most morally unsettling movies – allowed him to report absolute truth.[2] This is surprising, even shocking, coming from Kiarostami. After all, *ABC Africa* – the only recent Kiarostami feature we can reasonably safely call a documentary – seems to subvert distinctions between truth and artifice, fact and fiction, the real and the fake, the found and the staged, and so on (distinctions on which some definitions of documentary cinema rely[3]). The statements also jar with certain tropes that have become quite familiar in film and documentary theory: tropes which emphasise the constructedness of the film image, the partiality of the documentarian's claim to truth, the power relations silently bound up in the very act of attempting to report the facts 'neutrally', the inevitability of bias in a filmed account of events, etc.[4] Further, the statements sit uneasily with much of the academic criticism of Kiarostami's work, with its emphasis on the categories of uncertainty, partiality, and ambiguity, and which has lauded the director for the complex ways in which he draws attention to the tenuousness and contingency of cinematic claims to truth through reflexive formal techniques.[5] There are serious questions, in other words, about what to make of this. Were these critics wrong about what Kiarostami is up to in his films? Is there a way of taking seriously what he says here? Or is Kiarostami himself simply being disingenuous, hyperbolic, impulsive, and/or hubristic? I want to try answering the first two questions affirmatively: it is possible to take Kiarostami seriously here, and doing so will require us to nuance our understanding of the filmmaker's project.

Obviously this will turn on how we understand what 'absolute truth' might mean in this context. As such it is worth turning to the scene in *Ten on Ten* in which Kiarostami uses the phrase. Here we see images not only of the director in his car delivering his monologue to camera, but excerpts from *ABC Africa*. As he speaks of returning to Iran, watching the video footage, coming to decide that the ease and comfort displayed by his subjects could never have been achieved if he had used a 35mm camera, that the medium of video allowed access to absolute truth, we see: a child hiding shyly behind a roll of material; footage of Kiarostami himself videoing children as other children watch the footage as he records it; a group of children who play to the camera, pulling funny faces; more children scrambling about to try to get into (or out of) the frame; a woman's face caught in slow motion as she stares directly into the camera; one child jumping up and down in order to enter the shot. In other words what we see is not quite life 'as it really is' among Ugandan orphans, but rather a series of events that are intimately bound up with – indeed events that are in various ways the direct result of – the presence of the cameras in the village. One is tempted to say that we're not seeing life in this village as it is, but life as it is when it is acting up and showing off, responding to the presence of strangers, and performing for – or hiding from – digital images of itself. Not only is there no attempt to mask the artifice inherent in the act of videoing: in fact it is deliberately emphasised (as when, for instance, a shot of Kiarostami videoing is followed up with a shot of his collaborator Seifollah Samadian videoing Kiarostami videoing). So this truth must not be that of an objective account of the facts, if that means a report of how things stand externally to the reporter.

At the same time, however, I want to say that it really is a truth – and not, for instance, simply an acknowledgement of the irreducibly 'subjective' and/ or mediated nature of what it is to screen reality. In that sense, while *ABC Africa* fits in some respects with what Bill Nichols, in his influential taxonomy of documentary styles, called "the reflexive mode of representation",[6] it is nevertheless much more than another attempt at formally enacting a critique of "[r]ealist access to the world, the ability to provide persuasive evidence, the possibility of indisputable argument, the unbreakable bond between an indexical image and that which it represents".[7] In *Documentary Film Classics*, Rothman praises the documentaries on which he writes in the following terms: "They do not deny the possibility of revealing reality in the medium of film; they achieve such revelations even as they reflect on the conditions that make their revelations possible."[8] I want to read Kiarostami's achievement in *ABC Africa* in a similar way: not simply as problematising documentary truth, but also as revealing it, and as revealing it in problematising it. In *Ten on Ten*, Kiarostami quotes Nietzsche's *Beyond Good and Evil*: "That which is truly deep needs a mask."[9] It is this marriage of depth and surface, sincerity and masking, reality and artifice that I want to identify as essential to the documentary evidence presented in Kiarostami's movie. Such an identification may also make it possible to clarify aspects of the ethical and aesthetic problems inherent in documentary filmmaking more generally: the relation between fiction and fact; moral feeling and its connection to matters of fact; questions of evidence, rhetoric, and persuasion. If it helped to generalise, I would say that this is one subset of the problems stemming from that separation of fact and value which plagues – but also appears to have provided a condition of the possibility of – modern philosophy. Part of the intellectual depth of Kiarostami's cinema consists in how it can help us think differently here.

ABC Africa opens with a call: a phone rings as the letters A. B. C. are presented red on black, and rings again roughly in time with the appearance of AFRICA. The titles fade and we hear the sound of printing. The first image is of a fax arriving. The content is read in a woman's monotone. The fax from the Assistant President of the UN's International Fund for Agricultural Development (IFAD) confirms an invitation extended to Kiarostami to travel to Uganda to shoot a documentary on the Uganda Women's Effort to Save Orphans programme, an NGO set up in 1986 to provide aid to Ugandan children living in extreme poverty in a country devastated by colonisation, civil war, and AIDS. The idea is to give the plight of these orphans "greater relevance" and "draw much needed international attention" to it. So far, so standard: an internationally acclaimed director with significant festival clout, some experience in taking commissions, and a demonstrated interest in recording the lives of people (and particularly children) facing poverty and disaster is to travel to Uganda to shoot a film in order to raise international awareness about a terrible social, moral, and political problem. And certain early scenes of the movie come across as intelligible in these familiar terms, such as when we hear from an IFAD representative about the extent of the

Ugandan orphan problem (in 2002 there were estimated to be two million orphans in the country), or when the filmmakers visit a village where they are informed about the organisation's work in teaching local women – many of whom have taken on the burden of care for large numbers of orphaned children – skills relating to financial planning, obtaining an income, and so on. Nevertheless, Kiarostami's personal stamp is obvious from the start: we are treated, for instance, to a series of long takes shot from inside cars, and the movie seems to include more footage of relatively unimportant events than one would expect from a 'standard' documentary (by which I mean, something like IFAD might have been expecting him to make), including many extended takes of women and (especially) children singing, dancing, and playing (as well as some fairly mundane footage of the two filmmakers arriving at the airport, checking into their hotel, chatting to their driver, etc.). In a mainstream expository or observational approach,[10] we might expect that these shots would – if employed at all – be used as background, as a means of establishing setting and perhaps granting the viewer a connection to the ostensible subjects of the film; in Kiarostami's movie, however, the length and sheer quantity of them suggests they are in no way peripheral. Plus with their wobbly handheld framing, the freely associative way in which Kiarostami records them (letting himself be 'distracted'; following whatever turns up), and his use on them of some naff digital effects (including repeated 'snapshot' style freezeframes complete with fake shutter sound effects), these shots are surprisingly unserious, whimsical, and not a little touristic. In other words things are strange: this film is refusing to do what we expect (especially given its subject).

It is worth recognising that the footage presented in the final cut of *ABC Africa* was not originally intended to make it into the film at all. Rather, these images were merely intended as 'travel notes' taken down by Kiarostami and Samadian for the sake of getting an initial sense of their subject; the two were planning on returning to Uganda in order to make the real movie, but on getting home decided that the twenty hours of footage they'd taken was all they needed (with some serious editing work that, as Elena notes, took place over the course of eight months[11]). So this is a movie constructed out of notes for a movie that was never actually made. While this may explain some of the roughness and apparent "artlessness"[12] of the final product, it only raises further questions: why was Kiarostami happy with this preliminary digital footage? Why not go back and complete the original project? More generally, why has Kiarostami largely refused to follow through on the traditional tasks of documentary (presenting facts, gathering evidence, making an argument, persuading the viewer to a certain position, etc.)?

I want to point to two scenes that effectively transform the movie. They occur in near succession. First, the filmmakers visit a hospital in the town of Masaka (described in the film as the 'epicentre' of the AIDS pandemic). The scene is surreal and disturbing: entering the crude building, we see Catholic posters and a calendar promoting abstinence on the walls as we hear the cries of a sick child off screen; we see a series of terrible images in a ward for children; the crying child then appears for a moment, only to be quickly replaced by shots of a nurse joking and laughing; we get more freezeframes (this time of adult nurses, doctors, patients) with fake sound effects. Having already been made intensely aware of the presence of the cameras – and of the ethical questions surrounding these invasive sequences – we now enter a room where the body of a small child is being wrapped in a sheet. Nurses gather up the body; we follow it outside to see it placed on the back of a bicycle and taken away, we presume for burial. The setting then changes abruptly and we are presented with a long sequence featuring hundreds of singing schoolchildren – back on similar ground to be sure, but after the shift in tone occasioned by the hospital sequence it has been defamiliarised, rendered a bit uncanny.

After another road sequence, Kiarostami and his collaborator arrive at the building that is to accommodate them for the night. Following nightfall, we hear a long conversation between them as we view a thick swarm of mosquitoes gathering around an outdoor light. Now we are surprised: the light goes out as the electricity is cut. So begins the most intriguing sequence in the movie, in which Kiarostami and Samadian make their way toward their rooms by torch- and matchlight, musing on the difficulty of darkness and the problems it must cause each night for the villagers they have been videoing ("I can't think of anywhere in the world where sunlight would be more precious"). As we hear Kiarostami fumbling with and opening a door, there is the sound of thunder. As the rumbling builds the other sounds slowly fade away and the screen, which has been entirely dark (or close to it) for some eight minutes, is lit by a series of flashes of lightning – flashes lighting the silhouette of a tree. The sound of rain builds along with thunder cracks as the flashes continue. Then we are surprised again: this time by a dissolve to daylight, and the tree – accompanied by birdsong – now appears fully illuminated. The whole sequence is fascinating and powerful, and not just for the various ways in which it mimics the final video sequence from *Taste of Cherry*. Coming as it does in the middle of the film – and so shortly after the hospital scene – it signals quite clearly that Kiarostami's interest is not exclusively with the facts of the matter surrounding the plight of Ugandan orphans, but with something more ambiguous. As Olivier Joyard remarks, it is clear at this stage that "the deal with [IFAD] is off".[13] This is not to say that Kiarostami ignores the unbearable facts of life for Ugandan orphans, because he does present them; rather, it is to say that he never suggests that they are all he wants to show (even if they are essential to it). The minutes of darkness at the core of the film are connected to this. When the body is wrapped, and when the world reappears in that dissolve to light, the effect is emphatic as well as disorienting.

Kiarostami's question is not how to present the facts in the face of 'information overload' or so-called 'compassion fatigue', of how rhetorics of image and sound can be utilised in order to give those facts emotive purchase on the viewer. Indeed such a model seems to presuppose something that Kiarostami never does: that the viewer, whose sensibilities have been deadened, needs to be prodded and provoked into ethical affectivity. The problem with that model is not so much with the claim that our emotional responsiveness has been mortified, but with the aesthetico-ethical programmes that stem from making that problem central: programmes in which the filmmaker's task is to startle the viewer into responding (as in a certain avant-garde cinema, but also now in the aesthetics of shock sometimes employed in government health and safety campaigns), or to manipulate him, say by attempting to present systemic socio-political problems as moral games of good versus evil (for example, the farce of KONY 2012). These programmes share a commitment to the idea that the facts on their own are not enough, and need to be presented in such a way as to give them weight and punch. Part of the problem with such attempts at resensitisation, of course, is that they are desensitising: perhaps the viewer can be enlivened with shocks or spectacular manipulations, but eventually she will recoil again, becoming deader still (rather like the snail in Adorno and Horkheimer's *Dialectic of Enlightenment*, and which provides, for them, "[t]he true symbol of intelligence"[14]). The other part is with the moral non-cognitivism that may be implicit in that set-up, which takes ethical life to consist in emotional responses to – but which do not provide any rational grounding for making moral judgements regarding – the facts of which the world consists.

Wittgenstein clarified this in his 1929 lecture on ethics. Here he proposed a thought experiment: imagine an omniscient person – someone who knows every fact about the world since the beginning of time – decided to write a big book containing all his knowledge. Such a book would be perfectly encyclopaedic; it "would contain the whole description of the world".[15] Yet such a book, Wittgenstein argued, "would contain nothing that we would call an *ethical* judgment or anything that would logically imply such a judgment".[16] It would seem there is no fundamental difference between a proposition like 'she saw him' and one like 'she murdered him', no difference between 'the stone fell' and 'the stone killed'. In the world there are simply facts, and the moral distinctions we make between them are projections – or so the experiment may seem to show. But of course, it is not right to say that Wittgenstein rejected ethics or the possibility of a moral life; rather, he appears to have thought that the ethical has a different relation to the facts than many philosophers are in the habit of thinking. As such, this should not have to collapse into J. L. Mackie's error theory[17] or the kind of non-cognitivism espoused by the logical positivists and their inheritors;[18] nor should it force us into the claim that the facts need to be made sensational or spectacular. If a complete description of all the facts that make up the world would contain nothing of genuine ethical significance, then either our ethical life is based on non-cognitive emotional responses to what occurs, or it is bound up with something other than the facts. But what else could it be bound up with? What else *is there*?

I want to forward for comparison two, apparently competing sets of theoretical claims. On the one hand, we have the idea that the world, and the objects and relations it contains, exist independently of the representations we make of them, the truth of which is contingent on whether or not they represent those objects and relations accurately. On this model, one knows a fact if one's belief in its being true is justified by the relevant evidence – evidence which, moreover, will have to be located outside the mind and desires of the knower, if one is to avoid the various kinds of bias to which we can be prone. It isn't hard to see how moral non-cognitivism finds its feet from here: on this picture, the notion that there is a fundamental distinction between fact and value – such that statements about the latter lack robust truth conditions, and so must go without robust justification – seems perfectly natural, indeed inescapable, because it sets up facts as external to moral feelings and sensibilities. Distinguishing between facts on moral grounds will thus appear to tell us more about the person drawing the distinction than about the facts themselves: 'the punishment meted out was death by hanging' is in principle verifiable through objective inquiry, and so easy enough to account for; 'the punishment meted out was barbaric' may express a subjective attitude, but says nothing about the punishment *in itself* (where would we go looking if we wanted to verify it?). Value is something we bring to the facts, something interpreters overlay onto them, who thus *take the facts* in one way or another; as such, successful inquiry into the facts of matters will have to be carried out in 'value free' terms, lest one's view of them be clouded. Wittgenstein gives voice to the metaphysical picture underlying this intuition in the *Tractatus* when he writes: "In the world everything is as it is, and everything happens as it does happen: *in* it no value exists . . . ".[19]

The opposing set of claims looks something like this. The very idea of objective inquiry as outlined above is suspect, because it leans on something highly questionable: the assumption that it is possible for human beings to separate their representations of the world from their own subjectivities. Knowing, on this account, can never be pure in the way the claims in the above seem to imply; rather, it is always tainted by the knower's embedment in a political, historical, social, and cultural context. It is impossible for knowers to get outside their own perspectives to see things as they objectively stand (even if natural science must be granted a certain kind of privilege in this regard). Indeed, on this account, any claim to have achieved genuine objectivity is not only misleading, but should itself be regarded as political in a certain important sense. That is because it is an act of subterfuge: the would-be knower shrouds a subjective, politically determined claim in the garb of politically 'neutral' objectivity. Bias is not something we can convincingly claim to have sloughed off, because any truth claim is partly a function of the claimant's particular perspective; rather, the best we can do is to acknowledge our bias, and that our inquiries into the way things stand must always remain relative, to some significant extent, to our own particular epistemic standpoints.[20]

Though these sets of claims are in competition, they both share an underlying commitment to a certain understanding of objectivity. They understand it as requiring us to step out of our own subjective positions in order to view the world dispassionately. Like the description of the world given in Wittgenstein's thought experiment, which would consist of 'just the facts' and so contain no robustly normative content, an objective account is posited here as a neutral report of how things stand externally to the describer. Alice Crary details this notion of objectivity as follows:

> This idea is sometimes formulated in terms of a requirement to survey the world from a maximally abstract (i.e., dispassionate and dehumanized) vantage point . . . [T]o the extent that we take seriously the requirement for an abstract or non-subjective vantage point, we seem obliged to conceive progress toward an objectively accurate view of the world as involving a winnowing process that leaves ever fewer properties with an essential reference to subjectivity.[21]

Crary's metaphor of winnowing is clarifying: this notion of objectivity seems to require that we cast off the subjective elements of our engagements with the world in order to come to an accurate view of it. Despite their apparent differences, both sets of the theoretical claims of which I gave rough outlines above subscribe to this notion of objectivity. The difference, of course, is that the former set of claims implies it is attainable, while the latter set implies it is not. In both cases, getting access to the facts is contingent on a casting off of subjective elements: a casting off that, in the latter set of claims, is revealed as impossible.

Consider again the line from the *Tractatus* I quoted earlier, which channels the metaphysical picture underlying this notion of objectivity. It should be striking that the sentence relies on tautologies: everything being 'as it is', and happening 'as it does happen'. One wants to ask: how *could* things be other than they are, or happen as they do not happen? That is what is confounding about the picture Wittgenstein channels (and so about any debate which turns on it): in a certain frame of mind it seems highly intuitive, even inescapable; but when we try to flesh it out it starts to look beguiling. Just what is captured by the proposition that *everything is as it is*? If a determinate answer to this cannot be given, it is difficult to understand how the inference from it to the claim that there is no value '*in*' the world is supposed to work. Here are the outlines of another potential response to the theoretical debate I have sketched: not to say that one side or the other is right, but to say that both sides are beholden to an incoherent metaphysical picture. And this would apply equally to both, despite the fact that the latter set attacks objectivity: if the image of objectivity underlying the first set is incoherent rather than (true or) false, then the claims of the second set have been pitted against something insubstantial. If the picture of objectivity in question is incoherent, in other words, then it is not quite right to say that we cannot get outside our perspectives on the world to see things as they really are, because it is not clear what it would mean to 'get outside' our perspectives in this way, and so not clear what it means to be unable to. If a task requires something incoherent of us, 'failure' means something different – in fact it means much less – than if it asks something of us that we are unable to perform (think of the difference between asking someone without pen or paper to draw a circle, and asking someone armed with both to draw a square circle: in the former case, we know what it would be like to have the relevant means available). One could compare this with Donald Davidson's remark (which McDowell finds "very unsatisfactory"[22] for perhaps this reason) that "we can't get outside our skins to find out what is causing the internal happenings of which we are aware".[23] But what is the force of this 'cannot'? For what would it mean to get outside our own skins? Davidson can't mean it literally, because even a skinless creature would face the epistemic problem he outlines. But how *can* he mean it?

It is as though we are being asked to see the world without looking at it. And of course, it's not that we *cannot* see without looking. It's that we can give no sense to what it would mean to do it, and so no sense to what it means to be unable to.

In relation to the big book of Wittgenstein's thought experiment, we might ask: will the description of the world outlined in the book contain itself? If so, we fall into an infinite regress of descriptions, as the book will have to describe its own descriptions, and its descriptions of those descriptions, and so on *ad infinitum*; if not, it could never claim to be complete (unless the book itself somehow stands 'outside' the world it purports to describe – but then the world it describes could not be complete). For this picture to cohere, in other words, the act of description must both be included within and excluded from what it thus described. The dilemma I posed earlier between conceiving ethical life as grounded in merely emotional responses to the facts or something other than the facts may be a false one: it only found its feet because it was informed by this incoherent picture of a 'complete description of the world'.

Elena writes that, in *ABC Africa*, "[f]ar from trying to conceal his active role in shooting the film, Kiarostami demonstrates his interference with the real situation around him as soon as he possibly can . . .".[24] While he is right to emphasise Kiarostami's rejection of the procedures of mainstream documentary, there may be reason to doubt the coherence of the metaphysical picture that has nevertheless been presupposed here: that there exists an external realm of facts (what Elena calls a 'real situation'), and which the documentary filmmaker necessarily disturbs with his presence (what he calls 'interference') – a disturbance that is concealed in expository and most observational documentary, but which Kiarostami lays bare. On my reading, Kiarostami is not particularly interested in staging a confrontation between objectivist and anti-objectivist accounts of documentary evidence; his film does not require us to side either with the claim that objectivity is attainable if the filmmaker sticks to mind-independent facts, or with the claim that the act of filming always introduces an angle on the facts, a partiality attributable to the documentarian's own personal standpoint. Though it repeatedly acknowledges his camera, Kiarostami's film is not particularly worried about the stain of subjectivity, some idea that by filming the world, we are fatally altering a pristine or virginal set-up. There are other ways of understanding what it means for a documentary filmmaker to acknowledge the presence of his camera on a scene. For Kiarostami, we might say, the documentary filmmaker is simply part of the world he wants to record. The act of recording is not set up as an act of 'interference', at least if 'interference' means anything like 'intrusion' or 'incursion'. The presence of a camera affects what happens around it – how could it not? – but that does not diminish the reality of what is thus recorded. And of course, Kiarostami is fascinated by the effects of his camera on his subjects (effects that, nevertheless, he found to be different from the ones created when he shot with a film camera).

In a sense, then, Kiarostami's is a recording of recording: a recording of the very fact that the world, and the human beings in it, appear. To make appearance itself appear: this is the poetic task of his cinema. Acknowledging the camera does not necessarily entail acknowledging an inescapable partiality: instead it can entail acknowledging the fact that there is no metaphysical distinction to draw between reality 'in itself' and how it appears to a subject, between fact and value, or between knowing and moral sensibility; that value is just part and parcel of human experience, and so part and parcel of any inquiry into facts; but that it is much too much to say that we can therefore never overcome bias or partiality (indeed saying that would effectively undermine their status as meaningful concepts). Understanding Kiarostami's acknowledgements in this way – as acknowledgements of the appearance of his subjects and the world both before and because of his camera – is our best chance of coming to grips with the relationship between documentary evidence and moral persuasion at work in *ABC Africa*, and for making sense of his reference to absolute truth.

Perhaps it also gives a way of understanding the closing images of the film, in which the ghost-like faces of Ugandan children are superimposed onto the clouds we see from the window of the plane taking Kiarostami and his companions out of the country. These images may seem contrived and sentimental if we interpret them in terms of the moral plight of the individual children whose faces turn up: in disconnecting these children from their particular circumstances, such that each appears for a moment only to dissolve into another, the sequence will seem to be melting them into an amorphous mass, calling out for only the vaguest and most self-congratulatory moral affect from the viewer. But they do not have to be understood in this way. I would argue instead that the appeal of the face for Kiarostami comes from something very different; that what, for him, the face reveals, is human appearance itself: the face as *apparition*. In his essay on the face, Giorgio Agamben writes:

What the face exposes and reveals is not *something* that could be formulated as a signifying proposition of sorts, nor is it a secret doomed to remain forever incommunicable . . . Such a revelation . . . does not have any real content and does not tell the truth about this or that state of being, about this or that aspect of human beings and of the world: it is *only* opening, *only* communicability.[25]

Kiarostami's interest in faces is an interest in faces for their own sake: it is not about what they signify or mean (say, 'suffering' or 'the persistence of the human spirit'), but about their appearance as such before his camera; it is less about what the face expresses than the fact that it does express. Thus the kind of moral feeling he tracks throughout *ABC Africa* does not necessarily arise out of recognition of the hardship undergone by another, from coming to understand that experience, or grasp its meaning and significance – not, that is to say, out of the propositional or factual 'content' of these images (content that may or may not be genuinely moral, or emphatic enough to spur moral affect). Rather, it arises out of recognition that the faces on screen are, before anything else, communicating "pure communicability", the commonly shared "communicative nature of human beings".[26] It may be wrong, then, to name this feeling empathy – which is what distinguishes Kiarostami's imagery of faces from the images of destitute Africans some-times used, for example, in television commercials for various international charities. Rather than empathy, the images want to establish something closer to solidarity.[27]

If with its roughness and idiosyncrasy *ABC Africa* must remain a minor film in Kiarostami's *oeuvre*, it is also one of his most aesthetically (and perhaps politically) radical. Its philosophical interest consists in how it points to a way out of the metaphysics of objectivity and subjectivity, and so in how it asks us to rethink basic problems of documentary evidence. To say that the documentary filmmaker is part of the world he records is not to say he has no way of truly 'accessing' that world, of viewing it as it is 'in itself'. Nor is it to say he has a way. If we are always already *in* the world – if we are not just spectators – then the upshot is not that we can never attain objectivity. It is that moral claims are made on us regardless of whether our philosophies care to admit them.

Notes

1. Kiarostami goes on:

   Directing was spontaneously and unconsciously eliminated. By which I mean artificial and conventional directing . . . In this way the camera eliminates the artifice so implanted in the industry. It gives you the possibility of expanding the dimensions of cinema, and getting rid of the clichés, traditions, enclosed forms, and pretentious aesthetics. This camera gives the filmmaker an opportunity for experimenting without fear of losing the essential.

2. The Persian phrase translated as 'absolute truth' is 'حقیقت مطلق', which has particular theological connotations of a truth that is all-encompassing, fully developed, complete, etc.

3. And not only in 'naïve' or pre-theoretical models, but also – though of course with more sophistication – in the field of documentary theory, including for instance the classic work by Bill Nichols. In the context of a discussion of Jean Baudrillard's claims about simulacra, Nichols writes:

> Intriguing as these assertions are, I do not accept them. This book is devoted to another set of propositions, ones in which the separation between an image and what it refers to continues to be a difference that makes a difference. Our access to historical reality may only be by means of representations, and these representations may sometimes seem to be more eager to chase their own tails than able to guarantee the authenticity of what they refer to. Neither of these conditions, however, precludes the persistence of history as a reality with which we must contend. (*Representing Reality*, 7)

4. The articles in Renov's landmark collection *Theorizing Documentary* deal with these and similar problems. For example, see Renov's own piece 'Toward a Poetics of Documentary', which asserts that "[o]ur attempts to 'fix' on celluloid what lies before the camera . . . are fragile if not altogether insincere efforts" (26); Brian Winston's 'The Documentary Film as Scientific Inscription', which critiques the scientism of some direct cinema practitioners and calls upon documentary "to negotiate an escape from the embrace of science" (57); and Trinh T. Minh-ha's 'The Totalizing Quest of Meaning', which critiques "the aesthetic of objectivity and the development of comprehensive technologies of truth capable of promoting what is right and wrong in the world . . ." (94).

5. See Cardullo, *In Search of Cinema*, 52–60; Elena, *The Cinema of Abbas Kiarostami*, 170–1; Gow, *From Iran to Hollywood*, 18–39; Krzych, 'Auto-Motivations'; Mulvey, 'Kiarostami's Uncertainty Principle'; Saeed-Vafa and Rosenbaum, *Abbas Kiarostami*, 37–40.

6. Nichols, *Representing Reality*, 56–68.

7. Nichols, *Representing Reality*, 57.

8. Rothman, *Documentary Film Classics*, x.

9. Translated by Walter Kaufmann as "[w]hatever is profound loves masks" (*Beyond Good and Evil*, 240).

10. For definitions of these styles, see Nichols, *Representing Reality*, 32–75.
11. Elena, *The Cinema of Abbas Kiarostami*, 169.
12. Saeed-Vafa and Rosenbaum, *Abbas Kiarostami*, 39.
13. Quoted in Elena, *The Cinema of Abbas Kiarostami*, 170.
14. Adorno and Horkheimer, *Dialectic of Enlightenment*, 256–7.
15. Wittgenstein, 'Ethics, Life and Faith', 252.
16. Wittgenstein, 'Ethics, Life and Faith', 253.
17. See Mackie, *Ethics*. I am referring in particular to Mackie's famous 'argument from queerness', which runs as follows: "If there were objective values, then they would be entities or qualities or relations of a very strange sort, utterly different from anything else in the universe" (38). From this premise Mackie infers that objective values do not exist, such that when we speak or act as if they do, we are in error (see 38–42).
18. See for instance Ayer, *Language, Truth, and Logic*, 106–7. Since Ayer's book was published in 1936, non-cognitivism has been inherited and developed in more sophisticated ways. For example, see R. M. Hare's universal prescriptivism (see *Freedom and Reason*), and the expressivisms of Simon Blackburn (see *Ruling Passions*) and Allan Gibbard (see *Wise Choices, Apt Feelings*). Though these accounts are more nuanced than Ayer's, they all rely on an idea that I take the thinking at work in *ABC Africa* to challenge: that it is impossible for moral judgements to make a justifiable claim to world-directedness and so full rationality, in the robust fashion in which judgements of fact clearly do.
19. Wittgenstein, *Tractatus Logico-Philosophicus*, 6.41 (86).
20. It is notable that claims like the ones outlined in these two paragraphs were deployed in both the manifestos and critical essays put forward in support of the cinéma vérité and direct cinema movements and in the critical and academic backlash against them that unfolded in the 1970s and 1980s. And of course, it is also notable the aesthetic procedures of *ABC Africa* resemble some of those employed in those movements, including its focus on 'ordinary' subjects, its lack of voiceover and general hesitance to make an argument, its interest in social and political issues, its exploitation of new filmmaking technologies, and so on. Making points that echo some of the ones Kiarostami makes in *Ten on Ten*, Peter Graham praised American directors who would later be associated with direct cinema in his 1964 essay on vérité:

> The Americans have made considerable technical advances: handy silent cameras; quick, precise exposure settings; fast film; portable recorders synchronized electronically with the camera. With this equipment they can

approximate quite closely the flexibility of the human senses. This opens up whole new fields of experience; they can follow their subjects almost anywhere, and because of their unobtrusiveness (they need no artificial lighting) people soon forget the presence of the camera and attain surprising naturalness. ('"Cinéma-Vérité" in France', 34)

Rhetoric like this soon began to seem highly contentious to many documentarians, critics, and theorists. As Jonathan Vogels writes in his book on the Maysles brothers:

> Theorists held that cultural and artistic bias of all kinds reduced the artist's search for truth to just another search, no more or less pure or authentic than any other. Indeed, authenticity was dismissed as a sociohistorical construct that was itself laden with subjectivity. These theorists argued that because every film and every filmmaker must have a distinct point of view, only films that openly acknowledge their own processes for negotiating these limitations and biases could be considered trustworthy documents. (*The Direct Cinema of David and Albert Maysles*, 142)

Or as Emile de Antonio said in 1982:

> There lies behind cinéma vérité the implication of a truth arrived at by a scientific instrument, called the camera, which faithfully records the world. Nothing could be more false. The assumption of objectivity is false. Filmmakers edit what they see, edit as they film what they see, weight people, moments, and scenes by giving them different looks and values. As soon as one points a camera, objectivity is romantic hype. (Quoted in Zheutlin, 'The Politics of Documentary', 158; see also Vogels, *The Direct Cinema of David and Albert Maysles*, 144)

It is telling that these debates turned on the presence of the camera, its effects on subjects, and then what it meant for practitioners of direct cinema (including the Maysles brothers, who turn up on screen on several occasions in their wonderful 1975 documentary *Grey Gardens*) to acknowledge their acts of recording. As Jay Ruby put it in 1977, in a typical anti-objectivist gesture: "To be reflexive is to reveal that films—all films, whether they are labeled fiction, documentary, or art—are created, structured articulations of the film-maker and not authentic, truthful, objective records" (quoted in Vogels, *The Direct Cinema of David and Albert Maysles*, 147). It is this kind of understanding of what it means to acknowledge the camera – and the theoretical commitments undergirding it – that I think Kiarostami's film challenges.

21. Crary, *Beyond Moral Judgment*, 20. Though she makes her case in different terms, I take my argument here to complement the ones made by Crary in her very important book *Beyond Moral Judgment*. As Crary shows, ditching this 'abstraction requirement' should not trouble the notion of objectivity, provided we conceive of objectivity in a sufficiently nuanced way (in her terms, it must be allowed to accommodate what she calls "problematically subjective properties" (15)) (see in particular 20–9).
22. McDowell, *Mind and World*, 16.
23. Davidson, 'A Coherence Theory of Truth and Knowledge', 312.
24. Elena, *The Cinema of Abbas Kiarostami*, 171.
25. Agamben, 'The Face', 92.
26. Agamben, 'The Face', 96.
27. In his reading of *Nanook of the North*, Rothman contrasts two impulses in Robert Flaherty's approach to filming: one which acknowledges the presence of his camera, and through that the humanity of his subjects, and one which denies the presence of the camera and so too its subjects:

> To be worthy of the humanity of his subjects, a filmmaker must acknowledge the revelations that emerge through filming them, through their encounters with the camera. As we have suggested, Flaherty at his most progressive proves willing and able to do so. But *Nanook of the North* also reveals the filmmaker's guilty impulse to deny his human bond with his subjects, to disavow what is revealed by, and to, his camera. (*Documentary Film Classics*, 14)

This is exemplary of another, in my view highly compelling way of understanding what acknowledging the camera can mean: not as an admission of irreducible partiality, but as a way of bringing to light one's 'human bond' with one's subjects.

CHAPTER 3

Ten: Everything there is to Know

Ten presents ten vignettes of varying lengths separated by fake leaders counting down from ten to one. Almost all the footage is taken from two stationary video cameras mounted on the dashboard of a car and trained on its front seats. The film's protagonist – played by Mania Akbari, a divorced artist with a young son called Amin – is a divorced artist with a young son called Amin. She features in each of the ten scenes, having intense conversations with Amin, her sister, a sex worker, a heartbroken woman, and two women on their way to mosque. She is Kiarostami's first post-Revolutionary female protagonist and – among many other things – perhaps a reply to the Iranian critics who had been attacking him for consigning women to marginal positions in his films.[1] With its starkness and severity, *Ten* employs a visual style startlingly different from the lyrical, contemplative, rural aesthetic for which the director was known (though of course, in certain ways it is also highly characteristic, especially for its violation of shot reverse shot conventions – that Kiarostami signature is taken to its next level here – and interest in what happens inside cars). The film's formal elements produce a minimalist rigour that forces us to consider the artifice of video while simultaneously creating a sense of realism: on the one hand, the set-up feels harsh and unnatural, at least when compared with the ease with which we are absorbed in films that employ continuity editing; on the other hand, Kiarostami's directorial presence is minimised throughout the movie, inviting us to indulge the impression that we are viewing reality unmediated.[2] Breaking the film into ten separate sections grants it an analytical aspect, such that we are able to study its parts in isolation, and reflect more acutely on the relations between them. The stationary cameras train our gaze very steadily on the characters, giving the film a discomfiting intimacy. The car itself provides a device for constraining and thereby clarifying the potentials for action and expression of the characters on screen as it opens the political, feminist question of the relation between public and private.

It is fair to say that there is something excruciating about this film: the viewer can feel trapped or pinned in place, anxious for a release from the severity of its framing and spare *mise-en-scène*. And of course, this is reflected in Akbari's situation: she is herself in search of lines of flight, struggling with the repercussions of her recent divorce from Amin's father (she interrogates the sex worker and the pious women she encounters with genuine curiosity, as though their lives might teach her how she could change her own). These features are crucial to the moral power of the film. Its formal conceits do not only provide a metaphor for the protagonist's own entrapment in a patriarchal society; they also force the viewer to face her situation with clarity and steadfastness. Given all this – and touching as it does on the sensitive topics of divorce, prostitution, abortion, pornography, and hijab – it is perhaps unsurprising that *Ten* was banned in Iran.[3] It is Kiarostami's most politically provocative film. It is also arguably the most significant from his mature experimental period.

Ten opens with a shot of the car's passenger seat as Amin climbs in. The first thing out of his mouth – coming just after an offer of ice cream from an off-screen Akbari – is a command: "We're late, get going." At almost twenty minutes, it is the longest of the film's scenes, and with its uncompromising depiction of the relationship between Amin and Akbari – and in particular of Amin's spitefulness, as well as the peculiar combination of worldliness and petulance that seems characteristic of him – it is probably also its most compelling. This is partly achieved by directorial fiat: the shot does not change for over fifteen minutes, leaving us to watch Amin as he argues with his mother. We are thus placed in claustrophobic proximity to him, forced to view not only what he says and how he reacts to what Akbari says, but also the bits in between, as Amin stares out the window, pulls faces, plays with his schoolbag, thrashes about in his seat, covers his ears in a huff, and so on. Primarily the two are clashing over Akbari's recent divorce. Amin, it becomes clear, thinks it was a selfish decision on her part; most of the scene is taken up with her defending herself, and trying to get Amin to appreciate her position. "You're like your father," she says at one stage, "he shut me away, destroyed me. He wanted me only for himself." Kiarostami's point will not be lost on the viewer: though just a boy of roughly nine, Amin has taken on the chauvinism of a much older, traditionalist Iranian male, and functions as a kind of mouthpiece for what we presume are his father's attitudes. When the argument reaches its acme Amin exits the car, and now the cut to Akbari finally comes, as she transforms from what Michel Chion has called an *acousmêtre*[4] into a rather beautiful woman. There is much to say about this decision to withhold Akbari from the screen for over a quarter of an hour. It means the cut to her surprises us. For the first fifteen minutes of the film, we could be forgiven for thinking that Amir is its protagonist, and that this is another Kiarostami film about a boy; the cut thus underlines the fact that Kiarostami has finally made a film about a woman. Perhaps it is also a ploy to shake Western viewers out of condescending complacency: to someone whose primary exposure to Iranian life had come through mainstream Western media, Akbari – with her makeup, designer sunglasses and clothing, and light headscarf (which sits a few inches back on her head, revealing a swathe of her hair) – will look quite shockingly 'modern'. It will take some time for the significance of all this to reveal itself, however. We are now given about two minutes of her driving, negotiating with another motorist for a parking space.

The second scene opens with an extended shot of a woman – Akbari's real-life sister Roya Arabshahi – waiting in the passenger seat. Nothing really 'happens' for nearly two minutes (though it is so excruciating that it feels much longer than this); instead we watch Arabshahi staring out the windows as she struggles in the heat, fidgeting with her (comparatively heavy) head-scarf and manteau, and fanning herself. The shot switches to the driver's seat when Akbari arrives with shopping; they talk about their family as she starts driving. As they make their way through the streets, Arabshahi gives Akbari directions (she warns her about a deep pothole, which Akbari hits regard-less). Arabshahi steers the conversation to Amin. She speaks of his aggressive behaviour with her own son, his disrespectful attitude toward his grand-mother, and how he uses foul language. "He needs to go his father's," she says. "He'll set him straight. He won't call *him* an asshole." One wonders if this isn't her way of condemning Akbari's attempt at independence. "It's not easy," Akbari responds. "It's not easy, but you have to try," says Arabshahi, before Akbari stops to offer a lift to an old woman, who declines. "I'll be like her one day," Akbari says. Arabshahi gives Akbari some more unsolicited advice about Amin and his father before Akbari drops her at her destination.

The third scene opens with Akbari pulling over to ask an old woman for directions. She ends up giving her a lift to Ali Akbar Mausoleum. As they speak along the way, the woman offers Akbari both literal and spiritual directions. "My husband is dead, my twelve-year-old son too," says the old woman. "I also sold my house to go on a pilgrimage in Syria." She shows Akbari prayer beads, claiming they are her only riches in the world. "I gave everything I owned to someone who had twelve daughters," she says. "I gave all my things. I swear, on the Imam Reza." Akbari is mostly impassive as she talks, though eventually responds with a sentence that shows a certain kind of connection between the two women, as different as they are: "Very good. The fewer ties you have, the better you live." When they arrive at the mosque, she declines the woman's repeated offers to wait with her car so Akbari can go inside to pray.

The fourth scene involves the film's only professional actor, hired because Kiarostami was unable to find a real sex worker willing to appear as such. Interestingly, we do not see the circumstances in which Akbari picks her up, as the scene opens in the middle of their conversation. Nevertheless it appears that Akbari has picked her up to talk, with the sex worker mistaking her for a trick. As they try to find a place where the woman can be dropped, Akbari presses her into conversation, and they speak frankly of sex, pleasure, men, money, and abortion. Akbari appears genuinely curious, but the woman admonishes her repeatedly for the moralism she perceives in her questioning. "You want to lecture me? An honest trade, a decent job . . .," she says with derisory laughter. "Who do you think you are, sitting at your wheel, lecturing me, guiding me?" "Don't you ever grow fond of the men you sleep with?" Akbari asks. She goes on: "Do you fall in love? Don't you like to have feelings before making love?" "I used to need them," the woman replies. "But I need them so much that . . . That's your problem. You're all clinging to your men. You cling to your husband." Eventually the woman tries to get Akbari to see the economics of her own relationship: "Who bought you that necklace? You see. And that night, he gave you . . . [Y]ou have the give and take too." Throughout the conversation we see only Akbari, though when the woman exits the car we do get a view outside it: we watch from behind as she crosses the road and enters another vehicle.

In scene five, Akbari picks up a young woman outside a mosque. We quickly learn that Akbari has been attempting to pray, as the pair discuss the mausoleum's rules regarding chadors: Akbari has just been turned away because she failed to bring one with her, despite being let in without a chador the day before (now it is Friday, however: the holy day of the Iranian week). The young woman says she visits the mosque once or twice a week; Akbari says it is not yet a habit for her. "But I came yesterday," she says, "and I wanted to come today as well." Along with the word 'yet', this statement leads one to wonder about the effect her conversation with the pious old woman might have had on Akbari. "It's interesting," Akbari says – the same phrase she used repeatedly when pressing the prostitute to talk – "I never imagined that I'd come to a mausoleum one day to pray." The young woman says she once felt the same: she wasn't always a believer, and even now only describes herself as believing "to some extent". Akbari says a woman – once again we wonder if she means the old woman from scene three – told her that praying at the mosque would see her wishes granted. The young woman says her own wishes haven't been granted yet, and she has been praying at the mosque for ages: she wants to be married, and has been praying for her lover to want the same. Akbari responds with her own story, saying her son has left her to live with his father after their divorce. "I don't know. I feel guilty at times," Akbari says, confiding that her feeling of guilt all but faded away when she first visited the mausoleum.

Scene six opens with Akbari picking up Amin from his father, who is parked across the street. Amin enters the car scowling and utters another command: "Get me to Grandma's." The pair soon argue over directions. The conversation turns to Amin's father's satellite television. It seems Amin is annoyed at not being allowed to watch it, and so craftily dobs his father in for using it to view pornography, in what seems a rare moment of collusion between mother and son.[5] After the next leader the car is very dark, and it is difficult to confirm who the woman in the passenger seat is (indeed – another signature – there are periods of complete darkness, presumably as Akbari drives beneath bridges or the like). Akbari's passenger – there are accounts of the film in which she is taken as the sister, as the young praying woman, and as an entirely new character with an undetermined relation to Akbari – has had her heart broken by the man who recently left her. Akbari is cold throughout the conversation, reproving the other woman for her failure to accept reality: "You can't live without losing. We come into the world for that." They decide on dinner; Akbari finds a park; another leader appears, then we are back with a happier Amin. At first the two manage to avoid shouting at each other, talking half-jokingly around the issue of Amin's father's new partner and whether she will make a prettier wife or better housekeeper. Ultimately it becomes an argument (again apparently provoked by a disagreement about directions), this time turning on Amin's assertion that Akbari works too much to be a good mother to him.

The ninth scene involves the young woman Akbari picked up in scene five. Her relationship has turned sour; the man she wanted to marry has refused her. For some reason Akbari is much more sympathetic to this woman, who pulls back her headscarf a couple of inches to reveal her newly shaven head. "It suits you," Akbari says, but does not hide her surprise: "Why?" she asks, as the woman shrugs and smiles. "Why did you do it? Let me see." The woman removes her scarf entirely. "What did you feel when you did that?" asks Akbari. "It felt great. I stopped crying. This is the first time I've cried since then," replies the young woman, as tears roll down her cheeks. This astonishing moment serves as the film's emotional apex: the brief final scene – which again features a scowling Amin on his way to his grandma's – is really more of a denouement. It concludes with a piano sequence from Howard Blake's *Walking in the Air* (another signature).

We can start accounting for the power of the film by reflecting further on the car. It is a formal device for physically separating the characters, and provides a claustrophobic structuring principle that grants the film a special intensity while simultaneously speaking to the protagonist's entrapment.[6] It also gets the viewer confronting a series of questions regarding the public and the private. For of course, the space of the car is an ambiguous one in this regard, a semi-private bubble one nevertheless finds in the street, where drivers in their bubbles interact with other drivers in their own. We are reminded of this again and again as the film unfolds, as intimate conversations are interrupted (sometimes for a few moments, sometimes for long periods) by what happens on the road. There is a problem being flagged about videoing, and the disconcerting 'realness' of the movie: what, exactly, are we *privy* to here? After all, part of the film's power stems from its intimacy, from how it gives the sense that the viewer has encroached upon private space. I want to say it presents exactly what reality television purports to, yet usually ends up travestying: human life in its ordinariness.

How is Kiarostami able to achieve this? The question is especially pointed considering many of the film's stylistic features — including the use of non-actors (who effectively end up 'playing themselves'), an obsession with faces, a focus on mundane personal problems, and a certain (implicit or explicit) promise that what one is watching just *is* real in some sense — are shared by the reality genre. The difference, I would venture, is that *Ten* makes a far more complex, far less bombastic claim to reality than does reality television. I am referring, first of all, to Kiarostami's commitment to revealing the possibilities and limitations of his own medium: the use of leaders, the austere visual style and lack of shot reverse shots, the radically 'unnatural' camera placement, etc. — the movie, as is typical of Kiarostami, constantly brings our attention to its own constructedness. At the same time, however, the film also displays a singular realism, evident in its refusal to use music, its refusal to *explain* anything, its refusal to couch what happens in narrative form, and in the unflinching detachment with which it treats its subjects, who appear to perform for long periods without directorial intervention. It thus forces opposing aesthetic procedures into a confrontation, inviting us on the one hand to read it as a reflexive experiment, and on the other as granting genuine insight into the lives of a series of real Iranian women. This is part of how it troubles the viewer's claims to know, as distinctions between the constructed and the natural, the scripted and the unscripted are called into question.

Reality television often seems to betray the worry that ordinary human life might *lack* the requisite realness and so need supplementation: the nature of its claim to the real, we might say, requires a certain disingenuousness about what it claims to show. One thinks here of the phrase 'raw emotion': what is sought is what was there *before*, the human element untainted by the dishonesty or fakeness we associate with film, video, and scripted performance. What results, of course, is usually shot through with tawdry sentimentality and/or base sensationalism, as the people on screen play up their 'personalities', and as producers and editors work to use whatever narrative, visual, or sonic devices they can to extract the maximum possible drama from their manufactured situations. The paradox of reality television is that it attempts to peel off artifice to reveal ordinary human lives, but what emerges is painfully dramatised, jazzed up, and stagey. Against such a thought of reality, Kiarostami shows that the real is not what appears when the artificial has been stripped away; rather, this notion of removing artifice in order to get to the reality beneath it is itself profoundly fantasmatic (not to mention probably sadistic) – and indeed ends up producing painfully inauthentic, cloying, emotionally pornographic, and/or trite images of human life. This gives a way of understanding Wittgenstein in the following passage:

> Nothing could be more remarkable than seeing someone who thinks himself unobserved engaged in some quite simple everyday activity. Let's imagine a theatre, the curtain goes up and we see someone alone in his room walking up and down, lighting a cigarette, seating himself etc. so that suddenly we are observing a human being from outside in a way that ordinarily we can never observe ourselves; as if we were watching a chapter from a biography with our own eyes – surely this would be at once uncanny and wonderful. More wonderful than anything that a playwright could cause to be acted or spoken on the stage. We should be seeing life itself. – But then we do see this every day and it makes not the slightest impression on us! True enough, but we do not see it from *that* point of view.[7]

I will return to this passage in the next chapter. Now I want to ask: what does an unobserved human life look like? The question is unhinged by a paradox like the one that I raised in relation to Wittgenstein's 'big book' thought experiment in the last chapter: that writing a book describing every fact in the world would mean falling into an infinite regress of descriptions. Once again the problem pertains to the position of the describer, and how the acts of observing and describing are themselves part of the world that is to be observed and described. It is as if what we crave is to see *without a point of view*, to see the world "from sideways on",[8] in the apt phrase employed by both McDowell and Mulhall. If this is a desire for reality, it is just as much a desire to get out of reality, to view the world from a position outside the world. Kiarostami demonstrates that the problem is not simply with an 'observer effect' – in this context, the fact that being filmed or videoed will change a person's behaviour – but the craven attempts at surmounting it, at finding or extracting a really *real* (sensational, emotional) reality beyond display or beneath all mediation. His realism is achieved not through (the pretension of) eliminating artifice, but through a complex foregrounding of it. The claim to the real is predicated on a renunciation of it. Or rather: of a certain fantasy of it.

Now it is worth invoking Noël Carroll's theory of documentaries as films of "presumptive assertion".[9] For Carroll, what distinguishes documentary films is how documentary filmmakers intend their films to be received by audiences. Both documentary films and fictional films have propositional content, in that both types of film ask the audience to entertain "situations",[10] understood as sets of propositions. A fictional film, however, asks us to entertain those sets of propositions as *unasserted*: as imaginative *suppositions* rather than assertions about the way things actually are. When we watch *Jaws*, for example, we "suppositionally imagine"[11] that a huge great white is terrorising Amity Island (itself a fictional place): we do not really believe that such a thing is happening, but merely suppose that it is in our imaginations, taking what Carroll calls a "fictive stance"[12] toward the propositional content of the film. When we watch a documentary, by contrast, we are asked to "entertain as asserted the propositional content of the text":[13] we are asked not to imagine the content of the film but to believe it.

If fictional films ask us to suppose that something is the case, and documentary films ask us to believe that something is the case, then we might give a general characterisation of reality television by saying that it wants to get us *believing in suppositions*. The content of the images and sequences it presents is not strictly believable, because they are shot through with the contrivances of fiction, as producers work to extract drama from their scenes and personality from their subjects. Yet on the other hand, the content is not quite imaginatively supposable either, insofar as the images and sequences certainly play what Carroll calls "the assertion game":[14] they are in the business of making claims about the actual world and the real people in it, rather than simply about a fictional one populated with characters. Reality television, in other words, asks us to believe in propositions that could only be imaginatively supposed, and hence produces images and sequences whose content we can neither believe in nor suppose. Rather than human life in its ordinariness, what we are thus given is a travesty of it, born out of the fear that the ordinary does have the drama required to compel our conviction. Neither fiction nor documentary, it corrupts the ordinary in a very particular way.

It would not take much to convert *Ten* into a documentary, in Carroll's sense of the term: all the audience would need are a few cues designed to let us know that the content of what we are watching is meant to be believed. For example, one could imagine Kiarostami employing a voiceover, intertitles, or some kind of introduction to lead us in this direction, perhaps by tipping us off that the women on screen are real people, maybe that they are unaware of being videoed, or that what happens in the car is unscripted. One could also imagine *Ten* converted into fiction, on Carroll's account of fictional films. We would need cues designed to let us know that what we are watching is meant only to be supposed: imagine, for example, if Kiarostami had employed continuity editing, doing away with the unnatural camera placement, the extended shot lengths, and the violations of shot reverse shot conventions (and perhaps removed the sequences in which very little happens, propositionally speaking, for long periods). By refusing both of these options, Kiarostami leaves us in an ambiguous position: we are not called upon to believe in the content of the film, yet nor are we simply asked to suppose it imaginatively; we cannot consistently take an "assertoric stance"[15] to it, but nor can we take a fictive one. Throughout the film, the epistemic status of what is conveyed on screen is undeclared.

So there is a sense in which *Ten* shares structural as well as stylistic features with reality television: both blur the line between documentary and fiction, forwarding content that can neither be believed nor imaginatively supposed; both leave the viewer in a highly ambiguous epistemic position; both thus (claim to) grant an insight into the ordinary. The difference is that reality television wants to get us believing in suppositions – trying to compel a belief that we cannot wholeheartedly offer – while *Ten* troubles the distinction between supposition and belief. In reality television, the ordinary is corrupted by the very artifice that its producers want to deny (artifice, we might say, comes back to bite them); in *Ten*, the ordinary is achieved not because artifice has been denied but because it has been allowed to emerge and confound us. By disallowing both the belief and the supposition of propositional content, *Ten* brings out something that may not be reducible to such content, and which makes a claim on us in virtue of that.

Consider again those two minutes in which Arabshahi waits for Akbari. She scratches, taps, and rubs her forehead; she bites her finger; she glances out the window; she rubs her nose and eye; she fans herself; she looks around; she rubs her chin; she pulls and picks at her cheek and lip; she tugs at her headscarf and manteau; she pokes her teeth; she chews her lip; she tongues the corner of her mouth. It's exactly the type of material that another filmmaker – or reality television producer – wouldn't think twice about leaving out. By leaving it in, Kiarostami forces us to confront something. Perhaps a nervous response to the fact of being videoed, or perhaps just the kind of thing one does while waiting for someone, thinking oneself unobserved, this fidgeting is both ordinary and agonising. These idiosyncratic tics and mini-gestures are difficult to watch, even a little unbearable: *boring* in both the usual and the etymological senses of the word. This nervous energy – call it *jouissance*, if you like – makes one think of that line from Pascal: "All human unhappiness [*malheur*] comes from one thing, which is not knowing how to sit quietly in a room."[16]

What kind of proposition about Arabshahi – the character and/or the person – is being imparted in these moments? That she is nervous? That she is waiting? That she is uncomfortable? That she is hot? That she is a fidgeter? That she is caught in an oppressive society? I suggest that none of these descriptions do real justice to the difficulty of what is screened here; that there would be a residue left over if we were to boil these moments down to their propositional content. Instead it is tempting to suggest that what is being imparted – along with these or similar propositions – is a proposition that is not really *about* her at all. Rather, one wants to call it the proposition *of* her, the proposition that Arabshahi is: to say that this is the energy of a woman strug-gling against – and of course *as* – the absolute particularity and immanence of her own life. As it is no proposition about her, it does not pertain to any specific feature (or set of features) of her or her particular situation. Unlike 'she is hot' or 'she is waiting', this proposition would not be contained in the set of propositions that would give a complete description of her; knowing everything there is to know about Arabshahi does not require that we also come to believe or suppose the proposition of her, which is instead implied by the ascription to her of any feature at all (being is not a real predicate). Any proposition about her could be analysed in terms of existential quantification: 'there exists an X *such that* Y is true of it'. So where do we locate the proposi-tion of her, if not in the totality of propositions about her? *Is* she simply the totality of propositions *about* her? That still fails to get at the specificity of this proposition, the sense that it picks out something 'more' than a mere group-ing of features. And crucially, there is something affecting about it, something that one cannot simply ignore or disregard.[17]

The words 'empathy' and 'sympathy' seem to overshoot the mark at this point (just as they did in relation to the faces screened in the closing sequence of *ABC Africa*): it's not quite that I sympathise with the particular experience or feeling that has befallen Arabshahi here. I want to say that I am affected by Arabshahi's auto-affection: that I am affected – that I cannot but be affected – by her affecting herself. This may sound a bit Spinozist, but this feeling is difficult to account for in the terms of his philosophy of emotion: on the one hand, it is not an active affect in the sense of leading to greater power; yet on the other, it is not passive because its cause is in no way external.[18] One could say instead it is the feeling caused by someone's *inability not to* persist in their being, someone's inability not to be active.[19] The early Levinas will be more helpful than Spinoza here: "It is . . . the being in me, the fact that I exist, my existing, that constitutes the absolutely intransitive element, something without intentionality or relationship. One can exchange everything between beings except existing."[20]

As with the moral feeling evoked in *ABC Africa*, this affection is not *exchanged* in the mode of sympathy (feeling *for* someone) where, as Adam Smith writes in his classic account of the concept, "we place ourselves in his situation, we conceive ourselves enduring all the same torments".[21] After all, in these moments Arabshahi is not simply facing circumstances that would be describable in propositions, and which I therefore may be able to conceive myself as enduring; she also endures something less specified. And as Smith acknowledges, there is nothing absolute about sympathy: I am always able to eschew the exchange, fail to respond, decline to place myself in the other's position. In his account, this occurs when there is a lack of approbation or disapprobation: if I feel that someone deserves his suffering or does not deserve his success, then I will not sympathise with him. The feeling in question here, by contrast, does not require that I imagine myself into Arabshahi's particular position or moral situation, which is what would open the possibility of a failure of imagination, perhaps through a lack of belief or a disinclination to suppose. Instead Arabshahi's squirming in her seat just *makes me* squirm in mine, without the requirement of imaginative exchange. It makes no particular moral demand on me, but it does make a demand; its claim is more general, more subtle, but also more absolute.

The philosophical temptation that opens here, of course, is to say that what is conveyed in these moments is not natural, that it is supernatural or metaphysical, perhaps something like a soul. Yet such speculation would actually seem to lead us away from what opened the desire to speculate in the first place: that what is imparted here strikes one as intensely physical and mundane. The adjectives I want to use for its effect on me include: pressing, harrowing, acute, piercing, and of course boring. There is nothing spiritual about it; rather, it pertains to the struggle of having and being a finite, biological body, to the terrible *thereness* of a singular human organism. There is something very private about what is displayed in these moments, and yet – insofar as it *is* a display, insofar as these are exactly the types of behaviours we engage in without realising it, behaviours we do not and cannot *own* – something very public too.

Note again the quote from Levinas, where he speaks of the fact of one's existence as something "absolutely intransitive", as something that can never be exchanged. There is a very radical notion of privacy at work here, as though human beings are burdened by something so intimate that it is literally unspeakable. It would seem to be borne out in the claim I made earlier about this scene, and how it appears to foreground something about Arabshahi that would elude our propositions, something that would not be captured in a complete description of all her features, something that would be 'left over' after all the propositional content was accounted for. One could also return here to the scene where the young pious woman removes her headscarf: the two and half minutes that go by from the woman's loosening to her replacing her headscarf are some of the most moving I have seen in a film, yet amongst the hardest for me to describe satisfactorily. At the same time, however – and this is where we should perhaps depart from Levinas – it is not as though there is anything ineffable about them, or even anything particularly mysterious about what happens: the woman has shaved her head in an act of defiance against the man who jilted her and the society in which she finds herself, with its arbitrary rules and myriad other brutal impositions on the lives of women; Akbari is taken aback but touched by what she has done; the two share a moment of intense solidarity. While we cannot say if these propositions are meant to be believed or supposed, there is nothing about the scene that can't be uttered, just as there is nothing incommunicable about what happens when Arabshahi waits: what is affecting about these scenes is *displayed*, just as it is in ordinary life, where what is most characteristic of us is constantly given up in the most mundane of ways, in mannerisms, posture, gestures, and voice. It is nothing *in particular*, but particularity itself, and it is hard to imagine anything more ordinary.

Consider again the question I raised earlier: should we understand Arabshahi's fidgeting as the kind of behaviour human organisms engage in when they think themselves unobserved, or as a nervous response to the fact of being videoed? It is like the question of whether we should believe or merely suppose what is conveyed propositionally about her wider situation (for example, whether she really thinks that Amin should go live with his father, or whether she would really wear such a dark, heavy headscarf and manteau on a hot day). In my reading, it is crucial that we cannot come to an answer in either case. Once again, the unmatched, even overwhelming sense of reality evoked in *Ten* emerges out of its highly complicated, indeed undecidable relationship with artifice. What the film troubles is the intuition that, in order to get to the real, we need to dig down through what is merely for show in order to find bedrock. What happens in it affects us despite and because of the fact that we do not know if we are meant to believe or merely suppose it. Perhaps it goes some way toward showing that moral feeling can emerge out of something other than entertaining propositions (which is not to say that it is therefore non-cognitive).[22]

Whence does our sense of the moral importance of a human being come, when human beings and the things that happen to them are nothing more than totalities of natural facts, in principle describable in a big book of propositions? More broadly (but also more pointedly): what happens to value once the world has become a totality of propositional content? Rather than showing us how we might answer these questions, *Ten* asks us to shift their weight. Rather than ask: *is there something essential about value that stands outside the reach of the totality of all true propositions, something that cannot be described?* we should ask: *what capacities for thinking and responding become opaque to us once we admit this notion of totality into our philosophising?*

Notes

1. Farahmand's 'Perspectives on Recent (International Acclaim for) Iranian Cinema' (published in the year *Ten* was released, and which therefore cannot be blamed for failing to consider it) is paradigmatic here. She writes that "as for the portrayal of women, [Kiarostami] simply avoids the issue, by using only a few female characters" (99); that "[i]n his construction of female roles, Kiarostami keeps conservatively in line with the religious belief that allocates a marginal position and a subordinate gender role to women." She goes on to criticise his portrayal of the "exoticism of village women" in *The Wind Will Carry Us* (100). Khosrowjah paints a more sympathetic picture, conceding that "before *Ten* Kiarostami's films were routinely criticized by many for their conspicuous absence of marginal place of their female characters", but acknowledging Kiarostami's stated position on the matter: that his avoidance of female characters and domestic spaces "was an ethical decision to avoid possible misrepresentations due to legal restrictions" ('Unthinking the National Imaginary', 160).

2. I take it that this is why Kiarostami refers to *Ten* as a "non-made film". "The filmmaker must make the least intervention possible", Kiarostami says. "You dare, you argue, you coach, but you don't intervene" (quoted in Winter, 'The Long Roads Home').

3. Saeed Zeydabadi-Nejad writes:

> The censors considered four of the ten sequences that make up the film, including one that features a prostitute, unsuitable for public viewing. The ban was followed by attacks in the conservative magazine *Sureh*, which accused *10* of encouraging prostitution and social corruption. (*The Politics of Iranian Cinema*, 125)

For accounts of the complicated post-Revolutionary history and practice of film censorship in Iran, see Devictor, 'Classic Tools, Original Goals'; Naficy, 'Poetics and Politics of Veil, Voice and Vision in Iranian Post-Revolutionary Cinema' and 'Islamizing Film Culture Iran'; Sadr, *Iranian Cinema*, 166–291; Farahmand, 'Perspectives on Recent (International Acclaim for) Iranian Cinema', 88–98; and ASL19, 'Censorship in Iranian Cinema'.

4. See Chion, *The Voice in Cinema*, 15–49.

5. The issue of satellite TV is a particularly significant one in Iran, where satellite dishes are illegal because they allow access to international media. Like many other things in the country, however, illegal does not mean unobtainable. On the contrary: satellite dishes are ubiquitous there, often displayed openly on building façades and rooftops. There is also a particular significance to satellite dishes for Kiarostami, because one plays a crucial (and amusing) role in his brilliant *Life and Nothing More*.

6. Shooting in a car also allows filmmakers to work in secrecy, as demonstrated recently in Jafar Panahi's 2015 movie *Taxi*. It was produced after the filmmaker was banned from making films, and is partly a homage to *Ten*.

7. Wittgenstein, *Culture and Value*, 6 (original emphasis).

8. Mulhall uses the phrase in an article on the *Tractatus* that engages with 'resolute' readings of the text, which try to take seriously two of Wittgenstein's most difficult claims about the book: that its own propositions are nonsensical; and that the point of it is ethical. In reference to the opening remark of the text (where Wittgenstein asserts that the world is all that is the case: that it is the totality of facts, not of objects), Mulhall writes:

> our difficulties here suggest that this, too, is a remark that could only be made from a God's eye view on the world, a view from sideways on, from which the way the world necessarily is appears as something that might have been otherwise . . . If, then, talk about the world as a whole must be transcended ethically, must it not also be transcended logically? ('Words, Waxing and Waning', 239)

McDowell uses the phrase in an article on moral non-cognitivism and the famous paradox of rule-following that emerges in Wittgenstein's *Investigations*. It comes in the context of a discussion of Cavell's reading of Wittgenstein, the view of rule-following it forwards (which McDowell says can produce a kind of 'vertigo'), and the view of rule-following it works to reveal as empty (which McDowell describes as 'platonistic'). He writes:

> The idea is that the relation of our arithmetical thought and language to the reality it characterizes can be contemplated, not only from the midst of our mathematical practices, but also, so to speak, from sideways on – from a standpoint independent of all the human activities and reflections that locate those practices in our 'whirl of organism'; and that it would be recognizable from the sideways perspective that a given move is the correct move at a given point in the practice: that, say, 1002 really does come after 1000 in the series determined by the instruction 'Add 2'. It is clear how this platonistic picture might promise to reassure us if we suffered from the vertigo, fearing that the Wittgensteinian vision threatens to dissolve the independent truth of arithmetic into a collection of mere contingencies about the natural history of man. But the picture has no real content. ('Non-Cognitivism and Rule-Following', 207–8)

9. See Carroll, 'Fiction, Nonfiction, and the Film of Presumptive Assertion', 207–12.
10. Carroll, 'Fiction, Nonfiction, and the Film of Presumptive Assertion', 205.
11. Carroll, 'Fiction, Nonfiction, and the Film of Presumptive Assertion', 206.
12. Carroll, 'Fiction, Nonfiction, and the Film of Presumptive Assertion', 207.
13. Carroll, 'Fiction, Nonfiction, and the Film of Presumptive Assertion', 207.
14. Carroll, 'Fiction, Nonfiction, and the Film of Presumptive Assertion', 195.
15. Carroll, 'Fiction, Nonfiction, and the Film of Presumptive Assertion', 209.
16. Pascal, *Pascal's Apology for Religion*, 105 (my translation).
17. J. M. Bernstein writes: "The *achievement* of cinematic realism is its capacity to make possible the perception of a thing's existence as what demands a response, as in need of a response as the fulfilment of its naked reality" ('Movement! Action! Belief?' 91).

18. See Spinoza, *Ethics*, Third Part, specifically definitions I–III (83–4).
19. Perhaps this is the mirror image of what Agamben calls 'potentiality', which he describes "not simply [as] the potential to do this or that thing but [as] potential to not-do, potential not to pass into actuality" ('On Potentiality', 179–80).
20. Levinas, *Time and the Other*, 42.
21. Smith, *The Theory of Moral Sentiments*, 12.
22. In 'Dogs and Concepts', Crary gives an account of visual experience as simultaneously non-propositional and conceptual, in McDowell's sense of the term. She writes:

> A good phenomenological case can be made against understanding experience as propositional. Consider the case of visual experience. In such experience, the world becomes visually present to us. And what thus comes into view is describable in propositions. But the descriptive possibilities are unlimited, and none in particular is given. If we are to accept these features of our ordinary understanding of visual experience without correction or qualification, then we can't think of experience itself as propositional. We have to adopt a view of experience that takes seriously the recognition that, as Arthur Collins put it in a commentary on *Mind and World*, "experience does not come as though with subtitles". When McDowell discusses his reasons for rejecting the idea that the content of visual (and other forms of sensory) experience is propositional, he says he wants to take at face value an observation that is closely related to the observation, just touched on, that in perceptual experience no particular propositional description of the world is simply handed down to us. He wants to take at face value that when we move from such experience to beliefs about the world we are not drawing inferences from given propositions. On the contrary, we ordinarily take ourselves to be arriving at beliefs about the world non-inferentially, by articulating, or rendering in propositional form, content that is visually revealed to us. (220)

On my account of *Ten*, it reveals something similar of moral experience, bringing out a moral claim that is neither propositional nor ineffable/non-cognitive. I return in detail to the role of propositions in experience in Chapter 7.

CHAPTER 4

Five: Artifice and the Ordinary

In the press kit released with *Ten*, Kiarostami invokes a story by Milan Kundera:

> Kundera tells a fascinating story that genuinely impressed me: he relates how his father's lexical range diminished with age and, at the end of his life, was reduced to two words: "It's strange!" Of course, he hadn't reached that point because he had nothing much to say anymore but because those two words effectively summed up his life's experience. They were the very essence of it. Perhaps that's the story behind minimalism too . . .[1]

Kiarostami must be referring back to this when, in the 2005 film *Around Five: Reflections on Film and the Making of* Five, he refers to *Five* as a 'one-word film': if *Ten* was an example of 'two-word cinema', *Five* takes its minimalist tendency even further. If in the spirit of this we were to give the five episodes titles, we might end up with something like: 'wood'; 'esplanade'; 'dogs'; 'ducks'; 'moon'. The first episode follows a piece of wood floating on small waves, which alternately push it up onto a beach and drag it back down into the shallow water. The second presents an esplanade littered with puddles of rainwater backgrounded by a distant beach where larger waves break; over the course of the episode, we watch a number of people (plus the occasional pigeon) walking past, and observe a conversation between a group of four old men. The third episode gives us another seaside scene, this time with a number of dark shapes – eventually revealing themselves as dogs – silhouetted in front of the waves. The fourth stands out for its comedy: here hundreds of ducks – proceeding in a long queue – waddle across a beach, only to turn around and come back again. The final episode offers a view from above of water at night reflecting a full moon, the sounds of toads, birds, a rooster, and a dog, the slow brewing of a thunderstorm, and eventually dawn. The movie is more than an ode to calm, the beauty of nature, and the dignity and drama of the ordinary (even if it is also that): it opens beguiling problems of cinematic truth and artifice.

Five's full title is *Five Long Takes Dedicated to Yasujiro Ozu*. What is the significance of the dedication? Though it might not have been especially obvious before the release of *Five* (especially seeing as Kiarostami is typically quite coy about his influences, tending to dodge the question in interviews), it's possible to see an influence from Ozu on much of his filmmaking. Both are interested in modernity, tradition, and the interplay between them, and in particular with tracking the effects of importing a 'Western' model of the modern into a non-Western context; both are concerned with human alienation, separation, loneliness, etc.; both are renowned for their recording of the quotidian. Yet these are common enough themes. In any case, even granting that Ozu's influence on Kiarostami's cinema is clear (such that, at the very least, we could explain why the director might wish to dedicate a work to him), it would be something of a stretch to locate these themes in *Five*, which has no characters, dialogue, or narrative (at least in the usual senses of these terms). Kiarostami himself makes a few connections when asked about this in *Around Five*: the use of the long shot; simplicity; respect for the audience and its intelligence, which in Kiarostami's terms means something like restraint, the avoidance of emotional manipulation (as he says, "[*Five*] is in contrast with the kind of cinema that Ozu strictly avoided" – by which I take him to mean Hollywood). And these three factors do combine in Kiarostami's movie to produce something like the kind of calm many associate with Ozu: a calm that, by its nature, goads the viewer into contemplation and reflection. More speculatively, we might also point here to that crucial scene in *Tokyo Story*, where the old man and woman finally admit – to each other and themselves – that they want to go home. Part of what drives their admission must be the dawning acknowledgement that the seeming generosity of their children – who paid for them to be sent to an expensive seaside resort – is artificial: more an attempt at getting their parents out of their hair than an expression of their love. And of course, all this happens at the beach, with the old couple sitting on a sea wall, taking breaks in their talk to gaze out toward the water. With its understated but merciless unveiling of the unhappy flimsiness of daily life in modernity, this is paradigmatic Ozu territory – and perhaps it is possible to read *Five* in similar terms. But what is the role of artifice here?

At the start of *Five*'s first episode a piece of mottled wood, less than a foot in length, sits on a beach at the edge of the water, lapped by the tips of breaking waves. There are three rough zones apparent: the drier sand of the beach at the bottom of the frame; the shallow, choppy sea at the top; and the intermediary strip of wetter sand in-between which, reflecting an overcast sky, disappears and reappears as the waves roll over it. After just over a minute a larger wave nudges the wood hard enough to start it rolling down toward the water; another comes and picks it up; soon it's floating (here is when it first becomes obvious that the camera is handheld, as it follows the moving object). The wood is buffeted by the waves like this for another few minutes, rolling up and down the beach, in and out of the water. Then it breaks. This happens not, as we might have expected, as it is hit by a wave, but as it rolls down toward the ocean (perhaps the weight of the wood causes the break, putting pressure on an edge as it rolls a bit lopsidedly). We thus end up with two bits of wood – one much smaller than the other and probably best described as a chunk – each with a yellowy-white fleshy interior exposed on one side. The larger piece is quickly pulled into the water by a wave while the chunk – not the right shape for rolling – remains on the shoreline. The two are separated like that for roughly thirteen waves, when the piece is swept completely off screen, leaving us alone with the chunk for about seventy-five seconds. When the piece appears again, it is fully afloat in the top right corner of the frame. This lasts for just under two minutes, then the piece floats out of the frame, exiting from the top. We watch the mostly stationary chunk for thirty more seconds, low strings introduce a synthesised woodwind melody, and the image dissolves to black.

At first blush, the episode appears to add weight to a certain rather canonical account of Kiarostami's cinema, where the filmmaker's primary concern is taken to be the dignity and, to some extent, the drama of the everyday. On such a reading, the episode is meant to draw our attention to the kinds of quotidian detail that, perhaps due to the deadening effects of habit, we tend to fail to register. The reading is supported by some of Kiarostami's own statements in *Around Five*: "If I was going to invent another title for *Five*," he says there, "maybe it would be *Watch Again*, or *Look Well*, or simply *Look*." Or, earlier: "I think we should extract the values that are hidden in objects and expose them by looking at objects, plants, animals and humans, everything. In my opinion, *Five* is the result of this way of looking at things." From this perspective, we could perhaps describe the intended effect of the movie as a cinematic version of Roland Barthes's *punctum*, which term he uses to describe the small detail of a photograph that, in virtue of its minor status relative to the *studium* (which is something like the overall meaning of a photograph, what draws one to it in the initial instance and calls out for interpretation), "rises from the scene, shoots out of it like an arrow, and pierces me".[2] On this account, Kiarostami would be trying to draw our attention to the details of everyday reality, which we are only too likely to miss – the happy accident of the breaking of the wood being exactly the kind of 'event' one might, on strolling down a beach, fail to so much as notice.

On second blush, however, we need to complicate this account, for it does not address the questions the movie continually raises about its own status. In relation to the driftwood episode, we have to ask: was Kiarostami simply lucky enough to stumble across a piece of driftwood and start videoing it before it reached breaking point? Are we expected to believe the same thing about the second 'event' in the episode, when the larger piece separates from the smaller chunk and floats away, leaving the chunk on the shore? What about when the piece returns, only to disappear once again? Questions of this nature must be asked of the other sequences in the movie too: why did the old men who meet and converse on the esplanade happen to stop just *there*? Why distract the viewer from the remarkable actions and interactions of the dogs in the third episode with a progressive dissolve to white? Why do the ducks waddle past in such an orderly line, and what made them return in the other direction? Was Kiarostami simply in the right place at the right time to catch a full moon, partially obscured by passing clouds, reflected in a body of water surrounded by such an impressive range of creatures on the night of a thunderstorm (which, moreover, built slowly and dramatically over the course of his shoot, climaxing at the perfect point)? Note that I am not suggesting we raise these questions from an *external* perspective on the movie, as though they might puncture the cinematic illusions *Five* wants to establish, spoiling our suspension of disbelief. On the contrary: on any attentive reading of the film, these questions raise themselves; they are *internal* to its aesthetic effect and its philosophical significance.

The problem rearing its head just now is a familiar one: the relationship of human intention to the aesthetic and epistemic capacities of photographic media. On Barthes's classic account, some photographic images have a particular aesthetic power. Unlike (say) paintings, photographs will sometimes capture seemingly insignificant details, features of reality that have little bearing on the overall meaning of the image but which can nevertheless have an overpowering effect upon the beholder. He names the effect *punctum* for its poignant piercing quality. One of his examples is a 1955 photograph of children in New York City's Little Italy taken by William Klein. the grinning, perhaps blind boy on the right of the frame has a (we presume toy) gun at his head, pointed by a woman whose face we cannot see. Part of the power of the image, for Barthes, stems from one very particular detail of it: the grinning child's "bad teeth", to which the theorist "stubbornly"[3] keeps returning. Crucially for Barthes's account, a detail achieves this effect in virtue of how it exceeds human intention, in the fact that it has been captured *accidentally*. "[T]he detail is offered by chance", Barthes writes, "the scene is in no way 'composed' according to a creative logic";[4] "[c]ertain details may 'prick' me. If they do not, it is doubtless because the photographer has put them there intentionally";[5] "the detail which interests me is not, or at least is not strictly, intentional, and probably must not be so".[6]

In emphasising these aspects of *punctum* I am following Fried who, in *Why Photography Matters as Art as Never Before*, tries to claim Barthes for the anti-theatrical tradition he traces back to Denis Diderot (and in which he places his own sixties art criticism). Theatricality, on Fried's Diderotian account, is the condition of artworks that have failed to manage successfully "the primordial convention"[7] that they are made for beholding. As he shows, the necessity of managing beholding was a determining force in the development of French painting in the eighteenth century, when painters such as Jean-Baptiste-Siméon Chardin were celebrated for their convincing portrayals of subjects so intensely absorbed in idle pursuits that the viewer's very presence before the painting was effectively denied. The idea is that by depicting intense absorption, Chardin (and certain of his contemporaries) was able to suspend the beholder's sense that she is viewing an artwork, and so her sense that she is viewing an artefact designed to elicit a response. A convincing depiction of absorption checks the fact that paintings are made to be beheld, and the potentials for staginess and manipulation it introduces. As Pippin writes:

> No one in these Chardin genre paintings appears to be acting for effect, taking account of how they look to others, looking to normative acceptance by an audience, aiming to please or entertain an audience, conforming to the 'normalising gaze' of an audience; and in just that sense too, *neither is the painting*.[8]

Crucial to Fried's account — and this is something that critiques of his 'formalism' miss — is that theatricality is emphatically not a timeless or ahistorical category; rather, it emerges out of a field of tensions that develops dialectically, such that what appears as perfectly untheatrical at one point in time may suddenly appear painfully contrived at another (this is how Rococo painters such as Jean-Antoine Watteau appeared to Diderot). By claiming Barthes as an unknowing representative of this anti-theatrical tradition, Fried makes an advance on those who understand *punctum* in a purely subjective fashion, in terms of how a particular detail engages a particular beholder in a particular way. It is not that Fried denies this subjective aspect of *punctum*, but he shows that this is not all there is to the concept, which turns just as much on the beholder's sense that the relevant detail — "that accident which pricks me",[9] as Barthes puts it — must not have been intended by the photographer. This is why Fried wants to claim Barthes as anti-theatrical:

> *punctum* is seen by Barthes but not because it has been shown to him by the photographer, for whom, literally, it does not exist . . . This is in keeping with Diderot's repeated injunction that the beholder be treated as if he were not there . . . that nothing in a painted or staged *tableau* be felt by the beholder to be there *for him*.[10]

Drawing its very power to prick or pierce a particular beholder from the fact that it is unintended, *punctum* is a guarantee of anti-theatricality.

This is the register in which my 'first blush' account of *Five* might have proceeded. And indeed, in *Around Five*, Kiarostami himself seems to invite a reading of his film in such terms when he comments: "There are moments in all my films that I must confess are not of my making. This is not humility. In my opinion, *Five* should be watched with this in mind . . .". Yet this statement only complicates matters further. It comes directly after a series of amusing and ambiguous statements about the piece of driftwood, in which Kiarostami gives (only partially to retract) an explanation for his apparent 'luck': the breaking of the wood was achieved with a small, remote controlled explosive hidden inside it, and the separation of the chunk from the larger piece by tugging the piece off screen and out to sea with an unseen thread! On the one hand, then, Kiarostami seems to affirm the role of contingency, implying that the events captured in *Five* really were lucky finds;[11] on the other, he also affirms the fundamental role of design and creative control in the making of the movie, implying that the events it captures were the result of cinematic contrivance, indeed special effects.

It may seem Kiarostami is simply being incoherent here, but he is intensifying the problems of artifice and contemplation that *Five* raises. By asking us, on the one hand, to watch *Five* in the knowledge that his films contain moments that are not of his making, while on the other drawing our attention to the possibility that the whole thing is highly controlled, Kiarostami forces a crisis in metaphysical notions of intention and contingency, the fake and the real, the artificial and the natural (in passing it is worth noting that *Around Five*, by refusing to resolve these matters, effectively extracts itself from the 'making of' genre, such that we cannot really regard it as an external commentary on the film either: it is itself a problem, rather than a solution to any problem).

Let's try accepting the latter reading of the movie, in which the events it captures were not the result of luck or patience on Kiarostami's part but instead were carefully contrived. On this account of the film, the breaking of the driftwood was planned from the start, and if Barthes is right about *punctum*, this would seem to disqualify the event from achieving it. But how much can we put down to planning here, even if we grant that Kiarostami exploded the driftwood by remote control? Here are just three significant elements that turn up after the break which it is difficult to regard as intentional: the way the first wave pushes both bits up toward the viewer, splitting them in either direction to reveal the striking colour of their interiors; the way the smaller chunk sits steadfastly on the beach, refusing to be pulled into the sea; how the chunk ends up marking the border between the middle and bottom zones of the frame, while the piece rolls up and down between the borders of the middle zone.

Let's now try to accept that Kiarostami did not explode the driftwood, and was simply lucky enough to start videoing it before it broke. Surely the mere fact that Kiarostami's camera follows the wood means we nevertheless have to regard his capturing the event as intentional in an important sense; surely the fact that the scene opens before the break and concludes after the disappearance of the larger piece – which grants it a certain structure – cannot be regarded as an accident. Regardless of which way we read the breaking of the wood, then, Kiarostami's film troubles any attempt at drawing a clear line between the intentional and the accidental, the planned and the contingent. If there is *punctum* in this film it is not the sort that Barthes had in mind: here the aesthetic effect of the movie is bound up not only with how it captures small contingent aspects of reality that could never have been intended by the director, but also – and more fundamentally – with how it forces us to question the metaphysical assumptions underlying our desire for access to a pure, unmediated chance event.

This questioning really is that: it is not a denial that chance events exist, or that there is a reality antecedent to human intentionality, or whatever. It is also not to deny that film possesses what Diarmuid Costello and Dawn Phillips call 'epistemic privilege': a special capacity for recording reality, held in virtue of its being "mechanical, mind-independent, agent-less, natural, causal, physical, unmediated".[12] It is to ask whether we really know what we mean when invoking these terms in a full-blown philosophical register. For this is what is presupposed by both affirmation and denial, and exactly what Kiarostami's film should lead us to hesitate before committing to. His strategy in *Five* works something like this: first, instil in the viewer – through the use of a highly minimalist, restrained, and contemplative aesthetic, and by recording events that, at first blush, seem very 'ordinary' – the notion that she is viewing unadorned, unmediated, everyday reality; second, goad the viewer – by employing little tricks designed to get her questioning the status of what she sees, and giving her plenty of time and space to contemplate them – into asking whether or not the events that unfold really are unmediated after all; third, press the viewer – by complicating her notions of intention, control, artifice, and reality – into acknowledging that she did not really know quite what she meant when she started asking after unmediated reality in the first place. It is not that there is no distinction between intention and accident (no difference between setting up a piece of wood to break or having been there to catch its breaking), but that, once we abstract away from our practices and conventions and their applications to individual cases, our words start to lose purchase. Kiarostami's film indicates that, try as we might, we are unlikely to find a general account of the epistemic privilege of photographic media. Or more accurately, it is not quite that we'll never find a general account, insofar as this implies we are *lacking* something. Kiarostami's achievement in this film is to have identified – and worked to undo – a certain fantasy: the notion that, for something to be regarded as really real, it has to be unmediated by human intention; the intuition – which in certain frames of mind can feel unshakable – that the presence of the human disturbs a reality which, were it not for the incursion, would have remained pristine. The demand for reality at work here turned out to be a paradoxical one: if the real is set up in this way, we can never be in touch with it, because touching it will spoil it.

At the same time, I want to say that the effect of the film is more than 'merely' deflationary: as well as undoing a fantasy, it *does* grant a certain access to a transfigured ordinary. Consider again the passage from Wittgenstein I invoked in the last chapter, where he speaks of the uncanny and wonderful effect of seeing life itself. Now Wittgenstein acknowledges that we often come across people unaware of our presence and thus unaware of being observed, and it does not have this effect. But as he says, "we do not see it from *that* point of view".[13] He goes on to compare works of art to "insipid photographs" of scenery, which are only interesting to the photographer who took them. He writes: "without art the object is a piece of nature like any other".[14] This is the distinction I think Kiarostami is trading on, though perhaps in a more fraught and heightened way than does Wittgenstein's passage: the difference between presenting the ordinary as it is in itself (whatever that would mean), and presenting it in or through an artwork. As Fried argues, perhaps what is crucial about Wittgenstein's thought experiment is the presence of "the theatre and its curtain",[15] the fact that art and indeed artifice are built into the very structure of this experience of the ordinary.

Thus I want to say that Kiarostami's ability to grant a kind of access to ordinary reality is in no functional way distinct from how he undoes a particular realist fantasy. He takes the acknowledgement of artifice so far that he forces a crisis in the very distinction between the real and the artificial, but in doing so he demonstrates something quite surprising: that this procedure is not opposed to, but actually a condition for this authentic experience of life itself; that a radical acknowledgement of a depth of artifice may be what it takes, now, for cinema to defeat the flimsiness I spoke of earlier, if only for a few moments. Again it is worth comparing Kiarostami's procedure with reality television: it also purports to go for life itself but – in claiming to bypass all artifice and all mediation – actually produces images and sequences that are unbearably contrived (Kiarostami's own point of reference here is Hollywood, which he tellingly denounces in *Ten on Ten* for being *pretentious*). The presence of the director and his camera on the scene in *Five* is no transgression of the fourth wall, and it does not simply distance us but complicates our absorption. As in *Taste of Cherry*'s infamous coda, Kiarostami is part of the world he records in *Five*. But how could it be otherwise?

Notes

1. Kiarostami, 'Kiarostami on TEN', 3.
2. Barthes, *Camera Lucida*, 26.
3. Barthes, *Camera Lucida*, 45.
4. Barthes, *Camera Lucida*, 42.
5. Barthes, *Camera Lucida*, 47.
6. Barthes, *Camera Lucida*, 47. It should be said that Barthes develops the concept in relation to photography, not cinema which – he notes in passing and without fully explaining himself – lacks the capacity for *punctum* because of its greater propensity for artifice (as he writes: "in the cinema, no doubt, there is always a photographic referent, but this referent shifts, it does not make a claim in favour of its reality" (76)). Yet *Five* is, of course, a highly 'photographic' film, in that it does away with precisely those aspects of cinema that Barthes more than likely had in mind here, including both montage and narrative. I return to the issues of cinema, photography, and medium specificity in the next chapter.
7. Fried, *Absorption and Theatricality*, 93.
8. Pippin, *After the Beautiful*, 84.
9. Fried, *Why Photography Matters as Art as Never Before*, 97.
10. Fried, *Why Photography Matters as Art as Never Before*, 100.
11. Barthes uses the term *trouvaille* (see *Camera Lucida*, 33).
12. Costello and Phillips, 'Automatism, Causality, and Realism', 2.
13. Wittgenstein, *Culture and Value*, 6 (original emphasis).
14. Wittgenstein, *Culture and Value*, 7.
15. Fried, *Why Photography Matters as Art as Never Before*, 80.

CHAPTER 5

Shirin: Absorption and Spectatorship

Shirin's title sequence consists of a shot of an illustrated version of the twelfth-century romantic epic poem *Khosrow and Shirin* by Nezami Ganjavi, the images dissolving in and out before us for nearly ninety seconds. The text on screen remains unchanged except for the larger words in the top centre, which credit the director and screenwriter, present the film's title, and inform us that the work is inspired by Nezami, based on the short story adaptation of it by Farideh Golbou. After the last dissolve we see the face of a woman sitting in a cinema, her features apparently lit by the screen before her – a screen we naturally cannot see – and on which her gaze appears to be trained. She glances off to her left as if to acknowledge someone sitting nearby, pops a snack in her mouth, chews, glances off again, then casts her eyes back on the screen. Behind her there is another woman watching the film, as well as an empty seat. This lasts for just over thirty seconds, before we are presented with another woman. She too is eating, chewing languidly with her mouth partly open, looking a little bored or perhaps aloof; she scratches her forehead; at one stage, she glances down at something. She gets about thirty seconds before we see another face, this time of a woman adjusting her headscarf. As she does so, the music (which started during the title sequence) quickly fades and is replaced by sound effects: water dripping; someone opening a door, and walking slowly in an echoing room. She settles back to watch, her head leaning to rest on her seat, cocked slightly to her right.

The movie continues in this fashion for the rest of its ninety-two-minute running time. We are shown face after face for varying periods; we hear the narrative develop through on-screen dialogue; we watch as the women respond to the screen and/or become distracted from it. Piecing together the story of the film they are watching from this is difficult, especially because there is no dialogue for large swathes of it, but it centres on a love triangle between the Sassanian king Khosrow Parviz, Shirin, an Armenian princess, and Farhad, a sculptor. Khosrow forces Farhad into exile, where he sends him false news that Shirin has died; Khosrow and Shirin marry, but Khosrow is murdered by enemies in his sleep. All of the 114 women are noteworthy actresses; all except for one – Juliette Binoche, whom we see on two occasions – are Iranian. Men only appear in the dark background. I recognised two of them: one of them is Homayoun Ershadi, who plays the protagonist in *Taste of Cherry*; another is Jafar Panahi.

As Sara Saljoughi shows, part of the fascination of *Shirin* consists in the web of references it weaves: it is a work of cinema based on a short story adapted from a poem; through its use of 114 actresses, it references the many hundreds of films in which they have appeared. Further, the film raises the issue of medium in a complex fashion: as a work of cinema based on two works of literature, it asks us to reflect on their unique capacities, and underscores the fact that "the history of Iranian cinema is deeply implicated with literature and poetry";[1] portraiture turns up too, as Shirin first learns of Khosrow after seeing a portrait of him, and vice versa; plus of course the film references sculpture through the character of Farhad. This is not to say that *Shirin* simply revels in a post-medium condition, however. The film is interested above all in cinema, and develops that interest in one of the most literal ways imaginable. As Kiarostami said in an interview: "I believe if you let go of the story, you will come across a new thing, which is the Cinema itself."[2] The invocations of other media could thus be taken not as some hyperbolic statement about the impossibility of distinguishing between media but as an attempt on Kiarostami's part to isolate cinematic elements through repeated acts of differentiation. As I want to argue, the elements he isolates are absorption and spectatorship, which the film inflects in politically provocative and philosophically sophisticated ways.

If this is right, then *Shirin* might be read in terms of Fried's account – developed in the opening chapter of *Why Photography Matters* – of photographic works dealing with cinema, cinemas, and movie audiences: Hiroshi Sugimoto's *Movie Theaters*, a remarkable series of photographs of films screening in empty cinemas; Cindy Sherman's *Untitled Film Stills*, in which the artist placed herself as a protagonist in a series of fake 'stills' from imaginary films; and Jeff Wall's 1979 *Movie Audience*, a set of seven lightbox portraits of people apparently absorbed in a movie. For Fried, what unites these photographers is a concern with the problematic of beholding, absorption, and theatricality as it comes to a head in the relation between the media of photography and cinema. But if Fried is right that Sugimoto, Sherman, and Wall respond "to the problematic status of movies . . . by making photographs which, although mobilizing one or another convention of movies (or the thought of movies), also provide a certain essentially photographic distance from the filmic experience . . ."[3] then Kiarostami's own response does not provide that distance. *Shirin* reflects on the problematic status of cinematic absorption *with cinematic means*, and it is hard to imagine a more absorbing treatment of it. For one thing the film discovers – or rediscovers – is that the human face and its expressiveness while absorbed is perhaps the very paradigm of an absorbing object. Yet at the same time, it does not allow us to be 'innocently' absorbed, insofar as the film also provokes a confrontation with cinematic spectatorship: we are absorbed in a cinematic image of people absorbed in a cinematic image; but through that, we are brought to consider their and our absorption.

Proceeding via a series of critical accounts of individual photographs, as well as extended engagements with Heidegger, Wittgenstein, Barthes, and Hegel, Fried's photography book makes a case for the claim that certain contemporary art photographers have inherited the problematic of absorption and theatricality discussed in the last chapter, which developed out of eighteenth-century French painting and became foundational for modernism. His broad explanation for this inheritance is deceptively simple: when new technologies made it possible for photographers to produce large-scale works in the late 1970s, "issues concerning the relationship between the photograph and the viewer standing before it became crucial for photography as they had never previously been".[4] As photographs began to be made for the gallery wall, in other words, photographers had to face (and face down) theatricality, because they were forced to consider the rhetorical modes in which their pictures addressed their beholders. Hence Fried's deployment of the category of 'to-be-seen-ness', which – like the category of 'facingness' he deploys throughout *Manet's Modernism* – is a specific mode in which a photograph can acknowledge theatricality. Further, however, the theatricality inherent in the very act of exhibiting artworks in gallery spaces was compounded by other problems specific to the medium of photography, taken up in different ways by the artists Fried turns to: the notion of artistic intention, crucial to the modernist paintings and sculptures Fried supported in his sixties criticism, is pressured by the apparent automatism of photographic apparatuses, a problem countered in the work of Thomas Demand, whose meticulously constructed paper and cardboard scenes "[throw] into conceptual relief the determining force . . . of the intentions behind them";[5] the standing of photographic indexicality – as we saw in the last chapter, perhaps a condition for *punctum*'s defeat of theatre – is problematised in the case of digital works, as is clear in the images of Andreas Gursky, many of which "are intrinsically not, at least not in their entirety, the record of anything that could have been seen in the real world by a human observer or indeed a mechanical recording instrument";[6] problems of naturalness, artifice, authenticity, and posing come to a head in photographs of human subjects whenever they are aware of being photographed, as cleverly highlighted in Wall's *Adrian Walker, Artist, Drawing from a Specimen in a Laboratory in the Dept. of Anatomy at the University of British Columbia, Vancouver,* which depicts a subject absorbed in his task of drawing in what is nevertheless a situation that "appears patently staged".[7]

Hence Fried's claim that the photographers he champions have inherited the concerns of modernist painters and sculptors in an 'essentially photographic' way. In each of these cases, the problems of beholding, absorption, and theatricality are given particular, medium specific inflections: inflections that see the artists working not simply to negate theatricality but to manage it through its reflexive acknowledgement.[8] Like *Shirin,* Wall's *Movie Audience* depicts a series of people in a movie theatre, their faces apparently lit by the screen they are watching, which naturally we cannot see. Fried quotes from a text Wall wrote to accompany a 1984 exhibition of the work:

> When we go to the cinema, we enter a theatre (or what remains of a theatre) which has been re-installed in a monumentalising machine. The huge fragmented figures projected on the screen are the magnified shards of the outmoded thespians. This implies that the film spectator has also become a fragment of society which acquires identity through its repetitious accumulation; in this process it becomes an "audience." The audience is not watching the product of the action of a machine; it is inside a machine and is experiencing the phantasmagoria of that interior. The audience knows this, but it knows it through the labour of trying to forget it. This amnesia is what is known culturally as pleasure and happiness. On the other hand, the utopia of the cinema consists in the ideal of happy, pleasant lucidity which would be created by the revolutionary negation and transformation of amnesiac and monumentalising cultural forms. Cinematic spectatorship is a somnambulistic approach toward utopia.[9]

With an uncharacteristically "tortuous, post-Adorno idiom",[10] Wall taps here into a set of powerful intuitions regarding cinematic absorption, which manage to render it both machine-like and dreamlike: on this account, the cinema is a giant mechanical apparatus designed to produce a phantasmagoria of images, in which movie audiences are led to lose themselves as if in sleep; further, the audience takes pleasure in that very loss, experiencing its own amnesia as a happiness; thus it could be said to be complicit in its own passivity – a complicity that would presumably also form the condition for achieving the utopian lucidity that Wall tracks in the last two sentences of the passage. Now Wall figures his own project in *Movie Audience* in rather similar terms, saying that the work is supposed to anticipate, even evoke, its own moment of trial and occlusion as modernist art, its own transformation into tyrannical décor. This is greatly facilitated by the lighting technology used to make the piece, which itself induces a kind of primal specular fascination or absorption which is in some ways antithetical to the conditions of reflective and artificial estrangement indispensable to the unhappy lucidity of critical modernism.[11]

So *Movie Audience* presents a structural echo of the "tyrannical décor" of the cinematic apparatus, in which mechanical means are used to create the conditions for self-forgetting. As Fried points out, however, the conditions of viewing the works are radically different from those that obtain in the cinema, on the intuitions Wall taps: "the fact that *Movie Audience* has been hung unusually high by Wall himself is on the side of estrangement rather than fascination – it is hard to lose oneself in an image considerably above one's head".[12] The inherent theatricality of the act of exhibition is thus in tension with the content of the images, which are designed to create a specular fascination: a tension underscored by Wall's decision to hang the transparencies in an unusually high position. The portraits evoke but do not invite cinematic absorption, with its occlusion of the problematic of theatricality. Here Fried is leaning on a point he made in his 1967 critical polemic 'Art and Objecthood': that cinema, because of how it absorbs audiences, "automatically avoids"[13] the issue of theatricality, as if sidestepping it. Unlike the Chardins that must employ absorptive motifs to defeat theatre, or the paintings of Édouard Manet that must acknowledge it through facingness, cinema is inherently absorptive and so does not confront this problematic; hence it cannot defeat but rather "escapes theater entirely".[14] This is the basis of Fried's more provocative claim regarding film, which I will not try to defend in full: "cinema, even at its most experimental, is not a modernist art".[15]

Before I go on to complicate this, I would like to dispel an obvious objection to Fried's account. It would run something like this: just as with painting, cinema has its share of highly absorbing films and filmmaking traditions (such as classical Hollywood) and its share of non-absorbing or distancing films and filmmaking traditions (such as European political modernism); just as with painting, cinema has its share of highly theatrical films and filmmaking traditions (such as early cinema) and its share of anti-theatrical films and filmmaking traditions (such as Dogme 95);[16] as such it is absurd to claim that cinema sidesteps theatricality, even granting Fried's account of it. The argument fails to attend to the radical nature of Fried's claim. One could start to respond by saying that the claim pertains to the mode of address of cinema *as such*, rather than the particular modes of address employed by particular films or typical of specific traditions: that cinema addresses its audience by absorbing it. But this is insufficient. On this account, even when cinema may appear to employ modes of direct address – such as when actors in early cinema "greeted the camera's gaze with gusto, employing glances, winks and nods",[17] or when Michel speaks to camera in Jean-Luc Godard's *Breathless* (1960) – the result will be neither theatrical nor anti-theatrical, for cinema *has no mode of address* in the strict sense. This is how we might distinguish it from works made for the gallery wall where, thanks to the pressures associated with the act of exhibiting an artwork, the question of address – and so the question of theatre – rears its head as a matter of course.

The idea is borne out by the ontology of film developed in Cavell's *The World Viewed*, whose preface acknowledged the influence of Fried in emphatic yet general terms ("I would have written a little book about film if Michael Fried and I had never met. But it would not have been this one"[18]), and which turns to him on a number of occasions as its arguments develop. Particularly relevant are Cavell's claims that film "screens me from the world it holds – that is, makes me invisible",[19] that movies reproduce the world "[n]ot by literally presenting us with the world, but by permitting us to view it unseen",[20] and that film "present[s] the world by absenting us from it".[21] We could also turn here to Cavell's investigations in that book (which read as if he were following up on Fried's 1967 suggestion that someone pursue "a phenomenology of the cinema that concentrated on the similarities and differences between it and stage drama"[22]) of the difference between the abyss established between actor and audience in a theatre and the abyss established between them in the cinema. For example:

> In a theater, the actors appear in person; it is part of the latent anxiety of theater that anything can happen to break the spell – a cue missed, a line blown, a technical hitch. The abyss between actor and audience is not bottomless, unless convention is bottomless. In a movie house, the actors are not present in person and the screen is metaphysically unbreachable; the abyss between actor and audience is as bottomless as time.[23]

If all this is roughly right, then there is a set of intuitions regarding cinema that may need to be reviewed: the notion that, as in Brechtian epic theatre, a certain kind of critical distance can be achieved through the employment of strategies designed to bring the audience's attention to the illusions inherent in cinema; the idea that one can break the 'fourth wall' in cinema in the way one can in theatre; the notion that the magic of movies consists in a kind of illusionism, where audiences are invited to participate in the fiction that what they see before them is real – a fiction it will be the task of the modernist filmmaker to reveal as such.[24] I will return to these claims at the end of this chapter, and again in the final chapter. Now I want to emphasise that this is not to say that nothing aesthetically significant is happening when Michel speaks to camera; it is just to say that bringing out just what is significant about it is going to be complicated (and cannot baldly proceed with terms borrowed, whether implicitly or explicitly, from theatre). In particular, it would require attending to cinematic absorption without presupposing it is a function of illusion.

This gives a way into Fried's claim, which I take to be accurate, that mediocre and even bad films can be perfectly acceptable and enjoyable to a modernist sensibility, while bad paintings, sculptures, and poetry are not: films are not in the game of defeating theatre; hence they are not forced to bear the same burden of seriousness;[25] hence bad films are not necessarily affronting in the way that (say) bad abstract paintings are, especially when hung in galleries.[26] On Fried's account, a modernist painting succeeds if and only if it compels conviction, if and only if it can convince the viewer that what she beholds represents a decisive response to the formal problems bearing down on the medium;[27] a film, on the other hand, does not have to respond decisively to formal pressures to succeed, and does not ask for our conviction when it does[28] (Rothman and Keane: "Movies do not have to establish the world's presentness, the way painting does. The world is simply there"[29]). This also gives a way into that philosophical watershed of Kiarostami's career as a filmmaker, the paradigm of his characteristic gesture: the coda of *Taste of Cherry*, which reveals the director and his crew. The discovery he makes here, as I understand it, is precisely that the 'reveal' does not cancel or even dampen one's response to the film: if it achieves a distancing, it is a distancing that does not trouble my conviction in the movie – whatever that would mean – but complicates my absorption in it.

In the first chapter of *Why Photography Matters*, Fried cites his remarks from 'Art and Objecthood':

> It is the overcoming of theater that modernist sensibility finds most exalting and that it experiences as the hallmark of high art in our time. There is, however, one art that, by its very nature, escapes theater entirely – the movies. This helps explain why movies in general, including frankly appalling ones, are acceptable to modernist sensibility whereas all but the most successful painting, sculpture, music, and poetry is not. [Basically, I was saying that this is why I could enjoy even mediocre movies whereas all but the greatest high art left me cold.] Because cinema escapes theater – automatically, as it were –

it provides a welcome and absorbing refuge to sensibilities at war with theater and theatricality. At the same time, the automatic, guaranteed character of the refuge – more accurately, the fact that what is provided is a refuge from theater and not a triumph over it, absorption [in the sense of the viewer's being absorbed in and by the movie] not conviction – means that the cinema, even at its most experimental, is not a modernist art.[30]

In 2008 he gestures toward qualifying this: "Today I perhaps want to qualify the final conclusion, but my basic claim, that the absorption or engrossment of the movie audience sidesteps, automatically avoids, the question of theatricality, still seems to me – very broadly – correct."[31] Though he does not explicitly say what led him to "perhaps want to qualify" his conclusion, he does add that his use of "automatically" is not meant to imply that

> the avoidance of theatricality I associate with movies results simply from the nature of the apparatus – the camera and projector – as distinct from the deployment of a host of techniques of acting, directing, scene-setting, lighting, photographing, sound recording, editing, and so on.[32]

In 2012's *Four Honest Outlaws*, Fried appears to take this a step further. Referring once again to those remarks from 'Art and Objecthood', now he writes:

> There are problems with this formulation, in particular with the use of the phrases "automatically, as it were" and "the automatic, guaranteed character of the refuge," both of which can be taken to imply, first, that it is simply the mechanical (in that sense the automatic) aspect of film that counts in this regard, and second, that *all* movies, even, as I say, "frankly appalling ones," provide the kind of refuge I was trying to evoke. The emphasis on the automatic and the guaranteed fails to make clear that the successful construction of what might be called a "movie world" is an extremely complex achievement, requiring the cooperative work of a large team of artists and technicians (in that sense there is nothing automatic or guaranteed about it), just as the reference to "movies in general" ignores the fact that such attempts at construction may fail . . . Nevertheless the basic idea – that there are countless successful movies, many of them mediocre or worse, and that such movies escape theatricality by involving or indeed immersing the viewer in their narratives (more broadly in their "worlds" . . .), and that therefore they cannot be said to defeat or overcome theatricality in the ways that "Art and Objecthood" maintains works of high modernist painting and sculpture crucially do – still seems to me to be right.[33]

So Fried is happy to acknowledge that there is nothing truly 'guaranteed', in the strict sense of the word, about a film's absorbing its audience. On such an account, the claim could not be that movies achieve absorption just in virtue of the nature of their physical apparatus; rather, absorbing viewers is a complex matter, often involving large teams of people; further, we might add, what absorbs and what does not will naturally shift over time as film conventions shift, along with audience tastes and expectations (think of the first-year student who finds classical Hollywood movies – paradigms of absorbing cinema – 'boring'; or consider the fact that quite a number of the women in *Shirin* appear distracted and/or otherwise disengaged from the screen). This is all obvious and straightforward enough. Importantly, however, Fried also wants to say that this will not upset his commitment to the idea that movies sidestep the problematic of theatricality. The point, I take it, is that when films do succeed at absorbing us, it is not because they have defeated theatricality: that 'failure' in this regard means something very different in cinema than it does in (say) pre-modernist painting, for example in a Chardin that success-fully deploys an absorptive motif. Movies are not exhibited but screened.[34] If I fail to be absorbed in a 'film world' (to use Fried's 2012 terminology) it is not because the director has failed to negate, manage, or face down the theat-ricality inherent in the act of screening. And it is not because I have somehow lost conviction in what I see on screen. After all, movies project reality – they are (as Cavell puts it) *"a succession of automatic world projections"*[35] – and it is not at all clear what it would mean to be convinced (and therefore unclear what it would mean to be unconvinced) by a sequence of world projections. This must apply equally but differently to film in its narrative and reflexive modes: when a classical Hollywood film fails to absorb, it just fails (it is an unsuccess-ful film); when Michel speaks to camera, I do not lose conviction in what I am seeing on screen, but am forced to reconsider the nature of my absorption.

After all, the account is not simply 'negative': if the absorptive propen-sity of film exempts it from the requirement of compelling our conviction through the defeat of theatre, this naturally also places cinema in a particular, ambiguous but in certain respects privileged position with regard to the problematic of absorption. It is not for nothing that the very first chapter of *Why Photography Matters* opens with an account of photographs of cinemas, movie audiences, and a set of fake film stills. Nor is it for nothing that one of its most compelling chapters treats a film at length: Douglas Gordon and Philippe Parreno's *Zidane*, a study of Zinedine Zidane's performance during a 2005 football match between Real Madrid and Villareal shot from seventeen synchronised movie cameras all trained on him, which Fried reads as laying bare "a hitherto unthematized relationship between absorption and beholding – more precisely, between the persuasive representation of absorption and the apparent consciousness of being beheld".[36] If film is an absorptive art then that does not imply it is unable to reflect on absorption; on the contrary, perhaps it implies it can do it with particular depth and perspicacity.

Let me turn to a central sequence from *Shirin*, which takes place just after the forty-two-minute mark, when the dying queen speaks with a distraught Shirin of the pleasures and agonies of the world, imparting some final advice to her before she is to take the throne. Part of what strikes as strange in it is the occasional incongruences between the audience reactions and the narrative that unfolds through the dialogue between Shirin and her aunt, the queen. One is led to wonder: is it really worth all these tears? And not just tears from one or two of the actresses: *all* of them are either weeping outright or have tears in their eyes. The queen is dying, but we are only halfway through the story: a long way from its dramatic and tragic climax, as anyone familiar with the conventions of tragic romance (or the work of Nezami, considered one of the greatest Persian poets) would know. And of course, the film the women are watching is clearly a rather unsophisticated, melodramatic, and maudlin one. Consider too that Kiarostami has deliberately chosen notable actresses here, and not his usual cast of amateurs and/or non-professionals. Would such sophisticated and worldly people – most of them immediately recognisable as such to an Iranian audience – really be *so* moved by such a film (consider, for example, Taraneh Alidoosti's expressions during her time on camera, which jar as particularly exaggerated)? The point is not that the answer is no: it is that the question arises in virtue of Kiarostami's preventing us from seeing the screen the women are watching. We don't know what they are seeing, so how are we to know if their responses are appropriate to it?

For in fact the women aren't really watching a film adaptation of *Khosrow and Shirin* at all. Indeed they aren't really watching much of anything: Kiarostami had them sit on a chair in his own house, stare at three dots on a sheet of paper above his camera, and emote for it.[37] Kiarostami even claims not to have decided on his imaginary film until after the conclusion of this process, after which point the dialogue was produced, a soundtrack created, and everything pieced together in post-production. So Kiarostami seems to have wanted to create a disconnect between the unfolding narrative and the women's responses to it, and thus between the spectator and those spectating on screen. After all, why not simply screen a real film, and have the actresses respond? It would have saved a lot of work.

Taking *Shirin* in formal terms as a reflection on absorption and spectatorship is not to downplay its political and feminist concerns. For of course it is crucial that this is a film about women's spectatorship in the context of post-Revolutionary Iran. This can be brought out with particular sharpness if we consider Mottahedeh's fascinating study of the effects of the modesty rules imposed in the wake of the Islamic Revolution. Explicitly designed to 'purify' Iranian film of decadent Western influences, these rules – which were both written and unwritten, formal and informal – proscribed any further depiction of unveiled women, and led to the removal of all images of such women – or, where this was unfeasible, their blacking out via magic markers – from domestic and international films already in circulation.[38] Veiled or not, women were not to be treated as sexual objects, and had to be shown as chaste. Mottahedeh's point is that this new cinematic regime did not simply have the effect of removing women from Iranian films – and then, when they returned to screens in the mid to late 1980s, of leading filmmakers to be very cautious about how they were depicted (usually from a distance, or after relegating them to the background of a scene). For Mottahedeh, they also transformed the underlying visual logic of Iranian cinema, which could no longer proceed on the basis of the scopophilia that feminist film theorists were then critiquing in the West. On the one hand, the modesty rules reinforced the male gaze, insofar as, by requiring women on screen to be veiled, they effectively set up the spectator as male. On the other hand, however, rules and attendant anxieties about the depiction of women led Iranian filmmakers to eschew the voyeurism of Hollywood film. Thus, she argues, "innovative codes and conventions were created in the Iranian cinema of the 1980s and '90s that resonate with a feminist negative aesthetics";[39] Iranian filmmakers adopted "the governmentally imposed veiled, modest, and averted gaze, producing the national cinema as a woman's cinema".[40] Evaluating Mottahedeh's claims – which, sweeping as they are, are grounded in a series of compelling analyses of the formal structure of canonical Iranian films – is beyond the scope of this book. My point is simply that her kind of analysis is not precluded but can in fact be deepened by bringing it to bear on the accounts of cinematic absorption I have been treating, and vice versa.

I want to bring out three interrelated thoughts here. The first pertains to the provocative nature of *Shirin*'s images of absorption in the context of Iranian film, where until relatively recently it has been rare to see close-ups of women's faces.[41] This is compounded by a range of factors, perhaps including Kiarostami's decision to include a number of actresses who made their careers under the Shah (the film concludes with a close-up of Hamideh Kheirabadi, who started appearing in films in the middle of the 1950s, and returned to the post-Revolutionary screen in 1985). As well as this, there are the sexual themes – and to some extent scenes – of the narrative, and the fact that the original story is pre-Islamic[42] (note that in 2011 the Ministry of

Culture and Islamic Guidance prevented a publishing house from reprinting a version of Nezami's poem[43]). There is the fact that the absorption of these women renders them vulnerable in a certain way, as they exhibit a range of unguarded expressions, tics, and gestures, thus placing the spectator in a voyeuristic position, as private moments are made public; this theme is borne out in the narrative too: when Khosrow first encounters Shirin in the flesh, she is bathing in a spring while lost in reverie:

> O water . . . water . . . embrace me, caress me with your droplets, hold me like a lover, take my breath away. O water, I have such thirst for you, keep your thirst for me. Immerse me in your kisses, O water. Who is there? Who are you? A stranger who like a thief spies on me at night? Was it he? Khosrow? The prince of Persia? What was he doing there?

The women are all wearing headscarves, but there is a sense in which their intense absorption threatens to unveil them (note that the men, when we see them, generally appear impassive). Indeed in many ways this aspect of the film does render it at least partly scopophilic in the sense the term was given in early feminist film theory:[44] it is of course important that these women are very beautiful, and that we as viewers are invited in no uncertain terms to take pleasure in that (at the same time, of course, it is crucial that we are nevertheless denied the pleasure of seeing the narrative unfold on screen). The problem of absorption is thus inflected politically in *Shirin* – the film's scopophilia, and its reliance on a visual logic that is in certain key respects indebted to Hollywood – demonstrate that it is a deliberate provocation.

The second thought complicates the first. By depicting an audience of women, the film challenges an unspoken tenet of spectatorship in both Iranian and Hollywood cinema. In this sense, the film can be read as celebrating the ironic outcome of the application of censorship and modesty rules that Mottahedeh identifies, where the anxious attempt to exclude female bodies from Iranian screens rendered Iranian film a women's cinema. Even as the movie partakes in a scopophilic logic, then, it also seeks to problematise it, as the viewer is brought to question the nature of his absorption, and the meaning of the absorption displayed on screen. In Kiarostami's film, the scopophilic regime of Hollywood is brought to bear on a scopophobic regime that was designed as a corrective to it. By rendering the spectator female, he plays on the contradictions inherent in that very dialectic, where scopophobia works to negate scopophilia but inadvertently produces something distinct from both. Hence the film, through absorptive means, brings to light not just cinematic absorption as such, but also the gendered, political inflections of

it and the tensions and resonances between them. This leads me to my third
thought: through the inclusion of Binoche (who went on to appear in *Certified
Copy*) Kiarostami also situates that dialectic in a transnational context,[45] demonstrating just how porous all this is.

Let me underline the confluences between the images of cinematic
absorption at work in the accounts I have been tracking in this chapter.
We have Wall's account, on which movie audiences are encouraged by the
cinematic apparatus to participate in their own passivity, entering a dreamlike
state in which they enjoy a phantasmagoria of images.[46] We have the classic
feminist accounts on which Mottahedeh draws, on which the visual logic of
Hollywood film is underpinned by an objectifying voyeurism, which places
the spectator in a highly asymmetrical, sadistic position with regard to what
he views. We have Fried's account, on which the theatricality inherent in
the act of exhibiting artworks is sidestepped by the cinema, which sets up
moviegoing as a kind of refuge. And we have Cavell's account, which may
be indebted to Fried's, and on which there is a 'metaphysically unbreachable' abyss between actors on screen and movie audiences, which allows
spectators to view the world unseen. These accounts share a certain picture
of spectatorship, where viewers are absorbed in cinematic images in virtue
of being separated from them, enjoying them voyeuristically; they share a
picture of the cinema as an apparatus designed to relieve us from a burden
of responsiveness to what we see. These are pictures drawn by scepticism,
which I have been describing in terms of a fantasy of taking a 'sideways on'
view of the world: a fantasy of seeing the world from an absolutely secure,
detached position, of viewing it from a standpoint outside it.[47] This gives a
way of fleshing out Cavell's claim, broached in my introductory chapter, that
film is a "moving image of scepticism".[48] But what, on these accounts, would
it mean to undo that sceptical fantasy?

Here the accounts diverge. For Wall (or at least for the Wall of this
particular text) and the feminist theories informing Mottahedeh's book,
successful modernist films bring spectators to lucidity, waking them from
their voyeuristic dream by directing their attention to the apparatus in which
they find themselves, leading them to confront their own spectatorship. For
Fried and Cavell, by contrast, there is an incongruity between this model
of modernism and the cinema, because cinematic absorption bypasses the
problematic of theatre. On their accounts, what takes place when (say) Michel
speaks to camera is not a direct address to the viewer, a means of breaking
the spell and drawing her out of her absorption, because the world on screen
is sealed, and the spectator thus sealed off from it. In this spirit, maybe one
could venture that when characters speak to camera, the wall between them

and the viewer is not thereby broken but emphasised: as if, in the opening scenes of *Breathless*, Michel does not address us but that which cuts him off from us; as if, to modify a couple of lines of Wittgenstein's, the fly is hitting against the wall of its fly bottle.

Perhaps *Shirin* gives us another way of figuring all this, and staking out the grounds of this divergence. For one of its discoveries is that the women on screen are absorbing in spite of the disconnect Kiarostami introduces between them and the audience who views them, and sets about subtly under-lining: that even when I am left wondering about whether the faces on screen are expressing genuine or appropriate emotion, I am far from unaffected by them. As with the moral claims emerging from *Ten* and *ABC Africa*, I find it very difficult to describe satisfactorily the majority of these expressions in propositional terms: I could say that one is 'sad', another 'pained', another 'exasperated', another 'bored', another 'apprehensive'. It's not that the words are wrong but that they are simplifying. What's moving about these faces is not that they convincingly express whatever deep or powerful emotion, but the fact that they express, and each in its own singular way. What we see on each one, and which the category of conviction is so ill equipped to capture, is something like expressivity itself. For it isn't quite that the women are 'acting', in the usual sense of performing a role. Perhaps what we see is the condition of acting, that which renders possible the act of performing.[49]

On Fried's account, cinema is not a modernist art, because there is no theatricality inherent in screening to defeat; on Cavell's account, the gap between audience and actor cannot be bridged by modes of direct address, because address in cinema means something very different from what it does in theatre; implicit in both accounts is the idea that the category of conviction has no firm purchase on cinematic images, because films consist of world pro-jections, and it is not clear how we could become convinced by them, short of mistaking image for reality. If for these reasons the task of reflexive cinema cannot be the defeat of theatre, then perhaps that task is better understood as the defeat of scepticism. The sceptical fly bottle may be unbreachable; in fact the desire to breach it may be part of what sustains it: in this context, we might say that the fly bottle *is* the thought that we need to break the fly bottle, to overcome scepticism through an experience of overwhelming conviction that grants an unmediated connection to what we see on screen. The rub of the sceptical picture of spectatorship is that one cannot be extracted from it like this, nor through being brought to confront the illusion manufactured by the cinematic apparatus, because both notions presuppose one of the ideas that gives scepticism teeth: that absorption is a function of conviction. But perhaps *Shirin*'s absorbing, absorbed faces can indicate an exit. They would do it in virtue of how they move us without convincing us, making a claim on us that upsets scepticism by drawing us out of our detachment, and leading us to rethink the nature of our absorption. Though this is very close to modernism – so close that it should allow us to retain, if in slightly modified terms, accounts of the project of critical modernism in cinema – it is perhaps more accurate to call it philosophy.

Notes

1. Saljoughi, 'Seeing, Iranian Style', 524.
2. Quoted in Saljoughi, 'Seeing, Iranian Style', 534.
3. Fried, *Why Photography Matters as Art as Never Before*, 13.
4. Fried, *Why Photography Matters as Art as Never Before*, 2.
5. Fried, *Why Photography Matters as Art as Never Before*, 271.
6. Fried, *Why Photography Matters as Art as Never Before*, 166.
7. Fried, *Why Photography Matters as Art as Never Before*, 41. Fried goes on to quote Wall's own account of the production of the work, in which he asked the subject to 're-enact' a moment from his practice as a draughtsman:

   > he and I collaborated to create a composition that, while being strictly accurate in all its details, was nevertheless not a candid picture, but a pictorial construction . . . There was such a moment in the creation of his drawing, but the moment depicted in the picture is not in fact that moment, but a re-enactment of it. Yet it is probably indistinguishable from the actual moment. (41)

8. In this sense, the photographers Fried champions are participating in the problematic handed down to them from Manet, rather than from the comparatively 'naïve' (pre-modernist) French anti-theatrical tradition Fried identifies in *Absorption and Theatricality*. The crux of Fried's account of Manet is that, by the early 1860s, the problems of beholding that French painters of a Diderotian stripe had been negotiating became insurmountable, as their anti-theatrical, absorptive strategies lost their efficacy. The claim, in other words, is that Manet's work registers the coming to a head of a *crisis of beholding* in which "the primordial convention" (*Absorption and Theatricality*, 93) that paintings are made for beholding could no longer be convincingly denied. Instead Manet's approach was more complex, indeed dialectical: to acknowledge explicitly the presence of the beholder, but to do so in such a way that disorients him, calling into question the relation it establishes with him even as it establishes it.

In 1863's *Olympia*, for instance, the subject of the painting seems to stare directly at the beholder, violating a fundamental tenet of anti-theatrical painting; yet her stare is highly ambiguous and questioning, challenging and confrontational. Combined with the painting's bizarre narrative structure and its acknowledgement of the flatness of the canvas – achieved by refusing a robust sense of depth, in a deliberate counterpoint to the sophisticated illusion of perspective created by Titian's *Venus of Urbino*, the painting after which *Olympia* was modelled – Manet's painting does not allow the viewer to forget she is looking at an artwork. More than this, it is as if the painting stages in a nearly explicit way a new sense of the fraughtness of that very act, as if it registers a crisis not only of beholding but of the ontological status of artworks more generally.

In Fried's terms, the beholder of a Manet is placed in an "ontological double bind" (*Manet's Modernism*, 344) in which his own presence before the piece is both affirmed and interrogated. In the process, fundamental questions are forwarded about what it means to behold an artwork, and so perhaps what it means for something to be an artwork in the first place. Manet thus liquidates the Diderotian tradition of anti-theatrical painting, such that defeating theatre through the depiction of absorbed figures would no longer be a viable option. But this would not liberate painting after Manet from the problem of beholding or the wider "concerns of that tradition . . . least of all when a final step in a formalist-modernist evolution would purport to go beyond painting into Minimalist objecthood" (*Manet's Modernism*, 407).

Here Fried subtly broaches a crucial issue that I have been unable to treat in this chapter: the aesthetic standing of the minimalist (or as he preferred to call it 'literalist') artworks produced by Donald Judd and his contemporaries in the 1960s, and against which Fried's polemic in 'Art and Objecthood' was directed. The key claim in this polemic, of course, was that literalist artworks fail to compel conviction because of their failure to manage – indeed because of their open embrace of – theatricality.

9. Quoted in Fried, *Why Photography Matters as Art as Never Before*, 12.
10. Fried, *Why Photography Matters as Art as Never Before*, 12.
11. Quoted in Fried, *Why Photography Matters as Art as Never Before*, 12.
12. Fried, *Why Photography Matters as Art as Never Before*, 12.
13. Fried, *Why Photography Matters as Art as Never Before*, 13.
14. Fried, 'Art and Objecthood', 164.
15. Fried, 'Art and Objecthood', 164.
16. For a useful taxonomical account along these lines (which nevertheless

does not address Fried's claim regarding theatricality and cinema at length, even though one of its key arguments – that "the dialectical tensions" between absorption and theatricality on display in certain of Manet's paintings "is also precisely the characteristic of a cinema that is modern" (242) – would seem to challenge it directly), see Rushton, 'Early, Classical and Modern Cinema'. As well as Fried, Rushton's account draws heavily on Tom Gunning's classic essay, 'The Cinema of Attractions'.

17. Gunning, *D. W. Griffith and the Origins of American Narrative Film*, 261.
18. Cavell, *The World Viewed*, xxv.
19. Cavell, *The World Viewed*, 24.
20. Cavell, *The World Viewed*, 40.
21. Cavell, *The World Viewed*, 226.
22. Fried, 'Art and Objecthood', 171, fn. 20. Fried suggests the following as examples of the kinds of differences he has in mind: "that in the movies the actors are not physically present, the film itself is projected *away* from us, and the screen is not experienced as a kind of object existing in a specific physical relation to us . . .".
23. Cavell, *The World Viewed*, 229.
24. Richard Allen gives a perspicuous characterisation of this set of intuitions in his description of the theoretical commitments regarding illusion at work in 'Anglo-French Film Theory of the 1970s and Early 1980s' (*Projecting Illusion*, 7):

> Mass culture – classical Hollywood cinema – was deemed illusionistic and manipulative, and an alternative filmmaking practice was celebrated in which cinematic illusion and the pleasures of narrative involvement it afforded were eschewed in favor of the cerebral pleasures of films that sought to foreground the manner of their construction and undermine the effect of cinematic illusion. (9)

25. Cavell writes:

> Movies from their beginning avoided (I do not say answered) modernism's perplexities of consciousness, its absolute condemnation to seriousness. Media based upon successions of automatic world projections do not, for example, have to establish presentness to and of the world: the world is there. They do not have to deny or confront their audiences: they are screened. And they do not have to defeat or declare the artist's presence: the object was always out of his hands. (*The World Viewed*, 118)

26. Cavell: "in the case of films, it is generally true that you do not really like the highest instances unless you also like typical ones" (*The World Viewed*, 6).

27. In a crucial footnote to 'Art and Objecthood', Fried writes:

> essence – i.e., that which compels conviction – is largely determined by, and therefore changes continually in response to, the vital work of the recent past . . . the task of the modernist painter is to discover those conventions that, at a given moment, *alone* are capable of establishing his work's identity as painting. ('Art and Objecthood', 169, fn. 6)

28. Though this is not the place for it, it would be rewarding to trace in detail the highly complicated development of the categories of conviction, absorption, and theatricality throughout Fried's writing, from his 1960s criticism, through his art historical studies of the 1980s and 1990s, to *Why Photography Matters*, which mixes the historical with the critical. For our purposes, what is particularly notable about this development is the shifting role of conviction in it. In pre-modernist painting of the French anti-theatrical tradition, the artist's goal pertains to content: the convincing depiction of absorbed figures. In the context of modernist painting, the artist's goal is to compel conviction in the artwork as a whole through decisive responses to formal problems posed by the art of the recent past. In the photography book, however, the category of conviction is mostly absent. What to make of these shifts?

    One could speculate on the roles of abstraction and indexicality here: perhaps the increasing abstractness of modernist art – to put it baldly, the fact that it does not 'realistically' depict reality but concerns itself with problems of form – is what summons the full-blown problem of conviction. Photography, however, has a special relationship to reality, born (as I have argued) in virtue of its apparent automatic indexicality. In the case of photography, then, perhaps the category of conviction loses purchase because photographs (like traditionally 'realistic' paintings) are (thought to be) *of* the world. In the case of film, perhaps the case is even clearer, insofar as movies consist of world-projections, and becoming convinced by them would have to mean mistaking cinematic images for reality.

29. Rothman and Keane, *Reading Cavell's* The World Viewed, 199.

30. Quoted in Fried, *Why Photography Matters as Art as Never Before*, 13 (see 'Art and Objecthood', 164 for the original remarks).

31. Fried, *Why Photography Matters as Art as Never Before*, 13.

32. Fried, *Why Photography Matters as Art as Never Before*, 13.
33. Fried, *Four Honest Outlaws*, 182.
34. Cavell writes:

> Movies from their beginning avoided the shadowing of seriousness by exhibition, because they are simply not exhibited (or performed), but distributed and screened and viewed. One print of a movie is as full and authentic an instance of it as any other, so long as it is fair and complete. It is not a substitute for an original, but its manifestation. (*The World Viewed*, 122)

35. Cavell, *The World Viewed*, 72 (original emphasis).
36. Fried, *Why Photography Matters as Art as Never Before*, 230.
37. Anne Démy-Geroe writes:

> When Debra [sic] Young filed a review for the Hollywood Reporter from Venice after the film's premiere, she described *My Sweet Shirin* as "simply a parade of close-ups of 113 Iranian actresses who are watching a film which only exists in the mind of the viewer." Unusually for a film review, she detailed Kiarostami's working method. "Kiarostami has stated that the actresses are staring at three dots on a sheet of white cardboard off-screen, while imagining their own love stories; he chose the Shirin narration only later, after he finished filming." The Variety review also filed from Venice, by Ronnie Scheib, follows this almost verbatim. This focus on the technical nature of the film and on noting the almost incidental use of the Shirin story for the soundtrack is typical of the film's reviews and even Kiarostami can be found in interview on YouTube describing the process. It is clear that he was deliberately focusing attention on this aspect of the film in his Venice and subsequent media interviews. ('Persian or Islamic?' 149–50)

38. See Naficy, *A Social History of Iranian Cinema Volume 4*, 111–14.
39. Mottahedeh, *Displaced Allegories*, 4.
40. Mottahedeh, *Displaced Allegories*, 4–5.
41. Saljoughi writes:

> Because he is filming in Iran, Kiarostami is required to observe, at a basic level, the modesty laws by exhibiting women in veils. But his lengthy meditation on the female face as it careens through various emotions offers a bold challenge to the law's emphasis on not looking at women, at avoiding a spectator–image relationship based on the fulfillment of the desiring male gaze. ('Seeing, Iranian Style', 533)

42. In 'Persian or Islamic?' Démy-Geroe argues that *Shirin* is "protesting the suppression of pre-Islamic culture" (149).
43. See Démy-Geroe, 'Persian or Islamic?' 153.
44. The classic work here, of course, is Laura Mulvey's 'Visual Pleasure and Narrative Cinema'.
45. Saljoughi writes:

> The inclusion of Juliette Binoche functions to both include Kiarostami's subsequent film *Copie conforme* (*Certified Copy*, 2010) . . . but also locates Iranian cinema in a global context. Binoche's face thus serves as an index for European cinema in the same way that the Iranian actresses' faces point to the work of Kiarostami's colleagues at home. ('Seeing, Iranian Style', 526)

46. The account is reminiscent of psychoanalytic 'apparatus theory' as deployed by Christian Metz and Jean-Louis Baudry, to which it may well be indebted. I return to these accounts in Chapter 7.
47. David Macarthur writes:

> Since film is reality projected and screened, a displaced reality that we view from outside it – a position in which we (the audience) are essentially unseen – then the moral of recovering the world which film seemed to achieve is at the expense of our total absence from the recovered world; which is another way of saying that the renewed intimacy with reality is achieved, paradoxically, at the cost of a skeptical relation to it. ('What Goes Without Seeing')

> Schmerheim brings out the imperious elements of this sceptical set-up when he recommends

> understanding the traditional skepticist position as a *desire for control*. The craving for generality, the desire for a detached, all-encompassing view of the world underlying the skepticist position is a desire for control, because a world I know everything about is a world I can control, a world subjected to my will to power. (*Skepticism Films*, 87)

48. Cavell, *The World Viewed*, 188. Later, Cavell writes: "I have spoken of film as satisfying the wish for the magical reproduction of the world by enabling us to view it unseen. What we wish to see in this way is the world itself – that is to say, everything" (101–2).
49. It would be interesting to compare this display of expressivity with Fried's 1967 account of the sculptures of Anthony Caro:

they defeat, or allay, objecthood by imitating, not gestures exactly, but the efficacy of gesture; like certain music and poetry, they are possessed by the knowledge of the human body and how, in innumerable ways and moods, it makes meaning. It is as though Caro's sculptures essentialize meaningfulness as such – as though the possibility of meaning what we say and do alone makes his sculpture possible. ('Art and Objecthood', 162)

CHAPTER 6

Certified Copy: The Comedy of Remarriage in an Age of Digital Reproducibility

There is an aporia with two aspects at the heart of *Certified Copy*. The first pertains to narrative, and whether the protagonists are married; the second pertains to genre, and whether we can take this film as a genuine instantiation of what Cavell has called a 'comedy of remarriage'. The movie, which opens with a lecture on the importance of reproductions of works of art, will not let us solve either puzzle, but it won't let us give up on them: it repeatedly invites while consistently rebuking attempts at resolving them. This is especially frustrating because the puzzles are intertwined (such that resolving one might mean resolving the other). As it frustrates us, *Certified Copy* forwards the ambiguities of belonging and judgement that haunt concepts of genre, showing their bearing on questions of experience, authority, and scepticism.

In 1981's *Pursuits of Happiness*, Cavell – pre-empting in some ways the subsequent acceptance of popular culture as a field worthy of academic study – performed rich readings of Hollywood romantic comedies made between 1934 and 1949, taking them, if not quite as works of philosophy, then as philosophically serious works demanding philosophy's attention. He identified a subset of romantic comedies – more specifically a subset of screwball comedies – as members of a particular genre (or we might say – though it is notable that Cavell does not – subgenre). He calls it the Hollywood comedy of remarriage, including in it *The Lady Eve* (1941), *It Happened One Night* (1934), *Bringing Up Baby* (1938), *The Philadelphia Story* (1940), *His Girl Friday* (1940), *Adam's Rib* (1949), and *The Awful Truth* (1937). The Hollywood comedy of remarriage, Cavell says, distinguishes itself from a traditional romantic comedy "in casting as its heroine a married woman; and the drive of its plot is not to get the central pair together, but to get them *back* together, together *again*".[1] There are more convergences, some of them surprisingly specific: intense and virtuosic yet sometimes brutal repartee between the main characters, often turning on philosophical discussion regarding "the problem and the concept of identity";[2] concern with education broadly construed, and in particular the education of the woman by the man; a childless heroine; a hero and/or heroine from a sophisticated social milieu, perhaps from what people once called 'society'; a sense that the couple speak their own language, appearing unintelligible to the wider world; a certain reflexive tendency to raise the problem of the relation between actor and character, particularly regarding the principal woman; a concern with the idea of the public (often presented via the figure of the newspaper); the father of the female protagonist taking the side of her desire, rather than siding against it as he does in Shakespearian comedy; an ending that takes place in what Cavell calls, using words drawn from Northrop Frye's Shakespeare criticism, 'the green world': a location out of the city that might allow a different future for the couple by granting them a different view on their shared past, "a place of perspective in which the complications of the plot will achieve what resolution they can".[3]

Importantly, the understanding of genre at work here does not rely on the assumption that members of a particular genre must, if they are to be claimed as such, necessarily share a delimitable set of features. As Cavell acknowledges, here he seems quite close to Wittgenstein, who wanted show that our taking something as a certain type of thing – our knowing what a particular thing is – is not always contingent on our knowing the necessary and sufficient conditions of that thing's betokening its type. Famously, Wittgenstein made his case with the metaphor of family resemblance.[4] To be identifiable as a member of a family, a person need not share all the features characteristic of members of that family: you may have your grandfather's nose, your mother's eyes, and your father's gait, etc.; your sister may have your mother's eyes, and your father's nose and sense of humour, etc. – yet you are both recognisable as siblings. But Cavell goes further than Wittgenstein in acknowledging the complexities that now emerge. After all, we might say that people are recognisable as members of particular families not just because of what they share with other members, but also because of the way in which they fail to share distinctive features, or because of how they share them differently (for instance, Lisa Simpson's being recognisable as a Simpson is not just the result of her being yellow and having bizarre hair, but also of the ways in which she demonstrates her *non-belonging*, most obviously through her intelligence: she is, as we might say, 'the smart one'). This brings out something important about Cavell's understanding of genre: it depends not just on a film's sharing features with the other members, but also on the way in which it might *stand out* from the broader set – a standing out that displays more than brute dissimilarity.[5] In *It Happened One Night*,[6] for example, there is no arriving at a 'green world'; instead "what happens takes place 'on the road'". Yet this, Cavell argues, is *made up for* in the film, in particular in its "commitment to adventurousness", in how it shows that "a state of perspective does not require representation by a place but may also be understood as a matter of directedness, of being on the road, on the way".[7]

He writes:

> members of a genre share the inheritance of certain conditions, procedures and subjects and goals of composition, and . . . each member of such a genre represents a study of these conditions, something I think of as bearing the responsibility of the inheritance.[8]

This logic of genre may violate our intuitive notion of the logic of belonging (which holds that membership in a set just means possessing the particular feature, or set of features, definitive of it), but this does not make it weak or arbitrary. Genre membership asks not less but more of its members than other forms of belonging, and it asks especially much of those films that eschew certain generic features. Because members of a genre *"are what they are* in view of each other",[9] when a member of a genre eschews a particular feature, it must *compensate* for the eschewal (Lisa Simpson doesn't have the stupidity characteristic of the other members of the family, yet her intelligence is also stupid in its way, leading her as it sometimes does into pedantry and arrogance). This is part of how Cavell accounts for the obvious and important point that a genre should allow *new* members, new members that do not simply repeat the features of previous members – in which case they would fail to be really new – but rather extend them in repeating them. Each genuinely new member of a genre puts that genre to the test: it is not just the realisation but also (and more primarily) the *investigation* of its possibilities, an experiment with its own generic inheritance. The exceptions that emerge within a genre have their own specific way of proving its rules.

What draws Cavell to the remarriage comedy? It is not just its concern with problems of knowledge – as I have argued, that is typical of cinema in general, just part of this medium's inheritance – but the particular manner in which it understands and responds to them. Specifically Cavell reads the narrative drive of these films in terms of the "overcoming of sceptical doubt"[10] – yet this is a very particular sort of overcoming. Unlike in Descartes, doubt is not to be quashed here with certainty, and is not figured in terms of answering sceptical questions, or providing solutions to sceptical problems. The claim, rather, is that remarriage comedy pits epistemic knowledge against acknowledgement, and both of these against problems of love, sex, conversation, ordinariness, diurnality, fantasy, fidelity, and desire. Hence the idea, which runs right through *Pursuits of Happiness*, that these films have a particular flair for charting the vicissitudes of the problem of other minds. "The conversation of what I call the comedy of remarriage . . .", Cavell writes, "leads to acknowledgement; to the reconciliation of a genuine forgiveness . . .".[11] The couple in remarriage comedy must move through a certain crisis of knowledge toward a resolution based in acknowledgement. Unlike in more traditional romantic comedy, what brings the couple (back) together is not a change in circumstance or removal of an external obstacle, but the overcoming of internal obstacles. The moral of such comedies is that the satisfaction we seek is inadequate to our real need. It is not quite that we are forever sealed off from one another, can never know one another, but that the problem of other minds is not simply epistemic, that the other claims me differently. As Cavell writes: "the achievement of happiness requires not the . . . satisfaction of our needs . . . but the examination and transformation of those needs".[12]

I should reiterate that I do not necessarily want to claim *Certified Copy* as a comedy of remarriage. Rather I am interested in the particular questions it raises about film in general, this genre in particular. The film is so reflexive, so aware of itself as a film, that it puts Cavell's account into question – and not simply by challenging any particular generic ascription. It does it by forcing its viewers into a heightened state of uncertainty: an uncertainty that refracts the scepticism that Cavell says remarriage comedies work to overcome. Reading this film in terms of Cavell's philosophy of remarriage comedy, then, will reveal part of what is at stake in it – specifically, what is at stake in the possibility (or otherwise) of a contemporary instantiation of the genre. The problem the film poses is whether it is or indeed *can* be a remarriage comedy at all – and so the extent to which the particular mode of sceptical overcoming dramatised by these films still registers with us.

The movie opens with James Miller (played by the English opera baritone William Shimell) arriving late to Tuscany to speak on his new book. Entitled *Certified Copy*, the work presents an argument on the relative value of originals and copies, particularly in relation to art. In Miller's words, the aim of the book is to "try and show that the copy itself has worth in that it leads us to the original and in this way certifies its value". During his talk there is another late arrival: it's Juliette Binoche, who is not directly named in the film, which credits her as 'She' (or rather 'Elle'). Binoche doesn't only arrive late; she also leaves early, apparently deciding that her son – he is about ten years old – is being too disruptive. She hands a note to the book's Italian translator and leaves just as Miller is about to outline his theory of the four criteria of authenticity. Shortly after we watch Binoche and her son talking in a café. She is speaking about the book and her interest in it, trying to explain why she purchased six copies and left her phone number with his translator in the hope of arranging a meeting. The boy teases her for what he claims is the ulterior motive: "You like this James and you want to fall in love with him."

When Binoche and Miller meet the following day, it seems the boy was onto something. Miller comes downstairs into Binoche's antique shop, and she immediately seems flustered, if not defensive at his suggestion they leave town for the day. She nevertheless agrees, and so begin some visually spectacular scenes in which the pair make awkward, sometimes surprisingly testy philosophical conversation as they drive through beautiful towns and countryside. She seems keen on impressing Miller, taking him to see a nice church ("Did you get married here?" he asks, but receives no answer as Binoche is interrupted by a phone call), and then to see a famous Tuscan painting, itself a copy of a Roman fresco. Despite its beauty, Binoche points out (with the help of a guide speaking to another group, whose words she translates for Miller), the piece was found some fifty years ago to be an eighteenth-century copy, and not the Roman fragment it had been taken for. The work – still proudly on display despite this fact – doesn't really seem to impress Miller, who walks away as if bored by it (later he has to be prodded into acknowledging that he wished he had known about it before completing his book).

After the museum sequence, the couple order coffee in a café. As their drinks are prepared Binoche, having missed this part of Miller's talk, asks him to tell her about the event in Florence that gave him the idea for the book. Miller says it came after he witnessed a conversation between a mother and her young son as they stood beneath a copy of Michelangelo's *David* in the Piazza della Signoria. Miller was watching the pair because he recognised them, having seen them walk past his hotel on numerous occasions over the duration of his stay. He remembered the pair for the peculiar way in which they proceeded through the streets: the mother always walking one block ahead of the boy, yet repeatedly turning back to confirm his presence behind her. "She always had her arms crossed just like you," says Miller. The occasion in the piazza was the first time he had seen the pair side by side. Binoche, who has been looking surprisingly wistful or even hurt throughout the story, now says that it "sounds very familiar", and cries. Miller apologises awkwardly, and asks if Binoche knew them. "I wasn't very well in those days," she says. Miller goes on: "The mother was telling her son something about the statue. You know it's only a copy – the original's in the Academia – but the mother hadn't told the boy that. I'm sure. Am I right?" Binoche doesn't answer. "The boy was looking up at the statue as though it was a genuine, original, authentic work of art," Miller finally says, before being interrupted by a call, heading outside to take it. Now the waitress takes the chance to come up and speak with Binoche. "He's a good husband," she says. Binoche does not correct her, instead appearing to play along. She asks how the waitress knows that; the waitress says she can just tell. Thus develops a striking exchange, as Binoche complains of her husband's self-centredness, his obsession with his work, and how she barely sees him, while the waitress keeps trying to convince her to be happy with him. When Miller comes back inside Binoche informs him the woman has mistaken him for her husband. Miller seems to play along too, trying to explain and justify himself to the older woman.

The film has changed: for (most of) the remainder of the movie, Binoche and Miller seem to *keep on* playing along. Now they speak to each as though they really have been married for fifteen years, bickering about Miller's laziness on their anniversary, Binoche's sentimental fixation on romance, Miller's inability to simply enjoy his wine, and so on. When they visit another church they come across a young couple who've just been married, and argue over whether or not to pose with them for a photo: the couple want a picture with a happy older couple for good luck; Miller, apparently characteristically, seems not to want to indulge the perception – or perhaps Binoche's fantasy – that they are happy. As these scenes play out, the question naturally arises: is this is a story of two sophisticated strangers who, after being mistaken for a married couple, decide to act as one just for the intellectual and/or erotic thrill of it? Or are they a married couple who were pretending not to know each other, meeting and travelling through the Tuscan countryside as strangers as part of some elaborate intellectual and/or erotic game?

There is significant evidence to support the former reading. In the first part of the film, the pair really do speak like strangers, and the awkwardness between them seems unmistakably that of two middle-aged people who do not know each other wanting to get to know each other.[13] If Binoche's son is also Miller's, why does the boy appear not to know him? It can't just be that he doesn't know who his father is, because Binoche repeatedly attacks Miller for failing to spend *enough* time with his son. Also, we might ask, why does Binoche have to give Miller so much background information when describing his disappointing behaviour on the previous night? When she mentions it he appears at first not to know what she is talking about, so she has to explain: "You came back after a fortnight away . . . when I came out of the bathroom you were fast asleep, snoring." She is speaking to him just like they are acting here, giving him the kind of expository information that, in bad novels, plays, and films, gets relayed between characters as a pretext for filling in the audience.

Yet there is at least as much evidence for the second reading of the film. There is the exchange about Florence, in which the two appear to be skirting around something they will not say. There is the fact that Binoche breaks off her conversation with her son and storms out of the café right when he asks her why she didn't want Miller to sign a copy of the book using the boy's surname. There are the moments toward the start of the film when the boy comes up in conversation and Binoche becomes furious, seeming to break out of the character she seems to be pretending to be. This is to say that neither interpretation is satisfying: neither will make this film cohere.

The interpretive crisis created by the viewer's oscillation between these two mutually exclusive, necessary impossibilities comes to a head in the film's final scenes. Miller follows Binoche out of a church – they pass an elderly couple on the way – and they talk at the base of some stairs. Miller says Binoche has changed: she never used to go to church. Was she praying? Binoche says she wasn't: she just wanted to be on her own to remove her bra, which was sitting uncomfortably. He apologises, rather solemnly. She accuses him of having failed to notice earlier when she had put on lipstick and earrings; she says he never sees her. She then asks if he remembers the hotel in which they spent their wedding night. "Was it near here?" he asks, and she confirms it was. He points at one nearby. "Keep looking," she says, then as he looks around goes inside the building directly behind them, where she asks for the key to room nine – the room, she explains, in which she and her husband stayed on their wedding night. She goes upstairs. Miller follows her. When he arrives an off-screen Binoche – after insisting he keep the light off – instructs him to look out the window. As he does so, there is a cut to Binoche. "Remember?" she asks him. "No," he says. Binoche: "You don't remember? Don't you remember anything? I can't believe you've forgotten." She tells him to look out the other window, again asking if he sees and remembers. "You know I have a bad memory," he says. "It's not fair to test me like this." Binoche, now lying on the bed, says she can remember everything. She goes on to say that Miller hasn't changed at all: he is just as gentle, just as attractive, just as cold. Miller says Binoche is more beautiful than ever. "If we were a bit more tolerant of each other's weaknesses, we'd be less alone," she says. Soon she's asking him to stay. "I told you," says Miller to a hurt Binoche, "I have to be at the station by nine." He then enters the bathroom and stares into the mirror (and the camera), repeating the set-up of an earlier scene in which we watched Binoche applying lipstick. Bells ring out from the church we half see through the window behind him as he takes stock of his reflection (sometimes meeting his own gaze, sometimes avoiding it). Eventually he switches off the light and exits the room, leaving us looking out the window. Now the credits roll: not from the bottom to the top of the screen, but from the bottom to the top of the oblong of light created by its frame.

     Abbas Kiarostami and Film-Philosophy

Let me run the film through the criteria for remarriage comedy I drew out of *Pursuits of Happiness*. First, *Certified Copy* turns on dialogue: it is basically one long conversation between the protagonists. This talk is also often philosophical, and sometimes explicitly – indeed often heavy-handedly – concerns problems of identity (and when it doesn't, it concerns them implicitly). Second, the film is concerned with education, although it must be said that it's not clear if anyone is really educated (Miller's annoying lecturing seems mostly ignored by Binoche; at the end of the film, the onus is on his learning, but – as I will argue – it's unclear if any has taken place). Third, the couple may not be from high society, but they are cultured and sophisticated (much more so than members of today's ruling class tend to be, themselves now in the disingenuous habit of dismissing educated and cultured people as 'elites'). Fourth, they often appear incomprehensible to the wider world (and to the viewer), as the people the couple encounter misunderstand them repeatedly (and as they use languages unshared by most of those around them). Fifth, the film basically turns on the problem of actor and character, indeed in a far more heightened and reflexive way than do Cavell's remarriage comedies (it is worth mentioning Kiarostami's choice to cast the inexperienced Shimell as the leading man: unsurprisingly he struggles to keep pace with Binoche, and her prodigiousness comes through more obviously as a result of the asymmetry). Sixth, and here is our exception, the heroine is *not* childless, and indeed the burden she bears because of her son is a crucial part of her character and the couple's apparent relationship (and its problems). Seventh, there is a concern with the public and publicity, not figured through the newspaper, but through the publication of an academic book. Eighth, there is the encounter between Binoche and Miller and the older couple in a square, where the man – certainly readable as a kind of father figure, or indeed father-in-law figure – gives Miller relationship advice ("When you walk together, just put your hand on her shoulder"): advice Miller follows, leading Binoche to rest her head on his – just like the woman in the statue at the centre of the square, about which they had just been arguing.

The ninth point is perhaps the most ambiguous: does the film end in a green world that provides a place of perspective? They are certainly out of the city, having fulfilled the desire voiced by Miller when the characters first met, and which flustered Binoche. But is this green world a place of perspective? What does the couple see here, and does it allow them to forgive by acknowledging, by achieving a new view of the problem of knowing the other? This is the question whose irresolvability makes the film so fascinating and infuriating. In the final shot, we watch Miller's face watching Miller's face from a camera that doubles as a mirror. Like Miller, we keep looking but keep failing to see; like Miller, we aren't sure who or what we are looking at, and the attempts and failures of looking and seeing that structure the image involve the viewer too. We might say it is a perspective doubled back on itself: a perspective struggling to keep itself in perspective.

We should bring this back to the exception of the child. "The absence of children in these films", Cavell wrote, "is a universal feature of them."[14] He puts this partly down to a question of narrative purification: for the remarriage comedy to have teeth, its characters must be facing the threat or reality of divorce; children would serve to make such a threat or reality less likely; so "the absence of children further purifies the discussion of marriage".[15] Yet of course, this is one of the more significant changes the institution of marriage has undergone since Hollywood's golden age: children can no longer purify the discussion, because they are often not enough to hold a marriage together (though the presence of children might make it more difficult, they do not nix the question of ending one). It is notable that Cavell calls this feature 'universal' – a claim that may seem to sit uneasily with his logically complex account of generic membership. But one can see why it is so crucial for him: for Cavell, it is not for nothing that remarriage comedy emerges right when the question of the whole point of marriage had been renewed, thanks to changes in American society, and the increasing currency given to the idea that marriage is not (or not primarily) about economic necessity. This is part of why I do not want simply to claim this film as a member of the remarriage genre. As it should lead us to wonder, what if its conditions of possibility no longer obtain in the same way, or at all?

In 2004's *Cities of Words*, Cavell makes a series of remarks about the contemporary "absence of full-blown remarriage comedy".[16] Naturally he does not deny that films continue to be made with "remarriage elements in them"; in this context, he cites 1987's *Moonstruck*, 1989's *Say Anything*, 1993's *Groundhog Day*, 1994's *Four Weddings and a Funeral*, and 1985's *The Sure Thing*, which he reads as making a number of references to *It Happened One Night*. But Cavell says the genre is "no longer what it was", and speaks of recent remarriage comedies as "fragments"[17] rather than instantiations of the genre (of course, this could also be framed in terms of copies versus real articles). He ventures a problematic two-sided explanation for this. The first pertains to a shift in "the role, or idea of, or faith in, education …".[18] If in classical remarriage comedy "an essential goal of the narrative is the education of the woman" – a goal that, moreover, requires "the man's lecturing"[19] the woman – then in contemporary fragments of the genre – where "the young woman may be presented as explicitly better educated in society's eyes than the man"[20] – this has been partially foreclosed. The second pertains to a related shift, which Cavell thinks has weakened the possibility of men being "given authority by their experience"[21] (presumably the very authority that would allow them to educate the female protagonists of the films).

It is not simply that the male protagonists in classical remarriage comedy were knowing and authoritative, or that education in these films was just a matter of the man imparting wisdom to the woman; rather, Cavell's point is that these men start out from a position of experience from which they preside over the education and so recreation of the woman, but through that find themselves educated and so recreated too.[22] The narrative arc of *It Happened One Night*, for example, is shaped in part by the piecemeal revelation of what lies beneath Gable's façade of gruff worldliness, which emerges through the holes Claudette Colbert pokes in that façade. Part of Gable's charm consists in his willingness to let her reveal him in this way, but also in how he maintains the façade despite her (how in poking holes in it, Colbert reveals the façade as part of him). Think of the famous hitchhiking scene, where Gable tries to instruct Colbert in the proper methods of flagging down a car, only to find himself being taught a lesson (the drivers all ignore his poor thumb; she hails a car in seconds by showing some leg). In this context, it is important that the scene would lose its humour if Gable did not start out in it by making a claim to be authoritative. That, in turn, is part of what gives the next scene its more unnerving sense of humour, as Gable reasserts himself by chasing down the bag thief who gave them a lift, beating and tying him up, and stealing his car.

Perhaps now we can see what Cavell means in *Cities of Words* when he asks us to compare Gable with John Cusack. He writes:

> It would be a contribution to understanding why the remarriage genre is no longer what it was, to understand the difference of texture in a comedy that features as its leading man Clark Gable in comparison with one that features John Cusack . . . Cusack's charm and wit are formidable, but they depend upon his conveying an air of actual youth, of innocence untried, to make him a candidate for the young woman's attention. The difference from classical remarriage comedy, with such men as Gable, Cary Grant, James Stewart, and Spencer Tracy, may be put starting with the fact that these men are given authority by their experience, by their having staked their innocence against the need of "taking place in society," so that their capacity for inventiveness, improvisation, allowing themselves to behave with their marriage partner in ways incomprehensible to the rest of society, are entered upon knowing that they are risking a certain standing in the world . . .[23]

In *The Sure Thing*, it is important that Cusack is clueless and awkward, and that the woman he pursues (played by Daphne Zuniga) is responsible and studious. The narrative arc of the film is shaped by their mutual education: through her he learns to take responsibility for his actions and feelings, coming to see women as something more than potential sexual conquests; through his example and demonstrations (he shows her, for example, how to shotgun a beer) she discovers a sense of adventure that sees her shirk the life of safety and conventionality she had prepared for herself. But the façade in which Zuniga pokes holes is all bravado, and it masks less gentleness than sexual anxiousness; she reveals it not as part of Cusack but as a flimsy fiction. If Gable is disarming because we know (as he does) he is both dangerous and gentle, then the Cusack of *The Sure Thing* is disarming because we know (as he eventually learns) he is disarmed. Consider how mannered it would seem if Cusack tried in earnest to inhabit the swagger of a Gable; how he repels the creep who stops for them not through an act of violence but through inhabiting a cliché in highly exaggerated fashion (and to hilarious effect). Cusack's charm comes not from his authority and willingness to forgo it but from his assured way of inhabiting his lack of it.[24]

Let me return to the final scene of *Certified Copy*. As Miller stands peering out (and reflected in) the hotel room windows, Binoche keeps asking him to look, but it is unclear if he succeeds in seeing ("Come, come and see this side. Look. Do you remember now? Right there, look. See?" "You know that I have no recollection"). When Miller looks in the mirror, the image figures not the accomplishment of self-knowledge through experience but an ambiguity of it; it is an image of refraction, dissipation, and loss as much as of reflection and attainment. What is in question here, as Miller peers with an expression that seems both resigned and puzzled, is whether he has been able to come to a new view of himself, his situation, and his relationship with Binoche. When we see the church through the mirror's reflection and hear the bells ring out, this could either be the sign of their remarriage, or a kind of mockery of the pair, a sign of what they've failed to renew (or begin). What is unclear, in other words, is whether this counts as "the achievement of a new perspective on existence; a perspective that presents itself as a place, one removed from the city of confusion and divorce".[25]

Now let me return to what it means, on Cavell's picture, to claim a film as belonging to a particular genre. As we saw, his is a logically nuanced account of generic membership, where a film can qualify as belonging to a genre not only in spite but also because of how it fails to share relevant features with other members of the set. This allows him to develop some remarkable critical insights, as his discussions of exceptions and their resultant compensations are among the most rewarding in *Pursuits of Happiness*. But to some ears, the notion of genre at work here will sound just impossibly lax, as though it renders generic membership arbitrary, and the act of claiming a film as belonging to a genre decisionistic.[26] Surely, we would say while in this mood, counting the eschewal of generic features as evidence *in favour* of a particular generic ascription is to undermine any rational foundations the act might have; surely it is to render such ascriptions unfalsifiable. As Carroll writes: "The difficulty here is in knowing how liberal we can be in postulating 'compensations'."[27]

Of course, there is a Cavellian response to this line of criticism. It is to concede (like Immanuel Kant) that the "determining ground" of judgements of this nature "can be no other than subjective";[28] but to insist (also like Kant) that this does not weaken their claims on us. On the contrary: it is what gives them their special sort of purchase, what makes them bear on us in ways that natural scientific statements do not. The subjectivity of such judgements is crucial to them because it puts the judge at stake in them: it is what makes them revelatory of the judge, and so what renders the act of judging a risky one. Convincingly claiming a film as a member of a particular genre, then, requires nothing more or less than persuasively articulating one's experience of the film and the genre in which one places it. If there is authority in this act, it cannot be the kind of authority we grant to statements in the context of natural science; critical practice, for Cavell, is about accounting for subjective experiences, and is grounded in them. Thus there is no determinate answer to the question of how liberal one can be in (say) identifying exceptions that prove generic rules, because there is no way of determining in advance what will persuade, no fail-safe procedure for sorting the convincing from the unconvincing. Cavell goes further:

> consulting one's experience and . . . subjecting it to examination, and beyond these . . . momentarily *stopping*, turning yourself away from whatever your preoccupation and turning your experience away from its expected, habitual track, to find itself, its own track: coming to attention. The moral of this practice is to educate your experience sufficiently so that it is worthy of trust.[29]

So criticism requires not only attention to one's experience and the hard work of giving voice to it;[30] it also requires the checking of that experience, a checking Cavell describes as education. Experience is not figured here as a dumb, purely 'biological', or causally determined substrate which it is the task of the critic to interpret and somehow articulate; it should itself be subject to the demands of education, trained to respond with sensitivity and honesty.

This is to say that criticism requires exactly what is put in question by *Certified Copy*, and particularly in its final scene: self-knowledge achieved through the education of experience.

Attacks on the rationality of aesthetic judgement like the one I outlined above exploit the fact that such judgements are based in feeling. They turn on the idea that a judgement based in feeling forgoes the claim to be binding on others, because it tells us not about objective reality but about the subjectivity of the judge. So the attack is underwritten by the sceptical picture of the relation between self and world that has arisen repeatedly in this book, in which the self is figured as standing outside the world, as something that views it from sideways on. Crary breaks this down into two related assumptions: "the *ontological* assumption that no genuine feature of the world can be subjective . . ." and "the *epistemological* assumption that we approach a view of objective reality by abstracting from any local or subjective perspectives".[31] On this notion of self and world, aesthetic judgements – such as Cavell's claim that *It Happened One Night* is a remarriage comedy despite/because of the fact that it does not end in a 'green world', or despite/because of the fact that it "diverge[s] from the formula of a woman remarrying her divorced husband"[32] – are not in the business of making rational claims on us, because they simply express a subjective feeling or experience. So to challenge this we need a different thought of experiential authority: one unbeholden to the fantasy of authority underlying sceptical selfhood, and the repudiation of feeling at work in it. To claim experiential authority in this way is not to claim objectivity in the sense given to it in the sceptical picture, but nor is it to throw in one's lot with a decisionism that denies all objectivity: it is to lean upon the idea that judgements based in feeling can reveal the world and how things stand in it.[33] In McDowell's terms, it amounts to a rejection of "the doctrine that the world is fully describable in terms of properties that can be understood without essential reference to their effects on sentient beings".[34] It suggests that coming to know the world is sometimes partly a function of coming to know oneself.

It is worth noting that, in some second-wave feminist philosophies, there is something characteristically masculine about the sceptical picture of selfhood I have been tracing and the notion of objectivity it supports. Such arguments proceed on the grounds that the picture has historically reinforced the notion that men have authoritative insight into how things stand, because they have been taken to be more adept at separating themselves from their feelings. Catharine MacKinnon, for instance, writes of feminism as a "critique of the objective standpoint as male";[35] in a discussion of Francis Bacon, Genevieve Lloyd writes of the "male content to what it is to be a good knower";[36] in a classic contribution to Marxist feminism, Nancy Hartsock writes of "abstract masculinity",[37] and "the male sense of self as separate, distinct, and even disconnected".[38] On these accounts, there is a deep connection between the idea that insight into how things objectively stand must be attained through the sloughing off of subjective elements and the idea that men are better equipped to separate themselves from their subjective biases.[39] If they are right, they may give us a way of understanding why, when this notion of objectivity starts to be revealed as the fantasy it is, it can seem to generate a crisis of male authority. The disconnected standpoint looks less and less inhabitable, but there appears to be no authority in the model of subjectivity against which it defined itself: if I can't know from a position of certainty and security, the sceptic says, I cannot know at all.[40]

Perhaps these accounts could also give us a way of understanding the crisis of knowledge portrayed in *Certified Copy*. During the Hollywood golden age, we might say, the notion that men have a particular authority stemming from their insight into objective reality had greater currency (the point could be put more strongly, of course: on the feminist accounts I have drawn on, it is figured as something like a structuring principle of patriarchal society). Hence the narratives of classical remarriage comedies could turn on how male protagonists are brought through conversation with their leading ladies to overcome the disconnection constitutive of sceptical selfhood, achieving a marriage of minds that draws them out of their position of isolation[41] – a process that, as we have seen, Cavell understands as contingent on the male protagonist's starting out from a position of experience and authority (a position that, despite himself, he will be educated into forgoing).[42] On Cavell's understanding of contemporary fragments of remarriage comedy, by contrast, something has begun to shift in the conditions of this set-up, such that male protagonists can no longer sincerely or convincingly inhabit that position of authority, and so do not start out experienced; hence his claim that the "absence of appropriate men" is the "more telling fact"[43] than the absence of appropriate women when accounting for the difference between classical remarriage comedies and their contemporary fragments.

In *Certified Copy* this is figured in a starker way. The film reveals Miller as so deeply out of touch with himself, with Binoche, and with the world that he is mystified by his own experience.[44] Further, the crisis facing him – and the failures of self-knowledge it engenders – are refracted in the viewer's own experience of the film. As it withholds the evidence we feel we need to ground our claims regarding the status of the pair, or whether it can be read as a genuine instantiation of the remarriage genre, it leaves us as well as Miller stranded in ambiguity. Are the couple married? Are they getting back together? Will Miller leave to catch his train, or will he stay and make love to Binoche? Is this a remarriage comedy? Is remarriage comedy still viable or even possible as a genre? Or have its conditions been negated by the historical and experiential changes wrought during and since the 1940s – changes pertaining to the roles of men and women, as well as a wider shift in our culture's exposure to images, and the infection of originals by copies? *Certified Copy* offers no answers to these questions. In forcing the demands of self-knowledge and overcoming back onto us, however, it opens another, perhaps more useful one: how might we rethink (or renew) the relationship between the cinema and us, its viewers?

Notes

1. Cavell, *Pursuits of Happiness*, 1–2.
2. Cavell, *Pursuits of Happiness*, 55.
3. Cavell, *Pursuits of Happiness*, 29.
4. See Wittgenstein, *Philosophical Investigations*, §67; 27–8e.
5. Though it directly evokes Cavell, this should differentiate his account of genre from D. N. Rodowick's in *Elegy for Theory*, which reduces it to a family resemblance concept in the Wittgensteinian sense (see 74–5).
6. Rex Butler makes an intriguing connection between this film (to which I will shortly return) and *Certified Copy*:

   We are reminded in some ways of that celebrated moment in *It Happened One Night*, in which Clarke Gable and Claudette Colbert suddenly pretend to be married to throw off the authorities looking for them, and from that point actually do fall in love. ('Abbas Kiarostami', 65)

7. Cavell, *Pursuits of Happiness*, 29.
8. Cavell, *Pursuits of Happiness*, 28.
9. Cavell, *Pursuits of Happiness*, 29 (original emphasis). The full passage shows how Cavell wants to distinguish his own account of the logic of genre from the Wittgensteinian concept of family resemblance. Cavell writes of those readers of Wittgenstein's *Investigations* who will

   sense a connection here, in the denial that what constitutes the members of a genre is their having features in common, with Wittgenstein's caution not to say of things called by the same name that they must have something in common [hence share some essence or so-called universal] but instead to consider that they bear to one another a family resemblance. But if I said of games, using Wittgenstein's famous example in this connection, that they form a genre of human activity, I would mean not merely that they look like one another or that one gets similar impressions from them; I would mean they *are what they are* in view of one another. I find that the idea of "family resemblance" does not capture this significance, if indeed it is really there. (29)

10. Cavell, *Contesting Tears*, 90.
11. Cavell, *Pursuits of Happiness*, 19.
12. Cavell, *Pursuits of Happiness*, 4–5.
13. Butler writes: "their conversation is stiff and awkward, full of the small misunderstandings and takings of offence that two single middle-aged people, attracted to each other but carrying the burden of failed relationships in the past, are perhaps prone to" ('Abbas Kiarostami', 61).
14. Cavell, *Pursuits of Happiness*, 58.
15. Cavell, *Pursuits of Happiness*, 58.
16. Cavell, *Cities of Words*, 154.
17. Cavell, *Cities of Words*, 155.
18. Cavell, *Cities of Words*, 155.
19. Cavell, *Pursuits of Happiness*, 84.
20. Cavell, *Cities of Words*, 155.
21. Cavell, *Cities of Words*, 154. In his hyperbolic but compelling way, Agamben outlines a similar thought in *Infancy and History* (see 15–17).
22. Thus it would be unfair simply to attack the Cavell of *Pursuits of Happiness* for assuming that it must be men who have the authority to educate women, and not the other way around. There is a deeper problem with Cavell's account, pertaining not simply to the sexist assumption that men are authoritative, but to his naïve deployment of the idea of male redemption through the love of the right woman.
23. Cavell, *Cities of Words*, 154. While I want no truck with its nostalgic tone, I find this passage illuminating. I will not say the same about the sentence that follows it:

> The absence of full-blown remarriage comedies accordingly suggests that men have become unable, or less able, with good spirits, to let their social station, so far as it is established, become jeopardized by acting on unexpected, awkward desires, as if the awkward were as such illicit—less able, we might say, to maintain their sense of identity without its ratification by social role. (154)

I find the idea that the difference between men now and men then pertains to the unwillingness of the former to jeopardise their social stations by acting on unexpected or awkward desires highly implausible. If anything, I want to say, we are now less convinced than ever by those who try to inhabit their roles too earnestly, for example by the young academic who invests in tweed and a pipe. For a brilliant account of contemporary awkwardness figured not as a function of the forsaking of social roles but as emerging from a crisis of sociality as such, see the discussion of "radical awkwardness" in Kotsko, *Awkwardness* (67–89).

24. Though the film's deployment of young protagonists is important in itself, this is more than a function of Cusack's youth in *The Sure Thing*. Consider the more recent *High Fidelity* (2000), where the narrative turns on a nearly middle-aged Cusack's resistance to commitment, figured as a refusal to grow up.

25. Cavell, *Pursuits of Happiness*, 17.

26. See Schmitt, *Political Theology*, 5–15.

27. Carroll, review of *Pursuits of Happiness*, 105.

28. Kant, quoted in Cavell, 'Aesthetic Problems of Modern Philosophy', 88 (emphasis removed).

29. Cavell, *Pursuits of Happiness*, 12 (original emphasis). He goes on: "The philosophical catch would then be that the education cannot be achieved in advance of the trusting." The 'philosophical catch' Cavell invokes here turns on how experience requires an education to be trustworthy, while education cannot proceed without a trust in one's experience. This apparent paradox must be part of why there is no way of fully grounding the authority of an act of aesthetic judgement.

30. In an interview with Conant collected in *The Senses of Stanley Cavell*, Cavell says:

> If you give up something like formal argumentation as the route to conviction in philosophy, and you give up the idea that either scientific evidence or poetic persuasion is the way to philosophical conviction, then the question of what achieves philosophical conviction must at all times be on your mind. The obvious answer for me is that it must lie in the writing itself. But in *what* about the writing? It isn't that there is a rhetorical form, any more than there is an emotional form, in which I can expect conviction to happen. But the sense that nothing other than this prose here, as it's passing before our eyes, can carry conviction, is one of the thoughts that drives the shape of what I do. (59)

31. Crary, *Beyond Moral Judgment*, 180 (original emphasis).
32. Carroll, review of *Pursuits of Happiness*, 104. Of course, we should also add to this list Cavell's overarching goal in *Pursuits of Happiness*: establishing remarriage comedy as an independent genre in the first place.
33. This chimes with Crary's account of making room for an alternative conception of rationality on which its exercise "necessarily presupposes the possession of certain sensitivities" (*Beyond Moral Judgment*, 119). It may also support one of the ideas developed in Sandra Harding's feminist epistemology: coming to an objective account of how things stand may actually require such judgements. As she writes:

    in a society structured by gender hierarchy, 'starting thought from women's lives' increases the objectivity of the results of research by bringing scientific observation and the perception of the need for explanation to bear on assumptions and practices that appear natural or unremarkable from the perspective of dominant groups. ('"Strong Objectivity" and Socially Situated Knowledge', 150)

34. McDowell, 'Aesthetic Value, Objectivity, and the Fabric of the World', 114.
35. MacKinnon, *Feminism Unmodified*, 54.
36. Lloyd, *The Man of Reason*, 17. As Lloyd argues in the closing pages of her book, this is a critique of a certain model of reason, not a rejection of reason *tout court* (see 109–10).
37. Hartsock, 'The Feminist Standpoint', 297.
38. Hartsock, 'The Feminist Standpoint', 295.
39. Naomi Scheman makes a similar link between Cavell's account of the sceptical condition of cinema spectatorship and the male conceit of disconnected knowledge:

    Cavell's account of the pleasure of movies similarly takes as definitive the wish . . . to be an unviewed viewer of the world. Cavell's account of this wish seems, however, more innocent and less political . . . For Cavell, what cinema grants us is not meant to be the power of the pornographer but respite from our complicity in the structuring of the world, "not a wish for power over creation . . ., but a wish not to need power, not to have to bear its burdens." The wish is granted by the total presentness to us of the world on the screen without our being present to it, neither implicated in it nor limited in our view of it by our particular placement in it.

> The innocence of this wish is, I think, misleading. The wish to be an unseen seer may be a wish for a less troubled relationship to reality, but that relation has been troubled in large measure by the cultural placement of epistemic authority precisely in the eyes of an unseen seer: movies grant us the opportunity not to notice the extent to which we are supposed to work at pushing the world away in order to view it truly. The world of the scientist doesn't contain the scientist, but his absence from it is neither innocent nor effortless . . . Kant may have tried to tell us that the world is always our world, but we haven't really learned it, and we go on trying to spy on it: no wonder we are lured by the promise of a world we don't have to hide behind a curtain to see. (We see it, in fact, when the curtain is pulled aside.) ('Missing Mothers/ Desiring Daughters', 86)

Though this could be read as a critique of Cavell, I hope my accounts in this chapter and the previous indicate how it might be taken as a critical deepening of his philosophy of cinema.

40. As in previous chapters, we find at the heart of scepticism not simply a rejection of knowledge, but a kind of *oscillation* between certainty and defeat. For an extended discussion of the role of gender in Cavell's account of scepticism, see Viefhughes-Bailey, *Beyond the Philosopher's Fear* (particularly 83–124).

41. Cavell describes the situation facing Gable's character in *It Happened One Night* as follows:

> What is the matter? Why can he not allow the woman of his dreams to enter his dream? But just that must be the answer. What surprises him is her reality. To acknowledge her as this woman would be to acknowledge that she is "somebody that's real, somebody that's alive," flesh and blood, someone separate from his dream who therefore has, if she is to be in it, to enter it; and this feels to him to be a threat to the dream, and hence a threat to him. (*Pursuits of Happiness*, 100)

42. If this interpretation and extension of Cavell's account holds good, it will trouble at least one aspect of it: the idea, which I elided with ellipses in the long passage from *Cities of Words* quoted above, that the "standing in the world" forgone by the male protagonists of classical remarriage comedy has been "costly for them" to establish. On my reading, the standing of these men was precisely the opposite of costly for them to establish: it was handed to them merely in virtue of their being born with the right genitals at the right time (which is not to imply that forgoing it will cost them nothing).

43. Cavell, *Cities of Words*, 154.
44. This is why I want to resist Butler's reading of the film as a celebration of the "contingency or unmooredness of roleplay, of being free of all responsibility" ('Abbas Kiarostami', 73). Indeed with its emphasis on freedom from responsibility, this strikes me as an apt description of the disconnection from the world and others characteristic of the sceptical condition. That said, one would be hard pressed to find a better description of Kiarostami's project as a whole than the one with which Butler concludes his essay: "Kiarostami is a great spiritual director, but the spirit is only reality and is only to be accessed through reality. There is only reality and nothing more" (75).

CHAPTER 7

Like Someone in Love: The Suspension of Belief

Like Someone in Love opens in a swanky Tokyo bar. We see a woman with bright red hair doing something on her phone; a man in a suit sitting, eating, smoking, and drinking with two women; a man in a suit standing, smoking, and talking with two women; more well-dressed men and women milling about in the background. As lounge music plays, we hear a woman's voice: "I'm not lying to you. When did I ever lie to you?" As she continues it becomes clear that the speaker is not in the frame (though we keep checking the faces of the women on screen to confirm this). When this mystery is abruptly resolved with a cut we see she is a slight young woman (played by Rin Takanashi), sitting alone at a table. Her name is Akiko, and she has been talking on her phone. She insists again on her honesty: "I swear to you I'm telling you the truth." Akiko tells her interlocutor – apparently a jealous boyfriend – that she is at Café Teo. The man orders her to go to the bathroom, where he demands she count the tiles; it seems he intends on counting the tiles at Teo himself to catch her out. Akiko is not at Café Teo but Bar Rizzo, where she works as a hostess.

After Akiko returns from the bathroom a man in a crisp white shirt joins her at her table. He wants to give her some relationship advice. He says her dishonesty will only cause her further pain and eventually destroy her ("Everything should be made clear from the beginning," he says, "so that lines are not crossed"). As they talk it becomes clear he is her boss, which is to say pimp. He has a job for her tonight. Akiko says she doesn't want it: she is too busy with exams, plus her grandmother is in Tokyo and wants to visit her before she leaves in the morning. But the man insists. He says her excuses are lousy; that there is no point spending such a short amount of time with her grandmother anyway; that the job is very important and involves a man for whom he has great respect; that considering her past refusals of work she does not have a choice in the matter; that she will not regret it. Akiko shrieks at him: "I'm not going, I told you!" It could be the film's strangest moment. Akiko is off screen for the line, which sounds so exaggerated that it hits a false note. When we cut back to Akiko, she looks demure; if it weren't for the shocked, staring faces of those in the background of the scene one might be forgiven for thinking that the shriek came from someone else. By placing Akiko off screen at this important and, it would seem, uncharacteristic moment (not only for our early notions of this character but also for the film-maker himself), Kiarostami makes it a little difficult to believe it. And disturbingly, the pimp doesn't seem convinced either, calling her a cab she appears to enter willingly, without further discussion. Thus begins a long, visually stunning, and rather wrenching sequence shot mostly inside the car, where Akiko listens to five imploring voicemails from her grandmother, masochistically (and/or sadistically) asking the cabbie to drive past the waiting woman as she heads out to meet her client (which is to say john). Eventually, she falls asleep in the back of the car.

When the cabbie arrives at their destination, we see that the man (played by Tadashi Okuno) is old enough to be Akiko's grandfather. Perhaps in reference to Kurosawa's *Ikiru* – which starred Takashi Shimura as Kanji Watanabe – he is named Takashi Watanabe. Akiko heads upstairs and meets him in an apartment lined with books. As she enters, Takashi is finishing a phone conversation with a man seeking a translation from him (as will be revealed soon, he is a distinguished scholar). He lies about his plans for the night, saying he has to work. As Takashi notes down the text he is to translate, Akiko explores the room, and looks at a picture on the wall: it is a print of Chiyoji Yazaki's *Training a Parrot*, which depicts a Japanese woman in a kimono with a cockatoo on a swing, which the woman is teaching to speak. Takashi finishes his call and they get to talking, turning quickly to the painting. Akiko's uncle gave her a copy of it for her fourteenth birthday, telling her that it was a portrait he had painted of her; Akiko only worked out this was a falsehood two years ago. "My grandma used to tell me that the parrot seemed to be teaching the girl," Akiko says, adding that people used to tell her she looked like the young woman in the picture. She gets up to demonstrate, posing in front of the painting for the old man. "Now I see the resemblance," he says, as she pins her hair into a bun. "I didn't really believe it was me in the painting. My eyes are bigger, aren't they?" Now she grabs a photograph off the table next to her, suggesting the girl in it (perhaps the old man's granddaughter) resembles her. She stands and walks across the room and picks up another photograph, this time of the old man's wife. "Don't I look a bit like her?" she guilelessly asks. "Maybe," he says, before confirming he lives alone.

After directing Akiko to the bathroom, Takashi opens a bottle of wine and pours two glasses, which are sitting on a table set for dinner. When Akiko exits the bathroom, however, she does not return to him: instead she enters a bedroom. Though we cannot see her, we (along with Takashi) watch as items of clothing are flung into the doorway. The old man enters the room and asks what she is doing: dinner is ready and there is wine for them to drink. Akiko replies that she is sleepy. The movement of her feet beneath the covers (just visible through the doorway) confirms she is in bed. There is a shot change as the old man takes a seat: we watch him from front on, and see a nebulous reflection of Akiko in the television screen on his left. She appears to be sitting up, wearing what might be a negligee. He tries to convince her to come out for dinner, but she refuses. Her reflection shows her lying down. She asks him to join her, but he keeps insisting they head to the other room to eat, drink, and talk. The telephone rings and he steps out of the bedroom to answer it; he misses it; he peers out the window; he goes back to look at the Yazaki (Ella Fitzgerald's rendition of *Like Someone in Love* plays in the background). He snuffs out the candles he had set on the table. When the phone rings again, he ignores it and heads back into the bedroom. There is a shot of Akiko in bed, apparently asleep. Takashi unplugs the phone and switches off the bedside lamp. Now the scene changes, and we see the pair inside a car, with Takashi at the wheel and Akiko in the passenger seat. Though the previous scene ended with a shot of Akiko alone, both characters are very sleepy today. At one stage, while stopped in traffic, Takashi even nods off in the driver's seat.

After Takashi drops her outside her university, Akiko is approached by a man who grabs at her, getting up in her face. Takashi undoes his seatbelt as if to go out and confront the man, but Akiko pushes past him and enters the building. The man approaches the car and asks for a cigarette lighter. Takashi hands him the device and he steps away to smoke, as the two men warily regard each other. The younger man eventually asks Takashi who he is, inviting himself into the vehicle. He introduces himself as Noriaki, then asks Takashi about his relationship with Akiko. Takashi does not disconfirm Noriaki's suggestions that he is her grandfather. Noriaki says he is Akiko's fiancé, and Takashi ends up questioning him about his job, schooling, age, and experience in just the way a grandfather might. He also questions him about the confrontation he just witnessed. Noriaki shrugs it off, saying the pair have their altercations, before going on to explain why he wishes to marry her: "If I lose her, I won't find another like her." He complains about the previous night: how Akiko hung up on him, and refused to answer his questions. Takashi suggests that Noriaki lacks experience: "When you know you will be lied to, it's better not to ask. That's what experience teaches us." When Akiko returns to the car, she looks shocked to find Noriaki in the passenger seat, but plays along with Takashi's charade. We are over halfway through this spare film, but the basic narrative set-up is finally in place: the controlling Noriaki has no knowledge of the nature of Akiko's work, nor of the nature of the relationship between her and Takashi; Takashi's intentions regarding her are not entirely clear, but he seems bent on protecting her; Akiko may want to rid herself of Noriaki, but is unsure about Takashi.

Though its shocking abruptness has divided critics, I take the final scene to be the one which gives the rest of the film philosophical unity. Takashi is working in his study when he receives a call from Akiko, distressed. He drives out to pick her up. When he finds her, her lip is swollen and bleeding. We know the catalyst for this must be the event we feared all along: the abusive Noriaki has discovered the true nature of Akiko's work. When Takashi returns with Akiko to his apartment, we find Noriaki has pursued them. He rings the buzzer from the ground floor and appears on the intercom system. Takashi tries ignoring him. Noriaki starts screaming. We hear a crash, then he charges up the stairs and pounds on the apartment door. When this has no effect he stomps back down, and we hear him smashing up the professor's car (the very vehicle he fixed a few scenes earlier). He goes quiet for a moment and Takashi moves over to the double window, sheepishly looking out. After a few tense moments, the glass explodes, shattered by some object thrown up from the ground. Takashi falls to the floor as if hit and the credits roll.[1]

I contend that the double window is a metonym for the movie screen. There is its oblong shape, the fact that it appears as a rectangle of light, and how this shot positions us as looking up at it. There is the presence of the double curtains, with a layer of muslin drawn over the glass, and thicker drapes pulled out on either side. There is the fact that the smashing of the window takes place at the very end of the film, and the shockingly abrupt nature of this conclusion (which leaves so much unresolved), with the end of the window nearly coinciding with the end of the film itself (as Saeed-Vafa points out,[2] the film was originally called *The End*, which brings to mind the title cards displayed on screen at the conclusion of old movies). There was the nebulous reflection of Akiko undressing in Takashi's bedroom – a reflection that tellingly appears in a television screen (there are spectacular shots of reflections running right through the film, including the reflections of Akiko's pimp in the glass doorway of Bar Rizzo, which we see as she exits to catch the cab, and which coincide with the presentation of the establishment's neon sign, confirming beyond doubt that Akiko has been lying). The image also harks back to the final shot of *Certified Copy*, in which we are given a view out the window toward the nearby church, and where the credits rolled not from the bottom to the top of the screen but from the bottom to the top of the window frame itself, setting up that window too as a kind of screen. And of course, the fact that what is smashed is a window is itself important, because Kiarostami has been obsessed with windows for decades: as we have seen throughout this book, shots of characters peering out through car windows (often followed by point of view shots where the viewer takes on the peering) are one of his signatures, as are shots of characters reflected in windows and mirrors. As Nancy writes, in Kiarostami "the car window doubles the screen".[3] When someone looks out a window in a Kiarostami film, they initiate a complex mirror game with the viewer: as we view a character on a screen as they look through a screen, we are called upon to reflect on our viewing, to view our act of viewing someone viewing. When that window breaks, then, it is as if all those screens/windows have been broken too (the double window doubles the screen while doubling the windows that double the screen). Thus I read the breaking of the window here as a destructive recapitulation of all his mature works: a kind of *Aufhebung* of the gesture that found paradigmatic form in the coda of *Taste of Cherry*.

But what is the meaning of the break? It is crucial that this is a film about deception, whose tension turns on whether Noriaki will discover what Akiko does for work, and the nature of her relationship to Takashi. Consider the opening line of the film, and the thematics of the opening scene more broadly; consider the questions of identity and deception that arise regarding the Yazaki painting (which, through depicting the act of teaching a parrot to talk, itself intimates this very problem: if and when the parrot speaks, will it be really talking, or just parroting?). Takashi is engaged in deception too, having led Noriaki to believe that he is Akiko's grandfather; this same lie is not directly told but is nevertheless furthered by Akiko in her encounter with the professor's nosey neighbour, during which we also learn she resembles the man's mother very closely; there is also his lie to the colleague who called in search of a translation from him. Consider too the conversation the professor has with Noriaki about his car: Noriaki warns him about his timing belt, and how it could break at any moment. A timing belt is what synchronises the rotation of the crankshaft and the camshaft, ensuring the valves do not strike the pistons; when a timing belt breaks, it can easily destroy an engine. The threat of a broken timing belt is like the threat that Noriaki will discover the truth: both events will shatter the finely calibrated systems they support with a destructive release of energy. When the window breaks, then, it stands in for the breaking of all these deceptions. It could also be read as the metonymic shattering of the cinematic illusion itself.

That the cinema works on us in the way it does because it deceives or tricks us is intuitive. This Platonic idea is implicit in the notion that becoming absorbed in a film requires the viewer to suspend her disbelief. Coleridge was the first to articulate the notion in this way, when he wrote that his *Lyrical Ballads* aimed to "transfer from our inward nature a human interest and a semblance of truth sufficient to procure for these shadows of imagination that *willing suspension of disbelief* for the moment, which constitutes poetic faith".[4] Perhaps contrary to Coleridge's own intentions, we use the phrase today not just to refer to "persons and characters supernatural"[5] but to the process apparently involved in our enjoyment of fictions in general. As Anthony Ferri writes, if perhaps with some exaggeration: "we use Coleridge's 'willing suspension of disbelief' as the quintessential phrase identifying the essence of the viewing process".[6] The idea is that the pleasure cinema affords is a function of the illusion that what is happening on screen is real.

Versions of it were crucial in psychoanalytic film theories. In *The Imaginary Signifier*, for instance, Christian Metz famously argued that in the cinema, the spectator partakes in a "scopic regime"[7] in which he is made both "absent from the screen" and "all-perceiving" – "all perceiving as one says all-powerful".[8] Further, he argues that the experience manufactured by the cinematic apparatus involves a kind of disavowal on the part of the spectator:

> Any spectator will tell you that he 'doesn't believe it,' but everything happens as if there were nonetheless someone to be deceived, someone who really would 'believe in it' . . . This credulous person is, of course, another part of ourselves, he is still seated *beneath* the incredulous one, or in his heart, it is he who continues to believe . . .[9]

Metz's idea, of course, is grounded in a notion of the unconscious: while we consciously know that what we are watching is not real, there is nevertheless an infantile, irrational part of us that is duped. Hence, for Metz, the cinema must "remove the traces of its steps",[10] working to conceal the means by which it manufactures credulity. In "Ideological Effects of the Basic Cinematographic Apparatus", Jean-Louis Baudry makes a similar claim: the cinematic apparatus – "projector, darkened hall, screen" – effectively "reconstructs the situation necessary to the release of the 'mirror stage' discovered by Lacan",[11] in which the child's recognition of his body in the mirror spurs a misrecognition of himself as a coherent whole. Baudry's account of what happens during projection breakdowns is revealing:

> We should remember, moreover, the disturbing effects which result during a projection from breakdowns in the recreation of movement, when the spectator is brought abruptly back to discontinuity – that is, to the body, to the technical apparatus which he had *forgotten*.[12]

The disquieting effect engendered when a projection breaks down is offered here as evidence for a claim about how cinema absorbs us: when a projector breaks, we are brought abruptly out of our fantasising and back to the reality we had forgotten, like dreamers rudely awakened from sleep.

These and similar theories have come under sustained attack from cognitivists such as Carroll, Gregory Currie, and Berys Gaut. They regard the idea that the cinematic apparatus leads spectators of fictional films to believe in what they see on screen to be highly implausible. After all, these scholars argue, if spectators in cinemas really believed in the reality of what they see, they would respond to cinematic images very differently from how they typically do. We might presume, for instance, that non-psychopathic viewers would not take pleasure in horror films; we would not expect the viewers of a film like *Independence Day* to sit and watch the destruction of the world around them at the hands of an alien species while nonchalantly eating popcorn. Currie puts the point in an exemplary fashion:

> You have only to reflect for a moment on how you would react if you saw, or thought you saw, a threatening monster, or if you thought yourself alone in a house with an axe murderer, or I thought you were watching someone about to be attacked by an axe murderer, to see that your behavior in the cinema is quite unlike that of someone who really did believe in the reality of the fiction presented.[13]

Though the argument is obviously persuasive, perhaps its very obviousness should give us pause. Indeed the position Currie attacks here would probably be rejected – and for the same reasons – by a child of eight, who would be likely to be more than capable of telling you why the presence of a monster on screen does not imply the existence of monsters in real life (which is not to say she won't be scared of the monster on screen). Do film theorists who insist on the role of cognitive illusion really think that audiences in cinemas are duped into believing wholeheartedly in what they see on screen, in just the way they believe in the events of real life? As I indicated above, it would be better to understand their claims about belief in a more charitable way: as claims not about standard belief but some less rational version of it. Consider Metz's point that spectators will tell you they do not believe in what they see on screen: the claim is not simply that cinematic spectatorship involves cognitive illusion, but that the belief it engenders is of a special, disavowed kind. The cognitivist, of course, will now respond by questioning the empirical validity of the notion of the unconscious at work here.[14] I am not interested in intervening on either side of this debate. Rather, I am interested in the intuitions at work in it about cinematic images. In particular, I am interested in a deep intuition regarding how films move us, which is apparently shared by both sides here.

We have just seen that on classic psychoanalytic accounts, what happens in a film is entertained in beliefs (beliefs that may be disavowed, or held only unconsciously). In Chapter 3 we saw that, for Carroll, the content of a fictional film is not believed but imagined suppositionally by its spectators. In *Image and Mind*, Currie makes a similar argument: films affect us because they lead us to simulate imaginatively the events we see on screen. Fictions, Currie argues, engage our mental processes in "off-line" mode, by which he means they work by "severing the connections between our mental states and their perceptual causes and behavioural effects".[15] "With fictions," he claims, "what we acquire instead of beliefs is [sic] *imaginings* which simulate belief."[16] This notion of imaginative simulation, Currie argues, can resolve the paradox of fiction, or the problem of how we can be moved by events in whose reality we do not believe.

Because they do not rely on a problematic notion of cognitive illusion, the accounts of Currie and Carroll are perhaps more sophisticated than those of psychoanalytic film theorists. But the accounts share the assumption that, for a film to move us, we must be brought to entertain – whether through believing, supposing, or imagining – its propositional content. In a number of places in this book – most notably in Chapter 2's account of the particular form of solidarity engendered by *ABC Africa*, Chapter 3's account of how *Ten*'s troubling the distinction between supposition and belief allows something to emerge that is not captured by either, and in Chapter 5's account of how the faces of *Shirin* can move us without convincing us – I have sought to show that films can affect us otherwise. If those accounts hold good, in other words, we have reason to question the assumption underlying the cognitivist theories I have invoked, and the psychoanalytic theories against which they have been pitted (at least on the accounts of the theories forwarded for attack by cognitivists).

There is another, perhaps deeper reason to be dubious of these accounts, which it will take me some time to bring out. It is not simply that they may falsify the nature of our relation to cinematic images. It is also that they may falsify the nature of our relationship to reality. Consider what it is to be absorbed in ordinary life, outside the context of a viewing a film. Let's say you are sitting at your desk, involved in some work, and drinking coffee from a cup sitting next to your computer. Does your act of reaching for the cup to drink from it presuppose your *believing* that the cup is there? In a certain frame of mind, the idea may seem completely uncontroversial: why else would you reach for the cup? Surely we do not tend to reach for things we do not believe to be in reach! But there may be good phenomenological reasons for regarding this as confused. Consider the following from Carleton B. Christensen:

> I come out of my house and suddenly see *that* my recently departed visitor has thoughtlessly left the gate open, thereby potentially allowing my dogs to get out onto the street, where they could get hit by a car. Note how this example suggests an important phenomenological observation: I judge perceptually that *p* precisely when I am *not* oriented towards the things I 'see' in the way I need to be in order to set about doing what I have to do with them. For clearly, I am concerned to have the gate closed and the fact that I notice its having been left open at all indicates that I am aware of the significance this fact has for me (and, in particular, my dogs). Precisely because 'perceptual experience' in this apophantic sense does not orient me towards, or suitably set me up to engage with, the items I need to deal with, I might have to deliberate about what to do next.[17]

Drawing on Heidegger and Edmund Husserl – and responding to McDowell's influential account of the role of concepts in perceptual experience, to which I will shortly turn – Christensen forwards a nuanced description of the form of absorption characteristic of our being in the world. And it is obviously not that propositional content plays no role here. As the encounter with the open gate described in this passage demonstrates – where Christensen walks out of his house and judges perceptually that *p* (where *p* is 'the gate is open' or perhaps 'the gate has been left open') – it can play a pivotal role. The point is that judgements such as this do not play a constitutive role in perceptual experience: that Christensen only judges that the gate is open because the gate is not *supposed* to be open; that the gate's being open jars him into believing the proposition that it is. If the gate had not been left open, Christensen would not have needed to deliberate about what to do, nor would he have needed to make a perceptual judgement leading him to form this belief: he would simply have walked up to the gate, opened it, exited his garden, and closed it behind him. As Heidegger's phenomenology of our engagements with equipment indicates,[18] only in some circumstances, such as when something goes wrong in our dealings – for example, when one's hammer breaks, or the gate is left open when it shouldn't be – do we step back from the world, and enter the reflective, deliberative, intellectual mode of comportment proper to judgement-making and belief-formation. Though it may always be possible to give a partial rendering of our worldly engagements in propositional terms, such renderings miss the phenomenon of everyday absorption (or what

Hubert Dreyfus calls "coping"[19]), because of its pre-propositional elements. Our ordinary absorption in the world cannot be cashed out as propositional content except at the cost of something essential.

In 1994's *Mind and World*, McDowell advanced an account of perception which, in a Wittgensteinian spirit, was meant to dissolve sceptical problems regarding the bearing of the world and the mind upon one another. Scepticism can find its feet, according to McDowell, because of a "tension between . . . two forces".[20] The first force comes from what, following Wilfrid Sellars, he calls 'the Myth of the Given': the intuitive notion that, for the mind to be in touch with the objective world, it must be affected by "non-conceptual impacts from outside the world of thought",[21] which is often figured through some version of the idea of sense impressions. The problem with recourse to the Given, however, is that it effectively deprives us of what it was supposed to provide, because the notion of brute causal impacts from a realm external to thought – from what McDowell, again following Sellars, calls the 'space of nature' – undermines the justificatory force of what is delivered by it. If the idea of the Given establishes experience as in touch with the world, in other words, it achieves this at the cost of disconnecting it from what McDowell and Sellars call the 'space of reasons': the normative context in which our claims about the world can be vindicated, or "a logical space whose structure consists in some of its occupants being . . . warranted or correct in the light of others".[22] The point of appealing to the Given was to secure the mind's being in touch with the world, but it threatens to lead us headlong into the thought that "we have no convincing way to credit ourselves with empirical knowledge".[23] This is one of the ways in which scepticism sneaks into our picture of mind and world.

Another way, McDowell argues, is through a kind of recoil from the Given. This is the second force at work in the tension he identifies. It begins from an attempt to take seriously the lesson learned from the Given's failure to give us what we wanted: that purely causal, non-conceptual impinge-ments – "brute impacts from the exterior",[24] as McDowell puts it – cannot ground our knowledge of the world outside our minds, because they could never figure in justification. As we recoil from this idea, then, we may be led to give up the very idea of empirically derived knowledge, supposing that experience itself must be left outside the space of reasons. Thus Davidson's coherentism, which holds that justification for beliefs cannot be grounded in the "testimony of the senses",[25] and must instead be derived from other beliefs. "[N]othing can count as a reason for holding a belief", Davidson says, "except another belief".[26] The problem with this recourse to beliefs, accord-ing to McDowell, is that it leaves us trapped in them, as though they form a self-contained whole that can accept no rational influence from the world lying outside them. McDowell refers to the "confinement imagery"[27] that runs through Davidson's account, and to which I turned in Chapter 2, when I evoked Davidson's remark about our being unable to get outside our own skins: "Perhaps we can understand how Davidson can be so casual in this remark", McDowell writes, "if we take it that our literal confinement inside our skins strikes him as an analogue to a metaphorical confinement inside our beliefs, which he is happy to let his coherentism imply".[28] The rejection of the idea that we must ground our beliefs in the impingements of the Given, in other words, leads us back into the worry that our beliefs have no bearing on the world they were supposed to be directed towards. This is to say it leads us back to the very worry that made the Given look attractive in the first place. Hence McDowell's idea that a key symptom of being in the thrall of scepticism is a kind of oscillation between two opposing positions, neither of which seems to grant us purchase on reality.

It is worth pausing to recognise how McDowell's account of this sceptical oscillation chimes with the descriptions of scepticism I have been providing in this book. In *The Wind Will Carry Us*, we saw that the protagonist heads to Iranian Kurdistan in the hope of capturing a pre-modern tradition on camera: a tradition that he and his crew have set up as treasure-like. As I argued, he projects onto the villagers a fantasy of unmediated access to the world, but he finds this was a fantasy internal to his own world; thus he leaves without getting what he wanted. When I treated *ABC Africa*, I traced a different oscillation: this time between the idea that objectivity can be attained through the elimination of subjective elements, and the opposing thought that, because subjectivity cannot be elided, an objective stance can never be attained. In the account of reality television I developed in Chapter 3, I described a fantasy of capturing ordinary life by digging down through layers of artifice, and the seemingly paradoxical result of this procedure: images of the ordinary that are literally incredible. When the ordinary is figured as subsisting beneath mediation in this way, I tried to show, it sparks the thought that we have to cut through that mediation. But what emerges out of this are travesties of the ordinary. Chapter 4 turned to the idea that the aesthetic power of photographic media stems from their capacity to record events that could never have been intended by photographers or directors. Yet I argued this notion of something lying entirely outside the reach of directorial intervention is driven by a thought that is hard to make sense of: that if a human hand has been involved in an event, it will somehow spoil its claim to reality. If Kiarostami's procedure in *Five* achieves its goal, it will still the oscillation between a thought of pristine, untouched reality and the thought that, because accessing it would entail spoiling it, we must be completely out of touch with the real. In the chapter on *Shirin*, I treated the Cavellian idea of sceptical spectatorship, which is predicated on the notion that film grants us a connection with the world, but only at the cost of absenting us from it. The problem is that in being given what we want, we find ourselves losing it. In the last chapter, I followed the thought that, if the world cannot be known from a position of certainty and security, it cannot be known at all. As I tried to show, *Certified Copy* figures the consequences of this in terms of a crisis of experiential authority. In the sceptical conditions depicted and enacted by these films, we find ourselves faced not just with a loss of knowledge, but wavering between a thought of victory over scepticism and a thought of defeat by it, where the thought of defeat sparks a desire for victory that, in turn, leads us back into defeat.

Now McDowell's own attempt at stopping the sceptical oscillation is elegant: it is to recommend a picture of mind and world on which experience must have conceptual content. Here he draws on Kant's insight regarding spontaneity and receptivity, concepts and intuitions. For Kant, spontaneity is at work when we exercise our faculty of understanding: it is the power of knowing objects through the deployment of concepts. Receptivity is at work when we enjoy impressions through the faculty of sensibility: it is how we are able to obtain intuitions. Kant's insight was about the inextricability of these processes: that for knowledge to be possible, receptivity must be at work in spontaneity, and vice versa; in his justly famous phrase, "thoughts without content are empty, intuitions without concepts are blind".[29] A contentless thought would be a mere deployment of concepts without sensory intake to fill them out (this is what we see in Davidson, on McDowell's account of his coherentism); a blind intuition would be a bare sense impression that can make no rational claim on us (which is all the Given ended up offering us). McDowell's Kantian idea is that, to account for the bearing of mind on world and vice versa, we need to take it that perceptual experience is always already conceptual. That meets the need for rational constraint, because in experience we are receptive to the layout of the world; but experience can play a normative role in the space of reasons, because experiences come with conceptual content. This is how McDowell purports to dissolve the sceptical threat, releasing the tension between the force of the attraction of the Given and the force of our recoil from it. We are receptive to the world and so to the rational constraints it provides, but that very receptivity is permeated by concepts, and so spontaneity extends "all the way out"[30] to our empirical judgements. This implies there is no problem with asserting that experience can deliver knowledge of the world to us, nor with the idea that it can do it non-inferentially: "In experience one takes in, for instance sees, *that things are thus and so.*"[31]

Before we bring this back to the problem of how cinematic images move us, we should consider a problematic aspect of McDowell's early account. On the picture I just outlined, in experience we do not register bare bits of sense data, but how it is with the world. When I see my dog curled up asleep in the corner of my study, for example, I do not receive sense impressions that I must interpret and/or from which I must infer (which would allow scepticism to creep into the picture, as one is led to ask if those impressions can be trusted): I simply see *that* Champion Ruby is curled up asleep in the corner of my study. Yet this may imply something that sits uneasily with the phenomenological evidence I raised earlier in this chapter, which indicates that in our everyday dealings with the world, the making of judgements and the forming of beliefs tend only to take place in certain circumstances (such as when something jumps out as a disturbance, jarring me out of my absorption). The presence of Ruby curled up asleep in the corner of my study typically does not have this effect, because she often sleeps in here as I work: I see her in the room, but that does not mean I internally articulate it, indeed I usually pass over it without a moment's thought (by contrast, I would be jarred into immediate deliberation if I saw her in the front garden, because she is not allowed out there). The problem, in other words, is that the notion of conceptual content looks suspiciously like the notion of propositional content, and is thus in danger of reducing and so falsifying what absorbed experience is like. As Christensen says, McDowell remains "committed to the traditional conviction that to be conceptually contentful is to be *proposition-ally* contentful . . .".[32] This is also at the root of the criticism of McDowell advanced by Arthur Collins: that "the scene I take in perceptually will support a large and open-ended number of possible propositional descriptions and no one of them is essential or required . . . experience does not come, as though, with subtitles".[33] Part of the problem with taking experience as always already propositional is that it elides how experiences place no upper limit on what can be said about them: it's not quite that our propositions are not enough to describe a scene, but that there is always more to say. Experiences are inexhaustible in this way.

McDowell has been at pains to clarify and indeed modify this aspect of his account in more recent work, where he distinguishes his picture of perception as intrinsically conceptual from a picture of perception as intrinsically propositional. In 2009's 'Avoiding the Myth of the Given', he writes:

> Intuitions bring our surroundings into view, but not in an operation of mere sensibility . . . [T]he conceptual content that allows us to avoid the Myth is intuitional, not propositional, so experiencing is not taking things to be so. In

bringing our surroundings into view, experiences entitle us to take things to be so; whether we do is a further question.[34]

The difference may seem slight but it is crucial: experience is not taking things to be thus and so, but what *entitles us* to take things to be thus and so. In *Mind and World*, experiences were figured as delivering propositional content: perceptual content that can become the content of a judgement if the experiencer takes the perception at face value. As McDowell writes there: "*That things are thus and so* is the content of the experience, and it can also be the content of a judgement: it becomes the content of a judgement if the subject decides to take the experience at face value."[35] In 'Avoiding the Myth of the Given', by contrast, that things are thus and so is not the content of experiences, but something they make available for articulation. Experience delivers pre-propositional content that is nevertheless conceptual, which makes it immediately suitable for articulation in discursive activities like judgements. It does not come pre-carved into propositional form, in other words, but ready to be so carved. And of course, there is no limit on how it can be. The subtlety of this thought is perhaps part of why McDowell's descriptions of it can sound laboured: "intuitions immediately reveal things to be as they would be claimed to be in claims that would be no more than a discursive exploitation of some of the content of the intuitions".[36] The difficulty lies in avoiding two pitfalls: falling into talk of 'mere' or non-conceptual sense impressions, or into the intellectualist picture that would boil it all down to propositions. The former pitfall sees us appealing to the Given; the latter sees us "exaggerate the extent of the doxastic activity experience prompts in us . . .".[37] The account forwarded in *Mind and World* avoided the former mistake, but not the latter one. In avoiding it too, we avoid falsifying absorbed experience, and do not have to face the implication that rightly worried Collins: that in experience we somehow "acquire all the beliefs we would be entitled to by what we have in view".[38] This allows us to explain away a seeming paradox in the phenomenology I raised earlier, on which features of the world often do not register with us in propositional form unless they jar as remarkable in some way. If I do not first judge that *p*, someone might ask, how can I be jarred by it? Surely my being jarred by *p presupposes* my judging that *p*. But this is not a problem on this account of perception, because our intuitions reveal the layout of the world to us. When I am jarred by something unusual, I judge something that was already delivered for my perceiving. I carve out something that, in more usual circumstances, I would have left unarticulated.

This may allow us to rethink the paradox of fiction as it applies to cinema. Here is one of Carroll's formulations of it: "Emotional response is thought to require belief in the existence of its object; but with fictions we know that the Green Slime does not exist. So our fear in this case seems inconsistent with our knowledge."[39] As we have seen, the standard cognitivist response to such problems is to insist that emotional response does not have to require belief in its object, but merely that I suppose it, or simulate it in my imagination. The problem with such a response is that it falls into the intellectualist trap that caught the McDowell of *Mind and World*: the assumption that content must be propositional. Thus it is in danger of falsifying our relation to reality, because the entertainment of propositional content – whether through beliefs, judgements, simulations, assertions, or whatever – is just one, important but by no means central mode in which we engage the world. The very idea of a paradox of fiction betrays the assumption that belief is a necessary constituent of our worldly engagements. I do not have to believe in the existence of the Green Slime to fear it, just as I do not have to believe in the existence of my coffee cup to drink from it.

Drawing on my critical accounts of Kiarostami's films, I also said above that it is in danger of falsifying our relation to the cinematic image. Why can emerge more clearly now. Films, just like the rest of reality, make a range of conceptual content available to us. For us to be affected by that content, we do not have to carve it out in propositional form: as when we are absorbed in the world, in cinematic absorption we often do not need to articulate the content. This is why we can fear the Green Slime without considering its existential status: without believing in it, imagining it, or supposing it to be real. And for much of the time, this is how we do respond to films: we are absorbed in what happens, and are affected by it, all without having to articulate it propositionally.[40] This is not to say that cinematic absorption is pre-cognitive or merely affective (that would be to set it up as a version of the Given).[41] On this account, cinematic absorption is conceptual but pre-propositional: to respond to what happens on the screen, we do not need to infer from dumb data given to our senses; but nor do we need to articulate it in propositional terms. In Chapter 5 I argued that, on pain of giving teeth to scepticism, absorption should not be taken as a function of conviction. In the case of fictional films, one problem with that idea is that conviction would require belief in their propositional content (a situation that, as cognitivists are right to point out, would see us respond to films very differently from how we typically do). Perhaps now we can see there is a deeper problem. It is that this blinds us to the very phenomenon of cinematic absorption, and what is so uncannily powerful about cinematic images.[42]

Part of what is unsatisfactory about the accounts of Currie and Carroll is that they needlessly complicate what it is to respond to films. To be moved by them, I do not necessarily need to imagine or suppose anything. I can just respond pre-reflectively to what is there on screen. This does not mean propositional content is irrelevant to our experience of films (if that claim is not implausible enough in itself, then consider how it would be contradicted by all the discursive articulations of what happens in Kiarostami's films I provide in this very book). On this account, films deliver conceptual content ready for articulation: content we take in pre-reflectively and are moved by while absorbed, but which we can usually begin to articulate if called upon to do so.[43] This allows us to respect key aspects of what it is to talk about a film: that cinematic images contain more than we can formulate, overflowing our propositions; that a good critic may find content in them that we had not picked out; that images are inexhaustible. And of course, as in normal perception, cinematic spectators can easily move between these different modes of engagement, sliding ineluctably between non-propositional absorption and the explicit entertainment of propositions (indeed it would be a mistake to regard these two states as necessarily exclusive). In some cases, this will involve the entertainment of propositions about what happens in the movie (as when we notice that Akiko and Takashi are very tired, and so judge that they may have had sex the previous night). In some cases, this will involve awareness of the fact that we are watching a film (as when we note that Kiarostami is withholding crucial information from us, and so judge that *Like Someone in Love* is typical of his deliberately ambiguous style). In neither kind of case will problems or paradoxes regarding the reality of the fictional entities one sees on screen typically arise, as long as one is familiar with the conventions surrounding fictional films (as even eight-year-old children tend to be).

Sometimes questions arise regarding the propositional status of what happens on screen. This is typical of modernist films, which employ a range of techniques to get us questioning what we see, sometimes by provoking us into medium awareness.[44] And on the understanding of Kiarostami's work I have developed in this book, raising such questions is fundamental to his own directorial strategy. Consider what I have been describing as the paradigm of his characteristic gesture: the coda of *Taste of Cherry*, which reveals him and his crew. As I have argued, part of what is remarkable about it is that it does not simply distance us – puncturing our conviction in the film – but complicates our absorption in it. And there is something enlivening about it. Coming as it does after a shot of a man who may be killing himself, it casts a surprising light on the preceding story, imbuing it with what Butler very aptly calls "unexpected jubilation".[45] For psychoanalytic theory, the revelation of the director would have to represent a shattering of the cinematic illusion, rather like what happens when there is a fault with the projector, on Baudry's account of such events (consider the violence that is typical of some modernist techniques, as displayed, for example, in the opening sequence of Ingmar Bergman's *Persona*). But Kiarostami's coda brings about the very opposite of a rude awakening (though it is rightly described as an awakening). It troubles the propositional claims we might make about the film. We cannot say if Badii has died. We don't know if the scene counts as part of the preceding movie, or if that movie ended with Badii in the dark of his grave. We wonder if it has turned into a documentary of some sort. We cannot say if the soldiers are still in character, or what 'in character' means when one is watching non-professional actors, hired to play themselves. We try to understand the meaning of the director's presence on the scene. But we are not simply thrown out of the film. Rather, we are led to admit that we do not know what we are looking at. We are not thus distanced but disoriented and overwhelmed. The coda asks us to acknowledge that cinematic absorption operates on a level that precedes our judgements regarding, beliefs about, and knowledge of the world. It is enlivening because, in throwing us back on our absorption, it shows it is untouched by scepticism.

If we read the double window in Takashi's apartment as a metonym of the screen, then its shattering could be taken as the metonymic destruction of the cinematic illusion. This could be given weight by the fact that Noriaki smashes Takashi's window in an act of insane rage spurred by the discovery that Akiko has been deceiving him. On this interpretation, the break must be a gesture designed to force us to confront our own naïve belief that we were being told the truth (or perhaps our nagging doubt that we weren't), just as Noriaki did. Yet if the above is right, we should hesitate here. And of course, part of the problem is that this would align Kiarostami himself with Noriaki, as though the director is on board with his act of violence.

On my reading, Noriaki's act figures what we might describe as the sceptical underpinnings of the urge to overcome scepticism.[46] Kiarostami is presenting a lesson in what happens when we seek to root out and destroy deception.[47] We should read the break not as the shattering of illusion, then, but as the shattering of an illusion of it. What Kiarostami suspends is not simply belief but the belief in belief:[48] the idea that we *must* have believed in the first place, and the notion that propositional attitudes must be fundamental to how we encounter the world. This means that Deleuze's claim that the task of modern cinema is to "restore our belief in the world"[49] is right enough in spirit but in a deeper sense precisely wrong. The task of anti-theoretical film-philosophy is not to restore something that has been lost, but to show that we could never have had what we thought we lost, and so not simply that we do not have it, but also that we have not lost it. Absorption in cinema is literally uncanny. So it is with the world.

Notes

1. Kiarostami's procedure here corresponds exactly to Robert Baird's description of the cinematic "startle effect": a character is present; there is a threat off screen; then there is an intrusion into that character's personal space (see 'The Startle Effect').
2. Saeed-Vafa, 'Reflections on *Like Someone in Love*'. Saeed-Vafa also supports the idea that the window is a metonym for the screen, arguing that "the window of the old man's apartment becomes the screen/frame . . .".
3. Nancy, *The Evidence of Film*, 92.
4. Coleridge, *Biographia Literaria*, 6 (emphasis added).
5. Coleridge, *Biographia Literaria*, 6.
6. Ferri, *Willing Suspension of Disbelief*, 86.
7. Metz, *The Imaginary Signifier*, 61.
8. Metz, *The Imaginary Signifier*, 48.
9. Metz, *The Imaginary Signifier*, 72.
10. Metz, *The Imaginary Signifier*, 40.
11. Baudry, 'Ideological Effects of the Basic Cinematographic Apparatus', 45.
12. Baudry, 'Ideological Effects of the Basic Cinematographic Apparatus', 42.
13. Currie, *Image and Mind*, 24. See also the argument from Carroll and Seeley: "We don't flee danger at the movies, we don't attempt to help the injured, nor do we try to console the bereaved. No matter how you slice it, explanations of the qualitative, experiential grip of movies that appeal to an illusion of reality are dead in the water" ('Cognitivism, Psychology, and Neuroscience', 55). Gaut puts it similarly: "were [viewers] really under the illusion that they were in the presence of an axe-wielding maniac depicted in a horror film, they would flee the cinema" (*A Philosophy of Cinematic Art*, 63).

    Allen, by contrast, presents a compelling account of what he calls 'projective illusion' that preserves aspects of psychoanalytic theories, yet without committing to the claim that spectators are led to believe in the reality of what they see on screen. "When we experience a pictorial representation as a projective illusion," Allen writes, "we do not believe that what we see is real" (*Projecting Illusion*, 97–8). On Allen's account, in the experience of projective illusion, you lose awareness of the fact that you are seeing a film, that is, watching a recorded event that is staged before the camera. Instead of looking 'from the outside' upon something staged in this world, you perceive the events of the film directly or 'from within.' You perceive a fully realized though fictional world that has all the perceptual immediacy of our own; you experience the film as a projective illusion. (107)

14. Carroll takes this line in his reply to Warren Buckland's negative review of *Mystifying Movies* (see 'Cognitivism, Contemporary Film Theory and Method', 207–8).
15. Currie, *Image and Mind*, 149.
16. Currie, *Image and Mind*, 148. Elsewhere he writes:

> While fictions do not cause us to believe in the reality of the fictional story, they can engage us to the extent of causing within us the sometimes pleasant and sometimes unpleasant bodily states we associate with being emotionally moved by events. If fictions encourage simulations, and simulated beliefs and desires retain their internal connection to our bodily states, that is exactly what we would expect. (*Image and Mind*, 156)

17. Christensen, *Self and World*, 144 (original emphasis).
18. See Heidegger, *Being and Time*, SZ 63–113; 59–105e.
19. See Dreyfus, *Being-in-the-World*, 88–107. The difference between Dreyfus's account and the one forwarded here is that, following McDowell, I want to regard absorption as conceptual. McDowell and Dreyfus's debate on this issue is famous (see Dreyfus, 'Overcoming the Myth of the Mental' and McDowell, 'What Myth?'). For a collection of papers dealing with their important exchange, see Schear, *Mind, Reason, and Being-in-the-World*.
20. McDowell, *Mind and World*, xvi.
21. McDowell, *Mind and World*, 7.
22. McDowell, *Mind and World*, xvi.
23. McDowell, *Mind and World*, 15.
24. McDowell, *Mind and World*, 8.
25. Davidson, 'A Coherence Theory of Truth and Knowledge', 310.
26. Davidson, 'A Coherence Theory of Truth and Knowledge', 310; quoted in McDowell, *Mind and World*, 14.
27. McDowell, *Mind and World*, 16.
28. McDowell, *Mind and World*, 16.
29. Kant, *The Critique of Pure Reason*, B76 A52; 193–4e.
30. McDowell, *Mind and World*, 67.

31. McDowell, *Mind and World*, 9 (original emphasis).
32. Christensen, *Self and World*, 9 (original emphasis).
33. Collins, 'Beastly Experience', 379. This point supports the arguments developed in Chapters 2 and 3 that it is a fundamental mistake to take reality as a totality of propositional content.
34. McDowell, 'Avoiding the Myth of the Given', 269.
35. McDowell, *Mind and World*, 26 (original emphasis).
36. McDowell, 'Avoiding the Myth of the Given', 267.
37. McDowell, 'Avoiding the Myth of the Given', 269.
38. McDowell, 'Avoiding the Myth of the Given', 269.
39. Carroll, *The Philosophy of Horror*, 79.
40. Tarja Laine outlines a somewhat similar position in *Feeling Cinema*, which argues that "the process of emotional engagement with the film is a dynamic event of interaction" (11). Particularly relevant is her treatment of horror films, and her argument that they "scare through more immediate means than can be explained by spectators entertaining in thought, say, the impure properties of Count Dracula, or by their feeling concern for film characters in horrific situations" (12). Yet Laine bases her arguments on an ontology of cinema that contains metaphysical commitments that strike me both as implausible in themselves and as unnecessary for an account of cinema's affective powers, such as her claim that films should be understood as emotional agents which "feel about their subject matter and possess an emotional attitude toward the spectators" (3).
41. It would also be to make the mistake that causes such problems for Dreyfus's (otherwise highly compelling) account of absorbed coping. It sees him draw a sharp distinction between pre-cognitive, pre-conceptual absorption and detached, conceptually articulated reflection, and leads him to make implausible claims like the following:

    > After much experience, the chess master is directly drawn by the forces on the board to make a masterful move, and, in the same way, the kind person, as Sartre sees, is directly drawn to act by the force of the needy person's apparent need. In neither case does the master make his move *for a reason*. ('The Myth of the Pervasiveness of the Mental', 35)

    As McDowell shows (see 'The Myth of the Mind as Detached', 46), the absorption of a master in a game of blitz chess does not preclude his acting for reasons. If he pauses to reflect explicitly on what he is doing, he may indeed break his flow – but not because his acting in flow was somehow non-cognitive or purely perceptual. Rather, it is because he has actualised conceptual capacities that were already pervasive in his flow. I am arguing that the same goes for spectators in cinemas.

42. We could compare this account of cinematic absorption with Heidegger's treatment of worldly absorption in *Being and Time*. As Heidegger found, the difficulty is that philosophy, because of the intellectualist tendency that runs right through the tradition, is constitutively ill equipped to grasp the phenomenon in question. Like a star that vanishes as soon as one tries to focus on it, the phenomenon of absorption disappears when we try to grasp it theoretically.

43. As McDowell writes in one of his replies to Dreyfus's attacks on his alleged intellectualism:

> A *capacity* to step back from situations and consider whether features of them constitute reasons for thinking or acting in this or that way is a central element in what it is to have conceptual capacities at all. But that is not to say that the capacity for distance is actualized whenever conceptual capacities are in play. Exactly not: the capacity for distance is *not* actualized in unreflective perceptual experience or in unreflective intentional agency, but conceptual capacities are operative in both. ('The Myth of the Mind as Detached', 53; original emphasis)

This also indicates a way out of the rather tired debate in film theory regarding active versus passive spectatorship. On the one hand, it allows us to account for the undeniable power of cinematic images: the notion that, when they are absorbed in a film, spectators are in a profound sense given over to it. On the other hand, it allows us to account for the fact that, despite their being given over, spectators are not merely the passive dupes of what takes place on screen. Cinematic absorption is pre-reflective, but our conceptual capacities remain in play in it, ready to be actualised in reflection.

44. For a useful account of medium awareness that draws on insights both from cognitivism and a reconstructed version of psychoanalytic theory, see Allen, *Projecting Illusion*, 82–110. A significant difference between Allen's account and the one I am developing here, of course, is that his theory of cinematic absorption turns on the idea of illusion. "[T]he loss of medium awareness", as he writes, "is pre-requisite to the experience of projective illusion" (108).

45. Butler, 'Abbas Kiarostami', 72.

46. Considering the link between scepticism and masculinity I identified in Chapter 6, it should not surprise us that this act of violence emerges out

of a male desire for control. That said, the explicit depiction of violence is itself surprising, coming in a Kiarostami film. The only real precedents for it are in his pre-Revolutionary work, and especially *The Report*, which contains a harrowing scene of domestic violence perpetrated by its male protagonist.

47. This may give us a way of understanding the role of love in this film. First we should acknowledge that its characters seem in want of love. The professor is a widower or divorced or estranged from his wife; he calls a sex worker, but for something other than or more than only sex. Noriaki is not treated sympathetically in the film, but it's evident he is suffering, and perhaps from a kind of lovelessness: we could put his jealousy down to a function of his lack of love, or at least his inability to bear it (like Cavell's King Lear); he is brutal and controlling, but has been brutalised by a society that does not care for him, granting him little control over his own existence – as a young working-class man, it is clear enough that he cannot really keep Akiko (note the scene in which he confronts her at university: the extent to which he sticks out from the students) – which is perhaps part of what drives him to act in the way he does. Akiko herself treats her grandmother quite brutally, but she too seems to have been brutalised by circumstance, apparently compelled by financial strife into prostitution. Then there is the title, taken from the eponymous Ella Fitzgerald song to which Takashi listens in the initial apartment scene, and which also plays over the closing credits of the film. The lyrics:

> Lately, I find myself gazing at stars
> Hearing guitars like someone in love
> Sometimes the things I do astound me
> Mostly whenever you're around me
>
> Lately, I seem to walk as though I had wings
> Bump into things like someone in love
> Each time I look at you, I'm limp as a glove
> And feeling like someone in love

There are two ways of reading the song: to feel like *someone in love* could just mean being in the early days of falling in love, when you feel that something is starting to happen. Yet it could also have to do with semblance, with feeling *like* someone in love, with feeling something that resembles it, and in that sense isn't really it.

But the category of knowledge has an ambiguous application to love.

Consider the epistemic status of a declaration of love. It is perhaps more problematic even than the reports associated with sceptical threats of the problem of other minds: if it is true that when "I see someone writhing in pain with evident cause I do not think: all the same, his feelings are hidden from me" (Wittgenstein, *Philosophical Investigations*, 190e), then in love things are complicated. Here one can be mistaken in attributing the predicate 'in love' to oneself (Romeo and Rosaline); here it is not meaningless to say, 'I know I am in love' ('How?' 'I just *know*'); here the intensity of an emotional display can itself cast doubt on what we might presume (or hope) it is intended to convey (sometimes the louder you shout it, the hollower you sound). Wittgenstein again: "Love is not a feeling. Love is put to the test, pain not. One does not say: that was not true pain, or it would not have faded so quickly" (Wittgenstein, *Zettel*, §504; 89e; translation modified). It is not that love cannot be proven save through exceptional actions (gifts, sonnets, extravagant marriage proposals, etc.), but that this 'being put to the test' is crucial to it, and persists with it at all times. There is no way of proving it once and for all, and so the task it sets is continual. As a thought experiment, imagine it were possible to use neuroimaging to determine the intensity of feeling a subject has for a certain person. Even if one could establish scientifically that a particular man or woman arouses extreme desire and/or affection in the subject, then would this be sufficient to prove love? Are such feelings even necessary to love? Could we not, in certain circumstances, legitimately speak of it in their absence?

And why can't we say that Noriaki loves Akiko, and/or that Takashi does? To say that true love cannot exist in circumstances of insane jealousy or financial exchange would perhaps be too romantic. Yet at the same time it is clear that something isn't right for these characters.

48. To illustrate this one need only register the state of contemporary 'debates' regarding the existence of God, in which hapless theists end up looking like they believe in something for which there is no rational evidence (God as Russell's teapot). This is a way of understanding what the death of God means (God dies just as belief in God is reduced to believing in the existence of a particular entity). In modernity, we do not simply lose our belief; rather, we are saddled with a concept of belief that puts pressure on the lived experience of believing.

49. Deleuze, *Cinema 2*, 187 (see also 170–1). For an extended critique of the theological dimensions of Deleuze's claim about belief and modern cinema, see Bernstein, 'Movement! Action! Belief?' For a more sympathetic recent discussion of the claim and the responses it has provoked, see Sinnerbrink, *Cinematic Ethics* (52–79).

Bibliography

Adorno, Theodor and Horkheimer, Max. *Dialectic of Enlightenment*, trans. Edmund Jephcott (Stanford: Stanford University Press, 2002).

Agamben, Giorgio. *Infancy and History: On the Destruction of Experience*, trans. Liz Heron (London: Verso, 1993).

Agamben, Giorgio. 'On Potentiality', in *Potentialities*, trans. Daniel Heller-Roazen (Stanford: Stanford University Press, 1999), 177–84.

Agamben, Giorgio. 'The Face', in *Means without End*, trans. Vincenzo Binetti and Cesare Casarino (Minneapolis: University of Minnesota Press, 2000), 91–100.

Allen, Richard. *Projecting Illusion: Film Spectatorship and the Impression of Reality* (Cambridge: Cambridge University Press, 1995).

ASL19. 'Censorship in Iranian Cinema', in *Iranian Cinema in a Global Context: Policy, Politics, and Form*, ed. Peter Decherney and Blake Atwood (New York: Routledge, 2015), 229–42.

Ayer, A. J. *Language, Truth, and Logic* (New York: Dover, 1952).

Baggini, Julian. 'Alien Ways of Thinking: Mulhall's *On Film*', *Film-Philosophy* (7: 24, 2003), 12–23.

Baird, Robert. 'The Startle Effect: Implications for Spectator Cognition and Media Theory', *Film Quarterly* (53: 3, 2000), 12–24.

Barthes, Roland. *Camera Lucida*, trans. Richard Howard (New York: Farrar, Straus and Giroux, 1981).

Baudry, Jean-Louis. 'Ideological Effects of the Basic Cinematographic Apparatus', trans. Alan Williams, *Film-Quarterly* (23: 2, 1974–5), 39–47.

Bazin, André. 'The Ontology of the Photographic Image', in *What is Cinema? Volume 1*, trans. Hugh Grey (Berkeley: University of California Press, 2005), 9–16.

Benjamin, Walter. 'Franz Kafka', trans. Harry Zohn, in *Selected Writings Volume 2 1926–34*, ed. Howard Eiland and Michael W. Jennings (Cambridge, MA: Harvard University Press, 1999), 714–818.

Benjamin, Walter. 'The Work of Art in the Age of its Technological Reproducibility', trans. Harry Zohn and Edmund Jephcott, in *Selected*

Writings Volume 4 1938–40, ed. Howard Eiland and Michael W. Jennings (Cambridge, MA: Harvard University Press, 2003), 251–83.

Bernstein, J. M. 'Movement! Action! Belief? Notes for a Critique of Deleuze's Cinema Philosophy', *Angelaki* (17: 4, 2012), 77–93.

Blackburn, Simon. *Ruling Passions: A Theory of Practical Reasoning* (Oxford: Oxford University Press, 2000).

Buckland, Warren. 'Critique of Poor Reason', *Screen* (30: 4, 1989), 80–103.

Butler, Rex. 'Abbas Kiarostami: The Shock of the Real', *Angelaki* (17: 4, 2012), 61–76.

Cardullo, Bert. *In Search of Cinema: Writings on International Film Art* (Montreal: McGill-Queens University Press, 2004).

Carroll, Noël. Review of *Pursuits of Happiness: The Hollywood Comedy of Remarriage*, *The Journal of Aesthetics and Art Criticism* (41: 1, 1982), 103–6.

Carroll, Noël. *The Philosophy of Horror, Or, Paradoxes of the Heart* (New York: Routledge, 1990).

Carroll, Noël. *Mystifying Movies: Fads and Fallacies in Contemporary Film Theory* (New York: Columbia University Press, 1991).

Carroll, Noël. 'Cognitivism, Contemporary Film Theory and Method: A Response to Warren Buckland', *Journal of Dramatic Theory and Criticism* (VI: 2, 1992), 199–219.

Carroll, Noël. 'Fiction, Nonfiction, and the Film of Presumptive Assertion: Conceptual Analyses', in *Engaging the Moving Image* (New Haven: Yale University Press, 2003), 193–224.

Carroll, Noël and Seeley, William. 'Cognitivism, Psychology, and Neuroscience: Movies as Attentional Engines', in *Psychocinematics: The Aesthetic Science of Movies*, ed. Arthur Shimamura (New York: Oxford University Press, 2013), 53–75.

Cavell, Stanley. 'Aesthetic Problems of Modern Philosophy', in *Must We Mean What We Say?* (Cambridge: Cambridge University Press, 1976), 73–96.

Cavell, Stanley. 'The Avoidance of Love', in *Must We Mean What We Say?* (Cambridge: Cambridge University Press, 1976), 267–356.

Cavell, Stanley. 'Knowing and Acknowledging', in *Must We Mean What We Say?* (Cambridge: Cambridge University Press, 1976), 238–66.

Cavell, Stanley. *The World Viewed: Reflections on the Ontology of Film* (Cambridge, MA: Harvard University Press, 1979).

Cavell, Stanley. *Pursuits of Happiness: The Hollywood Comedy of Remarriage* (Cambridge, MA: Harvard University Press, 1981).

Cavell, Stanley. 'Declining Decline: Wittgenstein as a Philosopher of Culture', *Inquiry: An Interdisciplinary Journal of Philosophy* (32: 3, 1988), 253–64.

Cavell, Stanley. *Contesting Tears: The Hollywood Melodrama of the Unknown Woman* (Chicago: University of Chicago Press, 1996).

Cavell, Stanley. *The Claim of Reason* (Oxford: Oxford University Press, 1999).

Cavell, Stanley. *Cities of Words: Pedagogical Letters on a Register of the Moral Life* (Cambridge, MA: Harvard University Press, 2004).

Cavell, Stanley. *Philosophy the Day after Tomorrow* (Cambridge, MA: Harvard University Press, 2006).

Cheshire, Godfrey. 'Taste of Cherry', *The Criterion Collection*, 31 May 1999, <https://www.criterion.com/current/posts/55-taste-of-cherry> (last accessed 19 May 2013).

Chion, Michel. *The Voice in Cinema*, trans. Claudia Gorbman (New York: Columbia University Press, 1999).

Christensen, Carleton B. *Self and World: From Analytic Philosophy to Phenomenology* (Berlin: Walter de Gruyter, 2008).

Coleridge, Samuel Taylor. *Biographia Literaria, Or, Biographical Sketches of My Literary Life and Opinions*, ed. James Engell and W. Jackson Bate (Princeton: Princeton University Press, 1983).

Collins, Arthur W. 'Beastly Experience', *Philosophy and Phenomenological Research* (63: 2, 1998), 375–80.

Conant, James. 'An Interview with Stanley Cavell', in *The Senses of Stanley Cavell*, ed. Richard Fleming and Michael Payne (Lewisburg: Bucknell University Press, 1989), 21–72.

Conant, James. 'Must We Show What We Cannot Say?', in *The Senses of Stanley Cavell*, ed. Richard Fleming and Michael Payne (Lewisburg: Bucknell University Press, 1989), 243–83.

Conant, James. 'Throwing Away the Top of the Ladder', *The Yale Review* (79: 3, 1991), 328–64.

Conant, James. 'Elucidation and Nonsense in Frege and Early Wittgenstein', in *The New Wittgenstein*, ed. Alice Crary and Rupert Read (London: Routledge, 2001), 174–217.

Conant, James. 'The Method of the *Tractatus*', in *From Frege to Wittgenstein: Perspectives on Early Analytic Philosophy*, ed. Erich Reck (Oxford: Oxford University Press, 2002), 374–462.

Conant, James. 'Stanley Cavell's Wittgenstein', *The Harvard Review of Philosophy* (XIII: 1, 2005), 51–65.

Costello, Diarmuid and Phillips, Dawn. 'Automatism, Causality, and Realism: Foundational Problems in the Philosophy of Photography', *Philosophy Compass* (4: 1, 2009), 1–21.

Cox, Damian and Levine, Michael. *Thinking Through Film: Doing Philosophy, Watching Movies* (Chichester: Wiley Blackwell, 2012).

Crary, Alice. *Beyond Moral Judgment* (Cambridge, MA: Harvard University Press, 2007).

Crary, Alice. 'Dogs and Concepts', *Philosophy* (87, 2012), 215–37.

Currie, Gregory. *Image and Mind: Film, Philosophy, and Cognitive Science* (Cambridge: Cambridge University Press, 1996).

Dabashi, Hamid. *Close Up: Iranian Cinema, Past, Present and Future* (London: Verso, 2001).

Davidson, Donald. 'A Coherence Theory of Truth and Knowledge', in *Truth and Interpretation: Perspectives on the Philosophy of Donald Davidson*, ed. Ernest LePore (Oxford; Basil Blackwell, 1986), 307–19.

Deleuze, Gilles. *Cinema 2: The Time Image*, trans. Hugh Tomlinson and Robert Galeta (Minneapolis: University of Minnesota Press, 1989).

Démy-Geroe, Anne. 'Persian or Islamic? Depictions of Love in Contemporary Iranian Cinema', *The La Trobe Journal* (91, 2013), 149–57.

Derrida, Jacques. 'Signature Event Context', trans. Samuel Weber and Jeffrey Mehlman, in *Limited Inc* (Evanston, IL: Northwestern University Press, 1988), pp. 1–24.

Descartes, René. *Discourse on Method and the Meditations*, trans. F. E. Sutcliffe (London: Penguin, 1968).

Devictor, Agnès. 'Classic Tools, Original Goals: Cinema and Public Policy in the Islamic Republic of Iran (1979–97)', in *The New Iranian Cinema: Politics, Representation, and Identity*, ed. Richard Tapper (London: I. B. Tauris, 2002), 66–76.

Diamond, Cora. 'Throwing Away the Ladder: How to Read the *Tractatus*', in *The Realistic Spirit: Wittgenstein, Philosophy, and the Mind* (Cambridge, MA: MIT Press, 1991), 179–204.

Diamond, Cora. 'Ethics, Imagination and the Method of Wittgenstein's *Tractatus*', in *The New Wittgenstein*, ed. Alice Crary and Rupert Read (London: Routledge, 2001), 174–217.

Doane, Mary Anne. 'The Indexical and the Concept of Medium Specificity', *differences* (18: 1, 2007), 128–52.

Dreyfus, Hubert. *Being-in-the-World: A Commentary on Heidegger's* Being and Time, *Division I* (Cambridge, MA: MIT Press, 1991).

Dreyfus, Hubert. 'Overcoming the Myth of the Mental: How Philosophers Can Profit from the Phenomenology of Everyday Experience', *Topoi* (25: 1–2, 2006), 43–9.

Dreyfus, Hubert. 'The Myth of the Pervasiveness of the Mental', in *Mind, Reason, and Being-in-the-World: The McDowell–Dreyfus Debate*, ed. Joseph Schear (Abingdon: Routledge, 2013), 15–40.

Elena, Alberto. *The Cinema of Abbas Kiarostami*, trans. Belinda Coombes (London: SAQI, 2006).

Erfani, Farhang. *Iranian Cinema and Philosophy: Shooting Truth* (New York: Palgrave Macmillan, 2012).

Falzon, Christopher. *Philosophy Goes to the Movies: An Introduction to Philosophy* (London: Routledge, 2014).

Farahmand, Azadeh. 'Perspectives on Recent (International Acclaim for) Iranian Cinema', in *The New Iranian Cinema: Politics, Representation, and Identity*, ed. Richard Tapper (London: I. B. Tauris, 2002), 86–108.

Ferri, Anthony J. *Willing Suspension of Disbelief: Poetic Faith in Film* (Lanham, MD: Lexington Books, 2007).

Ford, Hamish. 'Driving into the Void: Kiarostami's *Taste of Cherry*', *Journal of Humanistics and Social Sciences* (1: 1, 2012), 1–27.

Fried, Michael. *Absorption and Theatricality: Painting and Beholder in the Age of Diderot* (Berkeley: University of California Press, 1980).

Fried, Michael. 'Art and Objecthood', in *Art and Objecthood: Essays and Reviews* (Chicago: Chicago University Press, 1998), 148–72.

Fried, Michael. *Manet's Modernism or, The Face of Painting in the 1860s* (Chicago: University of Chicago Press, 1998).

Fried, Michael. *Why Photography Matters as Art as Never Before* (New Haven: Yale University Press, 2008).

Fried, Michael. *Four Honest Outlaws: Sala, Ray, Marioni, Gordon* (New Haven: Yale University Press, 2011).

Gaut, Berys. *A Philosophy of Cinematic Art* (Cambridge: Cambridge University Press, 2010).

Gibbard, Allan. *Wise Choices, Apt Feelings* (Cambridge, MA: Harvard University Press, 1992).

Goodenough, Jerry. 'Introduction I: A Philosopher Goes to the Cinema', in *Film as Philosophy: Essays on Cinema after Wittgenstein and Cavell*, ed. Rupert Read and Jerry Goodenough (Basingstoke: Palgrave Macmillan, 2005), 1–28.

Gow, Christopher. *From Iran to Hollywood: Reframing Post-Revolutionary Iranian Cinema* (London: I. B. Tauris, 2011).

Graham, Peter. '"Cinéma-Vérité" in France', *Film Quarterly* (17: 4, 1964), 30–6.

Gunning, Tom. 'The Cinema of Attractions: Early Film, its Spectator, and the Avant-Garde', in *Early Cinema: Space Frame Narrative*, ed. Thomas Elsaesser (London: British Film Institute, 1990), 56–62.

Gunning, Tom. *D. W. Griffith and the Origins of American Narrative Film: The Early Years at Biograph* (Urbana: University of Illinois Press, 1994).

Harding, Sandra. '"Strong Objectivity" and Socially Situated Knowledge', in *Whose Science? Whose Knowledge? Thinking from Women's Lives* (Milton Keynes: Open University Press, 1991), 138–63.

Hare, R. M. *Freedom and Reason* (Oxford: Oxford University Press, 1965).

Hartsock, Nancy. 'The Feminist Standpoint: Developing the Ground for a Specifically Feminist Historical Materialism', in *Discovering Reality: Feminist Perspectives on Epistemology, Metaphysics, Methodology, and Philosophy of Science*, ed. Sandra Harding and Merrill B. Hintikka (Dordrecht: D. Reidel, 1983), 283–310.

Heidegger, Martin. *Being and Time*, trans. Joan Stambaugh (Albany: State University of New York Press, 1996).

Jarvie, Ian. *Philosophy of the Film* (New York: Routledge, 1987).

Kant, Immanuel. *The Critique of Pure Reason*, trans. and ed. Paul Guyer and Allen Wood (Cambridge: Cambridge University Press, 1998).

Kaufman, Anthony. 'Abbas Kiarostami Speaks about *Taste of Cherry*', interview with Kiarostami for *Indiewire*, 19 March 1998, <http://www.indiewire.com/article/abbas_kiarostami_speaks_about_taste_of_cherry> (last accessed 21 September 2015).

Khosrowjah, Hossein. 'Unthinking the National Imaginary: The Singular Cinema of Abbas Kiarostami', doctoral dissertation submitted to the Department of Art and Art History, University of Rochester (New York, 2010).

Kiarostami, Abbas. 'Kiarostami on TEN', in press release for *Ten* (New York: Zeitgeist Films, 2002), 3, <http://www.zeitgeistfilms.com/films/ten/presskit.pdf> (last accessed 18 February 2015).

Kotsko, Adam. *Awkwardness: An Essay* (Winchester: Zero Books, 2010).

Krzych, Scott. 'Auto-Motivations: Digital Cinema and Kiarostami's Relational Aesthetics', *The Velvet Light Trap* (66, 2010), 26–35.

Laine, Tarja. *Feeling Cinema: Emotional Dynamics in Film Studies* (New York: Continuum, 2011).

Levinas, Emmanuel. *Time and the Other*, trans. Richard Cohen (Pittsburgh: Duquesne University Press, 1969).

Lippard, Chris. 'Disappearing into the Distance and Getting Closer All the Time: Vision, Position, and Thought in Kiarostami's *The Wind Will Carry Us*', *Journal of Film and Video* (61: 4, 2009), 30–40.

Litch, Mary and Karofsky, Amy. *Philosophy Through Film* (New York: Routledge, 2015).

Livingston, Paisley. 'Theses on Cinema as Philosophy', *Journal of Aesthetics and Art Criticism* (64, 2006), 1–8.

Livingston, Paisley. *Cinema, Philosophy, Bergman: On Film as Philosophy* (Oxford: Oxford University Press, 2009).

Lloyd, Genevieve. *The Man of Reason: 'Male' and 'Female' in Western Philosophy* (Minneapolis: University of Minnesota Press, 1984).

Macarthur, David. 'What Goes without Seeing: Marriage, Sex and the Ordinary in *The Awful Truth*', *Film-Philosophy* (18, 2014).

McDowell, John. *Mind and World* (Cambridge, MA: Harvard University Press, 1996).

McDowell, John. 'Aesthetic Value, Objectivity, and the Fabric of the World', in *Mind, Value and Reality* (Cambridge, MA: Harvard University Press, 1998), 112–30.

McDowell, John. 'Non-Cognitivism and Rule-Following', in *Mind, Value and Reality* (Cambridge, MA: Harvard University Press, 1998), 198–218.

McDowell, John. 'What Myth?' *Inquiry* (50: 4, 2007), 338–51.

McDowell, John. 'Avoiding the Myth of the Given', in *Having the World in View: Essays on Kant, Hegel, and Sellars* (Cambridge, MA: Harvard University Press, 2009), 256–72.

McDowell, John. 'The Myth of the Mind as Detached', in *Mind, Reason, and Being-in-the-World: The McDowell–Dreyfus Debate*, ed. Joseph Schear (Abingdon: Routledge, 2013), 41–58.

Mackie, J. M. *Ethics: Inventing Right and Wrong* (London: Penguin, 1990).

MacKinnon, Catharine. *Feminism Unmodified: Discourses on Life and Law* (Cambridge, MA: Harvard University Press, 1987).

Metz, Christian. *The Imaginary Signifier: Psychoanalysis and the Cinema*, trans. Celia Britton (Bloomington: Indiana University Press, 1982).

Minh-ha, Trinh-T. 'The Totalizing Quest of Meaning', in *Theorizing Documentary*, ed. Michael Renov (New York: Routledge, 1993), 90–107.

Mottahedeh, Negar. *Displaced Allegories: Post-Revolutionary Iranian Cinema* (Durham, NC: Duke University Press, 2008).

Mulhall, Stephen. *Inheritance and Originality: Wittgenstein, Heidegger, Kierkegaard* (Oxford: Clarendon Press, 2001).

Mulhall, Stephen. 'Can There Be an Epistemology of Moods?' in *Heidegger Re-examined*, vol. 4, ed. Hubert Dreyfus and Mark Wrathall (New York: Routledge, 2002), 33–52.

Mulhall, Stephen. *Philosophical Myths of the Fall* (Princeton: Princeton University Press, 2005).

Mulhall, Stephen. 'Words, Waxing and Waning: Ethics in/and/of/the *Tractatus Logico-Philosophicus*', in *Wittgenstein and his Interpreters*, ed. Guy Kahane, Edward Kanterian, and Oskari Kuusela (New York: John Wiley and Sons, 2007), 221–47.

Mulhall, Stephen. *On Film* (London: Routledge, 2016).

Mulvey, Laura. 'Visual Pleasure and Narrative Cinema', *Screen* (16: 3, 1975), 6–18.

Mulvey, Laura. 'Kiarostami's Uncertainty Principle', *Sight and Sound* (8: 6, 1998), 24–7.

Naficy, Hamid. 'Islamizing Film Culture in Iran: A Post-Khatami Update', in *The New Iranian Cinema: Politics, Representation, and Identity*, ed. Richard Tapper (London: I. B. Tauris, 2002), 26–65.

Naficy, Hamid, 'Poetics and Politics of Veil, Voice and Vision in Iranian Post-Revolutionary Cinema', in *Veil: Veiling, Representation and Contemporary Art*, ed. David Bailey and Gilane Tawadros (Cambridge, MA: MIT Press, 2003), 138–53.

Naficy, Hamid. *A Social History of Iranian Cinema Volume 4: The Globalizing Era, 1984–2010* (Durham, NC: Duke University Press, 2012).

Nancy, Jean-Luc. *Being Singular Plural*, trans. Robert Richardson and Anne O'Byrne (Stanford: Stanford University Press, 2000).

Nancy, Jean-Luc. *The Evidence of Film: Abbas Kiarostami*, trans. Christine Irizarry and Verena Andermatt Conley (Brussels: Yves Gevaert, 2001).

Ngai, Sianne. *Our Aesthetic Categories: Zany, Cute, Interesting* (Cambridge, MA: Harvard University Press, 2012).

Nichols, Bill. *Representing Reality* (Bloomington: Indiana University Press, 1991).

Nietzsche, Friedrich. *Beyond Good and Evil*, in *Basic Writings of Nietzsche*, trans. Walter Kaufmann (New York: Modern Library, 2000), 179–435.

Orgeron, Devin. *Road Movies: From Muybridge and Méliès to Lynch and Kiarostami* (New York: Palgrave Macmillan, 2008).

Pak-Shiraz, Nacim. *Shi'i Islam in Iranian Cinema: Religion and Spirituality in Film* (London: I. B. Tauris, 1999).

Pascal, Blaise. *Pascal's Apology for Religion: Extracted from the Pensées*, ed. H. F. Stewart (Cambridge: Cambridge University Press, 1942).

Pippin, Robert. *After the Beautiful: Hegel and the Philosophy of Pictorial Modernism* (Chicago: Chicago University Press, 2014).

Price, Michael. 'Imagining Life: The Ending of *Taste of Cherry*', *Senses of Cinema* (17, 2001).

Renov, Michael. 'Towards a Poetics of Documentary', in *Theorizing Documentary*, ed. Michael Renov (New York: Routledge, 1993), 12–36.

Rodowick, D. N. *Elegy for Theory* (Cambridge, MA: Harvard University Press, 2014).

Rothman, William. *Documentary Film Classics* (Cambridge: Cambridge University Press, 1997).

Rothman, William. 'Film, Modernity, Cavell', in *Cinema and Modernity*, ed. Murray Pomerance (New Brunswick, NJ: Rutgers University Press, 2006), 316–32.

Rothman, William and Keane, Marian. *Reading Cavell's* The World Viewed: *A Philosophical Perspective on Film* (Detroit: Wayne State University Press, 2000).

Rushton, Richard. 'Early, Classical and Modern Cinema: Absorption and Theatricality', *Screen* (45: 3, 2004), 226–44.

Rybin, Steven. *Terrence Malick and the Thought of Film* (Lanham, MD: Lexington Books, 2012).

Sadr, Hamid. *Iranian Cinema: A Political History* (London: I. B. Tauris, 2006).

Saeed-Vafa, Mehrnaz. 'Reflections on *Like Someone in Love*', 14 May 2014, <http://www.jonathanrosenbaum.net/2014/05/40396/> (last accessed 2 November 2015).

Saeed-Vafa, Mehrnaz and Rosenbaum, Jonathan. *Abbas Kiarostami* (Champaign: University of Illinois Press, 2003).

Saljoughi, Sara. 'Seeing, Iranian Style: Women and Collective Vision in Abbas Kiarostami's *Shirin*', *Iranian Studies* (45: 4, 2012), 519–535.

Schear, Joseph (ed.). *Mind, Reason, and Being-in-the-World: The McDowell–Dreyfus Debate* (Abingdon: Routledge, 2013).

Scheman, Naomi. 'Missing Mothers/Desiring Daughters: Framing the Sight of Women', *Critical Inquiry* (15: 1, 1988), 62–89.

Schmerheim, Philipp. *Skepticism Films: Knowing and Doubting the World in Contemporary Cinema* (New York: Bloomsbury, 2015).

Schmitt, Carl. *Political Theology: Four Chapters on the Concept of Sovereignty*, trans. George Schwab (Cambridge, MA: MIT Press, 1985).

Schwitzgebel, Eric. 'Do People still Report Dreaming in Black and White? An Attempt to Replicate a Questionnaire from 1942', *Perceptual and Motor Skills* (96: 1, 2003), 25–9.

Sebald, W. G. *Vertigo*, trans. Michael Hulse (New York: New Directions, 2000).

Sinnerbrink, Robert. *New Philosophies of Film: Thinking Images* (London: Continuum, 2011).

Sinnerbrink, Robert. 'Re-enfranchising Film: Towards a Romantic Film-Philosophy', in *New Takes in Film-Philosophy*, ed. Havi Carel and Greg Tuck (Basingstoke: Palgrave Macmillan, 2011), 25–47.

Sinnerbrink, Robert. *Cinematic Ethics: Exploring Ethical Experience through Film* (Abingdon: Routledge, 2016).

Smith, Adam. *The Theory of Moral Sentiments*, ed. Knud Haakonssen (Cambridge: Cambridge University Press, 2002).

Spinoza, Baruch. *Ethics*, trans. Andrew Boyle and revised by G. H. R. Parkinson (London: Everyman, 1993).

Turvey, Malcolm. 'Is Scepticism a "Natural Possibility" of Language?' in *Wittgenstein, Theory and the Arts*, ed. Richard Allen and Malcolm Turvey (London: Routledge, 2001), 117–36.

Viefhughes-Bailey, Ludger H. *Beyond the Philosopher's Fear: A Cavellian Reading of Gender, Origin and Religion in Modern Skepticism* (Aldershot: Ashgate, 2007).

Vogels, Jonathan. *The Direct Cinema of David and Albert Maysles* (Carbondale: Southern Illinois University Press, 2005).

Wartenberg, Thomas. *Thinking on Screen: Film as Philosophy* (London: Routledge, 2007).

Weinberger, Stephen. 'Neorealism, Iranian Style', *Iranian Studies* (40: 1, 2007), 5–16.

Winston, Brian. 'The Documentary Film as Scientific Inscription', in *Theorizing Documentary*, ed. Michael Renov (New York: Routledge, 1993), 37–57.

Winter, Jessica. 'The Long Roads Home', *The Village Voice*, 11 March 2003, <http://www.villagevoice.com/film/the-long-roads-home-6411177> (last accessed 27 April 2016).

Wittgenstein, Ludwig. *Zettel*, trans. G. E. M. Anscombe, ed. G. E. M. Anscombe and G. H. von Wright (Berkeley: University of California Press, 1967).

Wittgenstein, Ludwig. *Culture and Value: A Selection from the Posthumous Remains*, ed. George Henrik von Wright and Heikki Nyman (revised edition of the text by Alois Pichler), trans. Peter Winch (Oxford: Basil Blackwell, 1998).

Wittgenstein, Ludwig. *Philosophical Investigations*, trans. G. E. M. Anscombe (Malden, MA: Blackwell, 2001).

Wittgenstein, Ludwig. *Tractatus Logico-Philosophicus*, trans. D. F. Pears and B. F. McGuiness (London: Routledge, 2001).

Wittgenstein, Ludwig. 'Ethics, Life and Faith', in *The Wittgenstein Reader*, ed. Anthony Kenny (Malden, MA: Blackwell, 2006), 251–66.

Zanganeh, Lila. *My sister, guard your veil; my brother, guard your eyes: Uncensored Iranian Voices* (Boston: Beacon Press, 2006).

Zeydabadi-Nejad, Saeed. *The Politics of Iranian Cinema: Film and Society in the Islamic Republic* (London: Routledge, 2010).

Zheutlin, Barbara. 'The Politics of Documentary: A Symposium', in *New Challenges for Documentary*, ed. Alan Rosenthal and John Corner (Manchester: Manchester University Press, 2005), 150–66.

Index

EU Authorised Representative:

Easy Access System Europe Mustamäe tee 50, 10621 Tallinn, Estonia

gpsr.requests@easproject.com

Printed and bound by CPI Group (UK) Ltd, Croydon, CR0 4YY

06/01/2026

02029805-0001